REVISING MYTHOLOGIES

The Composition of
Thoreau's Major Works

REVISING MYTHOLOGIES

The Composition of

Thoreau's Major Works

STEPHEN ADAMS and DONALD ROSS, JR.

University Press of Virginia   Charlottesville

THE UNIVERSITY PRESS OF VIRGINIA
Copyright © 1988 by the Rector and Visitors
of the University of Virginia

First published 1988

Library of Congress Cataloging-in-Publication Data
Adams, Stephen, 1948–
  Revising mythologies : the composition of Thoreau's major works
Stephen Adams and Donald Ross, Jr.
    p.   cm.
  Includes index.
  ISBN 0-8139-1185-0
  1. Thoreau, Henry David, 1817–1862—Criticism, Textual. I. Ross,
Donald, 1941–   . II. Title
PS3054.A33 1988
818'.309—dc19   88-801
                                                                        CIP

Printed in the United States of America

FOR

Warren and Margaret Adams

and for Carl Strauch

Contents

Acknowledgments

We are grateful to J. Lyndon Shanley for his helpful commentary on our drafts of the *Walden* chapters, and for his list of Journal sources to *Walden*. Kent Bales gave us insightful criticism of an early version of the manuscript. Elizabeth Witherell has helped, both in her role as editor in chief of the Thoreau edition and in providing corrections and criticisms of several drafts of our chapters. Wendell Glick read early drafts of the chapters on the reform papers and provided his insights. The Department of English and the Center for Programs in the Humanities at Virginia Polytechnic Institute and State University aided by giving Professor Adams released time and material support for a close scrutiny of Thoreau's lecture drafts and other materials. The National Endowment for the Humanities, through a Fellowship for College Teachers, allowed Professor Adams time for sustained work in 1983. The Graduate School of the University of Minnesota provided funds for a photocopy of Princeton's Journal transcripts, and the Composition Program and English Department at Minnesota helped enormously with the typing of the manuscript. The Princeton University libraries, Huntington Library, Henry W. and Albert A. Berg Collection (The New York Public Library; Astor, Lenox, and Tilden Foundations), Pierpont Morgan Library, Houghton Library at Harvard, and Concord Free Public Library supplied us with microfilms and transcripts of various manuscripts.

Some of these chapters have appeared, in different form, in other places. Parts of chapters 4 and 10 were published in "The Endings of *Walden* and Stages of its Composition," *Bulletin of Research in the Humanities* 84 (1981):451–69; an early version of chapter 5 appeared in *English Language Notes* 20 (1982):39–47. Adams's "Silence on the Mountain: The Hole in Thoreau's *Week*" (in *Essays on the Literature of Mountaineering*, Armand E. Singer, ed. [West Virginia Univ. Press, 1982], pp. 46–51) and "Looking for Thoreau's Dark Lady," (*Thoreau Society Bulletin*, no. 161 [Fall 1982]) cover some of the ground from chapters 3 and 6, while his essay "Thoreau Catching Cold: *A Yankee in Canada*," *ESQ: A Journal of the American Renaissance* 25 (1979):224–34, is the core of chapter 7. We are grateful to the editors of those journals for permission to use the materials. Finally, Ronald Clapper has let us cite his fine study of the *Walden* manuscripts. We commend his work to the attention of Thoreau scholars.

Abbreviations

Parenthetical references in the text are to the following editions of Thoreau's writings and other sources:

AM Manuscripts in the Houghton Library, Harvard University.

C *The Correspondence of Henry David Thoreau*. Ed. Walter Harding and Carl Bode. New York: New York Univ. Press, 1958.

CC Henry D. Thoreau. *Cape Cod and the Miscellanies*. Vol. 5 of *The Writings of Henry David Thoreau*. Boston: Houghton Mifflin, 1906.

CE *The Complete Works of Ralph Waldo Emerson* (Centenary Edition). 12 vols. Ed. Edward Waldo Emerson. Boston: Houghton Mifflin, 1903–04.

CL Walter Harding, "A Check List of Thoreau's Lectures." *Bulletin of the New York Public Library* 52 (1948):78–87.

CPL Manuscript of Thoreau's "Walking" in the Concord Free Public Library.

CW *The Collected Works of Ralph Waldo Emerson*. Ed. Alfred R. Ferguson et al. 3 vols. to date. Cambridge: Harvard Univ. Press, 1971–.

DHT Walter Harding. *The Days of Henry Thoreau*. Enlarged and corrected edition. New York: Dover Publications, 1982.

EEM Henry D. Thoreau. *Early Essays and Miscellanies*. Ed. Joseph J. Moldenhauer, Edwin Moser, with Alexander Kern. Princeton: Princeton Univ. Press, 1975.

Ex *Excursions and Poems*. Vol. 5 of *The Writings of Henry D. Thoreau*. Boston: Houghton Mifflin, 1906.

FD Linck C. Johnson. *Thoreau's Complex Weave: The Writing of A Week on the Concord and Merrimack Rivers, with the Text of the First Draft*. Charlottesville: Univ. Press of Virginia, 1986.

HM Manuscripts in the Henry E. Huntington Library, San Marino, Calif. References include the number of the

manuscript, the number or title of the division within the
manuscript, and, where paginated, Thoreau's page numbers
(recto and verso).

J   *The Journal of Henry D. Thoreau.* Ed. Bradford Torrey and
Francis H. Allen. Boston: Houghton Mifflin, 1906.

JMN   *The Journals and Miscellaneous Notebooks of Ralph Waldo
Emerson.* Ed. William H. Gilman, Alfred R. Ferguson, et al.
16 vols. Cambridge: Harvard Univ. Press, 1960–82.

L   *The Letters of Ralph Waldo Emerson.* Ed. Ralph L. Rusk. 6
vols. New York: Columbia Univ. Press, 1939.

LMHDT   William L. Howarth. *The Literary Manuscripts of Henry
David Thoreau.* Columbus: Ohio State Univ. Press, 1974.

MH   Manuscripts designated bMS Am 278.5 in the Houghton
Library, Harvard University. References include the folder
number within bMS Am 278.5 and, for paginated leaves,
Thoreau's page numbers (recto and verso).

MLJ   Manuscripts of Thoreau's Journals (vols. 22, 29, and 30) in
the Pierpont Morgan Library.

MW   Henry D. Thoreau. *The Maine Woods.* Ed. Joseph J.
Moldenhauer. Princeton: Princeton Univ. Press, 1972.

PJ   The *Journal* of Henry D. Thoreau. Ed. John C. Broderick et
al. 2 vols. to date. Princeton: Princeton Univ. Press, 1981–.

RP   Henry D. Thoreau. *Reform Papers.* Ed. Wendell Glick.
Princeton: Princeton Univ. Press, 1973.

S   J. Lyndon Shanley. *The Making of Walden with the Text of
the First Version.* Chicago: Univ. of Chicago Press, 1957.

T   Transcripts of Thoreau's journals. Through the generosity of
the University of Minnesota and Elizabeth Witherell, editor
in chief of the *Writings of Henry D. Thoreau,* we have used
photocopies of the typed transcripts of Thoreau's journals.
In quoting them we have used the transcriber's conventions
to indicate cancels and insertions. Words between ⟨ ⟩ marks
were inserted in pencil and words typed thus ~~thus~~ were
lined through.

W   Henry D. Thoreau. *A Week on the Concord and Merrimack
Rivers.* Ed. Carl Hovde, William Howarth, and Elizabeth
Witherell. Princeton: Princeton Univ. Press, 1980.

Wa   Henry D. Thoreau. *Walden.* Ed. J. Lyndon Shanley.
Princeton: Princeton Univ. Press, 1971.

REVISING MYTHOLOGIES

The Composition of

Thoreau's Major Works

1
Introduction

IN HIS JOURNAL for 9 May 1853 Thoreau reported on a day with
Mr. Alcott:

> Having each some shingles of thought well dried, we
> walk and whittle them, trying our knives, and admir-
> ing the clear yellowish grain of the pumpkin pine. We
> wade so gently and reverently, or we pull together so
> smoothly, that the fishes of thought are not scared from
> the stream, but come and go grandly, like yonder clouds
> that float peacefully through the western sky. When we
> walk it seems as if the heavens—whose mother-o'-pearl
> and rainbow tints come and go, form and dissolve—and
> the earth had met together, and righteousness and
> peace had kissed each other. (*J* 5:130–31)

Transferring this entry to a late draft of the *Walden* manuscript,
Thoreau gave the episode a new date (winter 1845–46) and new
mythical significance. Alcott became "the philosopher" who
helps "the hermit" survive and even profit from winter at the
pond. To the Journal entry Thoreau added, "There we worked,
revising mythology, rounding a fable here and there, and building castles in the air for which earth offered no worthy foundation" (*Wa* 269–70).

This passage from "Former Inhabitants; and Winter Visitors"
radiates allusions to other parts of *Walden*. The "fishes of
thought," for example, recall Thoreau's ambition to "fish in the
sky, whose bottom is pebbly with stars" (*Wa* 98) and later to cast
his line "upward into the air, as well as downward into this element which was scarcely more dense" (*Wa* 175). "Shall I go to
heaven or a-fishing?" Thoreau asks in "Brute Neighbors" (*Wa*
224); he eventually concludes that the dilemma is a false one,
since, as he discovers talking with Mr. Alcott and as he proclaims
in *Walden*, heaven and earth can merge. The metaphors of shap-

ing and constructing in this passage seem especially significant. The image of whittling "shingles of thought" looks back to Thoreau's urge to "improve the nick of time, and notch it on my stick too" (*Wa* 17); it anticipates the Artist of Kouroo whittling *his* magnificent stick (*Wa* 326–27). The castle building recalls Thoreau's house building at the start of *Walden* and prepares for his concluding advice about castles in the air: "Now put the foundations under them" (*Wa* 324). These images of shaping and making, along with the reference to revising mythologies and rounding fables, refer self-reflexively to the writing of *Walden* and they bring us to the purpose of our own book. For what insights they lend into his major works, we want to examine the shavings left from Thoreau's literary whittling, the stages by which his air and grounded castles grew, and the revisions that his mythologies underwent.

Thoreau spent much of his mature life revising the facts of his experience to turn them into mythology, and then revising the myths to turn them into texts. His transmutations, from world to world, and from word to word, are the subject of this book. This study examines the frequently complex evolution of Thoreau's major works—from their origin as ideas jotted in his Journal through the stages of lecture and essay to their publication (often many years later) in book form. Our approach is not usual for most writing about Thoreau, and is rare in American literary studies—we present detailed information about the composition and revisions of Thoreau's major works and explore some of the changes in interpretation that can result from knowing what took place. We also give some of the facts and a few conclusions about how the emerging books and essays interacted with one another in the confines of Thoreau's Journals or the existing drafts. Thus, the first draft of *Walden* (by no means the finished piece) is seen in its place as a work being written concurrently with both the second draft of *A Week* and a nearly polished draft of the first essay in *The Maine Woods*. Most thematic studies of Thoreau are almost perversely ahistorical; they easily ignore the passage of time and development of the author by quietly juxtaposing writings over a decade or more apart. In this regard, studies of Thoreau are similar to those of other nineteenth-century American authors, and quite different from studies of, say, British romantics, where scholars have more carefully preserved the chronologies of when a passage was drafted, revised, and finally published.

At the start of his writing career, Thoreau apparently was reluctant to revise. Emerson noted the young Thoreau's theory that "the poem ought to sing itself: if the man took too much pains with the expression he was not any longer the Idea himself" (*JMN* 7:144). Emerson also wrote to Margaret Fuller that "Henry Thoreau has too mean an opinion of 'Persius' [the early essay "Aulus Persius Flaccus"] or any of his pieces to care to revise them but he will give us Persius as it is, if we will do the revising" (*L* 2:280–81).

That Thoreau's attitude toward revising changed is indicated not only by his extensive practice but also by explicit comments in his Journals and correspondence. In December 1853 he wished for "some kind of india-rubber that would rub out at once all that in my writing which it now costs me so many perusals, so many months if not years, and so much reluctance, to erase" (*J* 6:30). The following March he discussed his method of correcting manuscripts, which involved "purifying" them rigorously and then returning to the rejected sentences "after the lapse of time" so he could "easily detect those which deserve to be readmitted" (*J* 6:146; see also *J* 6:179). He later wrote to the aspiring poet S. Ripley Bartlett, "I have found that the precept 'Write with fury, and correct with flegm' required me to print only the hundredth part of what I had written" (*C* 572). Revision for Thoreau became a crucial act of "seeing again"—of returning to past experience with new eyes for its meaning. He explains the principle behind revision when he talks of making two reports in his Journal: "first the incidents and observations of to-day; and by to-morrow I review the same and record what was omitted before, which will often be the most significant and poetic part. I do not know at first what it is that charms me. The men and things of to-day are wont to lie fairer and truer in to-morrow's memory" (*J* 9:306). As we hope to demonstrate, Thoreau's best works evolved over long periods during which he gradually discovered or created significance and poetry in incidents from his past.

This is a study of Thoreau's major writings: the longer works

(*A Week*, *Walden*, "An Excursion to Canada," *Cape Cod*, *The Maine Woods*) and some of the shorter excursions and reform papers ("Walking," "Life without Principle," "Slavery in Massachusetts," the John Brown essays). Examination of the other short works fills out the shape of Thoreau's literary career, the growth of his mind and parallel evolution of his style. We avoid complete readings of works where previous commentary seems convincing, where Thoreau's revisions were minimal (e.g., *Cape Cod* and *The Maine Woods*), where manuscript evidence of development has not survived ("Resistance to Civil Government"), and where we have little substantial to add. Our chapters are fullest and most detailed when our approach or access to unpublished or recently published materials sheds genuinely new light and suggests significant reinterpretation of texts (e.g., *A Week*, *Walden*, "An Excursion to Canada"). With the works that occupied Thoreau's attention over several years, and over several drafts, we have focused on the addition of new content, explicit changes in rhetorical stance, and general markers of organization in the texts. We have not tried to explore the minor revisions Thoreau made to the paragraphs and sentences of *Walden* or *A Week* or the essays where extensive material for further study exists—in the published Journals, the forthcoming volumes of the Princeton edition, and the lecture drafts. Thoreau revised *Walden* extensively at the paragraph level to integrate new material, whether that new material was retrieved from the early Journals or written afresh. At present, however, the body of data is enormous and the scholarly methods for generalizing about it not well defined.

At some points, the treatment of Thoreau's evolving works is limited by the manuscript evidence available. The scholar must depend on what pieces of paper have been preserved from Thoreau's Journals and draft stages of lectures, essays, and books. Some conclusions are necessarily speculative in places where manuscript evidence is lacking. Thoreau *might* have had the complete *Walden* in mind from the start; crucial leaves, especially for the second half of the book, may have disappeared, thereby distorting our sense of *Walden*'s development. But, as William Howarth has meticulously documented (*LMHDT*), Thoreau did preserve many drafts of his writings (especially for one who recommends the *"bonfire*, or purifying destruction" for one's unnecessary effects [*Wa* 67]). Thoreau's own numbering of the *Walden* leaves indicates which are missing and from what parts of the book. Also, Thoreau's voluminous Journals (practically complete from 1850 on) provide dates and early drafts for much of the material that he later worked into his published writings.

Overall, our study is meant as a continuum with previous scholarship, not a repudiation of it. It adds to the existing body of interpretation, complements it, rather than charting a pathway of triumphs and errors among the various critics. Anyone even remotely sympathetic to current literary theories knows that any commentary is a transient and incomplete effort to keep up with other streams of words. This is almost the only view possible in the face of theories that find all interpretations to be partial and transitory (and probably idiosyncratic). Dealing with Thoreau's texts as they changed (as they were written), we conclude that Thoreau, too, saw his own works in a dynamic and flexible way.

Hershel Parker has pointed in the correct direction, toward a "new scholarship" which makes the facts about composition and revision a part of the proper study of texts and which takes relevant biographical and textual evidence fully into account.[1] Parker urges us to see literary works in this broader and dynamic context, rather than focusing all of our interpretive energies on a fixed, authorized, and determined product. Our interpretations can thus point to writings whose meanings changed as they were being composed, and whose meanings are liable to further

---

[1] "The 'New Scholarship': Textual Evidence and Its Implications for Criticism, Literary Theory, and Aesthetics," *Studies in American Fiction* 9 (1981):181–97. Leonard Neufeldt, in *The House of Emerson* (Lincoln: Univ. of Nebraska Press, 1982), p. 15, discusses his interest in fostering "an examination of the genetic history of each work, insofar as that is possible, but also the genetic history reported by the sequence of Emerson's complete writings." Neufeldt cites a similar general request by Daniel B. Shea in "Emerson and the American Metamorphosis" from *Emerson: Prophesy, Metamorphosis, and Influence* (New York: Columbia Univ. Press, 1975), p. 31.

change as they are read by later generations. Parker invites us to consider literary texts as manifestations of the creating imagination, rather than as final Works that somehow got bound into matched sets at the ends of their creators' lives. A romantic view of a world of becoming rather than being is thus quite appropriate, especially for writers like Thoreau and Emerson, whose ideas were in flux—the praise of inconsistency in "Self-Reliance" and "Song of Myself" has its echoes throughout the middle of the nineteenth century.

To examine the development of Thoreau's works is to reevaluate his life as a writer. Two significant aspects of his intellectual history emerge. The first is his changing view of mythology, wherein he recapitulated a major trend in Western thought from the late eighteenth and early nineteenth centuries. That trend first began to see myth as an aspect of all civilizations and therefore worthy of respect, then to include Christianity with other mythic systems, then to see the possibility of conscious myth-making as an antidote to a world where scientific explanation appeared to be stripping life of wonder and separating man from nature. Myth finally assumed the status of a special source of truth and aesthetic power. Thoreau came through these conclusions gradually, and his views about mythology are often quite different even among the drafts of *Walden* and, especially, *A Week*.

Our second, related emphasis in reviewing Thoreau's intellectual history concerns a single event, with a single date, after which time his way of talking about the world changed. This is what we call his "conversion" to romanticism, a period during 1851 and 1852 when he began to use the formal terms regarding the imagination and poetry that had become commonplace in England and among his New England friends such as Emerson. We question the general assumption that Thoreau was fully romantic from his earliest years because he grew up in what is conventionally regarded as the romantic period (1790–1830 in England, 1820–1865 in America), or even that he was romantic from his first acquaintance with Emerson. Rather, his Journal, poetry, and essays from 1834 to 1846 reveal the influence of his schooling by men rooted in neoclassicism and the eighteenth century. These apprentice pieces show him regularly addressing such neoclassical topics as original genius, Ossian, the primacy of Homer, and the battle of the ancients and moderns. Thoreau is still searching for subjects, structures, and voices of his own. The works dramatize the clash of various perspectives from his formal and informal education; he experiments with different ways of exploring, organizing, and talking about his world. He does show familiarity with Transcendental themes and concepts, but he does not apply them consistently or with the full commitment that he would reveal later on.

Early in his career he follows the Emersonian method of piecing together essays from various Journal excerpts, but he does not yet fuse them successfully into organic wholes. As Margaret Fuller wrote of "The Service" (1840), "I never once feel myself in a stream of thought, but seem to hear the grating of tools on the mosaic" (*C* 42). Thoreau's dominant aesthetic at this stage is conservative and neoclassical, as suggested by his explicit comments on art (especially on imagination) and by his own practice. He separates observation and reflection and assigns to his readers a passive role as recipients of preformulated messages. Mythology in these early pieces tends to be ornamental, a showing off of his fine classical education, rather than the force it would eventually become for generating and shaping content.

The first draft of *A Week* (fall 1845) reveals that, even while he was living at Walden, Thoreau had not fully embraced the romantic vocabulary and concerns that would seven years later pervade the account of his stay at the pond. The book began as a tribute to his brother, John, and as an outlet for his writings after the *Dial* folded (1844). The first draft is a rather miscellaneous, unfocused piece that follows eighteenth-century conventions. As in the early essays, Thoreau's overt aesthetic theorizing is neoclassical, and he uses myth decoratively. But while he was drafting *A Week*, he was also exploring in his Journal Oriental writings that moved him toward a new aesthetic of freedom and flow—an aesthetic that approaches the romantic creation of flexible organic forms and a literature of discovery and process rather than of product.

Between his early and late work on *A Week*, Thoreau visited

Maine and climbed Mount Katahdin (September 1846). Although it did not scar him for life, as some critics suggest, the experience on Katahdin did prompt him to reevaluate his relationship with nature and his own earlier trip to Mount Agiocochook (the high point of his Merrimack trip). In his essay on the experience, drafted at the pond and completed soon after he left with the first version of *Walden*, Thoreau moves closer to a romantic travel writing which is shaped by a romance quest and which explores the epistemological and literary uses of mythology.

The Maine trip and his recreating it in prose influenced the meaning and structure of *A Week*. Later stages of *A Week* combine the neoclassical forms and concerns of the first version with significant new attitudes toward myth (as a structural device and mode of perception) and a progressive aesthetic. He added to the manuscript some earlier Journal entries on Oriental writing— reflections that help justify the experimenting that he did in the published *Week* (1849). Myth now becomes a way of discovering (or creating) significance in events from years ago, as Thoreau "re-vises" (sees again in a new light) his experience for meanings it did not at first reveal. Myth also becomes a way of structuring his narrative beyond mere chronology and of giving *A Week* a new purpose and direction. He now organizes his various thoughts and meditations around a romance quest for heaven, which he seeks on Agiocochook but ultimately locates on earth, in a *"purely* sensuous life" (*W* 382). And he now actively involves his readers in the creation of the work, challenging us at the end to undertake our own imaginative journey and compose "our own unwritten sequel" (*W* 392) to his book as it lapses into silence.

Just as *A Week* developed over many years while Thoreau revised his original experiences and discovered new meaning in them, so too did his masterpiece *Walden*. The draft that he took with him from the pond (1847) was essentially two lectures spliced together and supplemented with a series of brief essays on various topics. This first draft was primarily an exercise in social criticism: Thoreau exposed his neighbors' "desperate" lives and put forward his own program of leaving town for a self-sufficient life in nature. To that version he gradually added more short pieces, but the book still had no real center or focus beyond the initial long section of social criticism and then an appendix in which he surveys the seasons.

Thoreau set the manuscript aside for two years (from fall 1849 to early 1852) as he worked on other projects (lectures on "Walking" and his excursions to Canada and Cape Cod). Toward the end of that time he underwent what we call his conversion to romanticism—a period from 1851–52 when he became emotionally committed to the ideas, terminology, and literary figures of the romantic movement. These he had known all along, having grown up under Emerson and other Transcendentalists, but now for the first time he felt their full impact and made them genuinely his own. His Journal shows him rehearsing romantic tenets as fresh, new articles of his faith. For the first time he speaks of himself unambiguously as a Transcendentalist and adopts the vocabulary and concerns of the British romantics—for example, the originating imagination, sympathetic relationship with nature, and a Faustian quest toward an ideal goal.

His conversion seems to have helped Thoreau complete the draft of *Walden*, which had lain fallow for over two years. By adapting a somewhat standard romantic vocabulary he could translate his discoveries about the natural world into clear, Transcendentalist metaphors. In a crucial series of revisions he added mythical significance to his stay at the pond. As in *A Week*, he took on the role of the mythic hero of his own romance quest. He clarified what became the related major concerns of the book and evolved a narrative that would better shape it. In the first half, his narrative persona leaves society to seek an authentic life; imagination provides the direct apprehension of nature's divine essence that climaxes this initial quest. In the second half, which Thoreau revised most radically, the narrator assumes the roles of poet and mythmaker, recommitted to the world and seeking order behind the apparent chaos of experience—a quest that leads to his climactic discovery of organicism. In the course of its seven revisions, then, the book gained important new focus and meaning.

Walden represents the summit of Thoreau's literary career, as various forces came together at the right moment. He gained energy and inspiration from explicitly adopting romantic language. Romantic aesthetics gave him a flexible way of unifying and shaping diverse materials collected over time into a multisignificant narrative that leaves room for—and invites—the reader's participation in the creation or performance of the work. He revised carefully over many years and seven drafts, discovering and creating new meaning for his old experiences. He acted the role of his own Artist of Kouroo, writing to please himself (rather than publishers or popular taste) and create a perfect work of art. Finally, he felt as yet little urgency from the political concerns that were soon to distract him.

Works written before and after his conversion offer fascinating insights into the tensions Thoreau felt during this crucial period. The travel works, for example, display pressures of genre and audience consideration that kept them from reflecting his new orientation as thoroughly as does *Walden*. In these pieces, while Thoreau struggled to become a successful published author, he mines the rather straightforward travel materials that proved most popular on the lecture circuit and most in demand by editors of periodicals.[2] He does address concerns that pervade *A Week* and *Walden*, but he does not develop them as deeply or complexly. Writing for a popular market discouraged him from experimenting as radically with myth, combinations of genres, and the inner travel that makes his masterpiece so resonant. He concentrates instead on facts that would interest middle-class people who might want to travel the same routes. Also, he submitted these works to little "re-vision" (in the sense either of rewriting passages to improve them or of seeing his experiences again through fresh eyes as he returned to them over time). He did pare down his original Journal drafts of the travels to Cape Cod, Chesuncook, and the Allegash to give these narratives bet-

[2] Scholars have yet to develop William Charvat's pioneering work on how the literry marketplace affected American writers. See "Literary Economics and Literary History," *The Profession of Authorship in America, 1800–1870*, ed. Matthew J. Bruccoli (Columbus: Ohio State Univ. Press, 1968), pp. 283–97.

ter unity and focus, but he did not add much to the narratives—not nearly so much as he did to his first two published books. The travel works also display the beginnings of the "scientism" and social concerns that would gradually move Thoreau away from romanticism.

In "An Excursion to Canada" (written primarily from late 1850 to early 1852), Thoreau uses again his familiar quest structure, but the quest he describes is unsuccessful, as political and social concerns prevent the fertile perception of and relationship with nature that he celebrates in *Walden*. The account of Canada remained unsatisfactory to Thoreau the persona of the work and to Thoreau its writer (in a letter to Greeley he called it "insignificant" [C 294]). But the work is carefully, if not obviously, structured, and it offers a revealing preview of later writings in which social conditions at home turn even the landscape around Concord into hell.

In the long interstice between the third and fourth versions of *Walden*, and while he was drafting "An Excursion to Canada," Thoreau also worked on *Cape Cod*. Rather than repudiating his Transcendentalism, as some critics argue, this book was composed largely before Thoreau's conversion and his late revision of *Walden*. *Cape Cod* represents traditional aesthetic and scientific travel writing, although it is more sophisticated and challenging than most. It is structured rather conventionally, without the mixing of genres or mythological underpinning that characterize Thoreau's more ambitious works. In it he occasionally treats themes and concerns that he was to handle quite differently in *Walden*. The book shows him experimenting with various attitudes toward perception, history, and nature. His stance here is essentially pragmatic and fatalistic, in contrast to the mythic and imaginative approach he would soon add to *Walden*.

Although he drafted "Chesuncook" shortly after returning from his Maine trip of 1853, Thoreau did not polish it into essay form until after he had drafted "The Allegash" in 1858. Both pieces underwent comparatively little revision. Both contain brief sections celebrating imaginative perception of and empathy with nature, but these sections are dwarfed by the surrounding material, which is scientific and detached. Thoreau seems once again to be aiming for a popular market—for readers who wanted straightforward, entertaining travel stories without the distractions of Transcendental quests and meditations. This is mostly what he gave them, crafting informative and entertaining narratives out of his own observations and reading. His attitudes and role seem to have changed significantly by the time of these pieces. He travels the woods and rivers not as the spiritual quester and poet of *Walden*, but chiefly as a naturalist. He has abandoned his previous role as hero of his own mythic quest; now he is the observer of others who become the focus of what reduced mythological enhancement the narratives contain. He appears ambivalent about the destruction of the forests, anticipating a future America of barren deserts but hoping for potential value from the civilization that he sees encroaching on the wild. He also seems nostalgic for a period now passed when imagination could more often and easily transfigure the world.

Thoreau moved away from his heightened romanticism of the mid 1850s not only because he was writing for a popular market and was himself growing more secular and scientific but also because he was increasingly involved in social concerns, as the history of his political writing reveals. "Resistance to Civil Government" represents his early exploration of the individual's problematic relationship to the state, especially regarding slavery. Here Thoreau proposes individual moral purity as the ultimate solution, while hoping to influence the 1848 election. But at this stage the state does not essentially exist for Thoreau; he can imagine it away or simply attend to more important matters—getting his shoe fixed and picking berries.

The reform essays of 1854 emerge from the Transcendentalism that brought forth *Walden*, but they lack the energy, scope, and aesthetic control of Thoreau's masterpiece. "Life without Principle" and "Slavery in Massachusetts" show the darkening political scene moving Thoreau away from sacred, vivifying nature toward the distractions of the slavery question. Especially in the former, Thoreau surveys many familiar themes, but now nature and imagination no longer remove him easily from the political functions that should, he says, remain unconscious; instead, those functions become barriers to an authentic life. "Slavery in

Massachusetts" shows him all too conscious of social concerns that interrupt him in his daily life and spiritual aspirations, remove his serenity and thus his motive for going to the lakes, and turn the Massachusetts landscape into hell. In both, myth practically disappears as a structural principle and as a source of imaginative discovery. The essays remain basically propaganda, skillful expositions of prefabricated messages rather than exploratory voyages in which his readers become fellow travelers on Thoreau's quest for meaning that is created in the performance of the work. The John Brown essays provide a new mythical hero for Thoreau but one quite different from the role he himself played in his earlier works. These pieces are moving, effective political rhetoric, but they are written with limited aims. They do not involve very much of Thoreau's previous life, or even the contemporaneous life that he was leading in the environs of Concord and recording in most of his Journal entries for the late 1850s and 1860s.

These Journals are source books for what were to be Thoreau's next major works. "The Dispersion of Seeds," "Wild Fruits," and "The Fall of the Leaf" are extensions of the project that he conceived while making crucial revisions in *Walden*: to "make a chart of our life, know how its shores trend, that butterflies reappear and when, know just why this circle of creatures completes the world" (*J* 3:438; cf. *Wa* 225). But for various reasons (including ill health, his failure to establish much of an audience for his published work, his increasing secularization, and his basic satisfaction with his life observing nature and recording his findings privately), Thoreau did not get far into these works. His late Journals remain collections of closely observed natural facts, but those facts rarely blossom into poetry, as he hoped they would.

He did manage to abstract from his late projects three essays ("Autumnal Tints," "The Succession of Forest Trees," "Wild Apples") and one lecture ("Huckleberries") that recover some of the old *Walden* feeling of man and nature united in a wonderful organic process. But the material lacks freshness, as if Thoreau had lost much of his emotional energy and sense of new discovery. The concerns in these essays seem nostalgic (especially in "Wild Apples," which Thoreau compiled in 1860 out of Journal entries mostly from 1850–52). The last essays do not go far beyond themes treated in his earlier masterpiece. They demonstrate Thoreau moving back to a decorative use of mythology, and away from portraying himself as the hero of his own unifying and shaping quest romances. Nature is the hero of these last pieces, and Thoreau appears as its skilled observer. They offer much objective reporting of what this sensitive naturalist saw, with occasional brilliant commentary on nature's relation to the life of man. But now man and nature connect less frequently while the scientific side of Thoreau moves to the fore; flashes of imaginative insight become rarer than they were in the early and mid–1850s. The last essays, however, represent only a small portion of what Thoreau might have written had he been able to work over his Journal materials as thoroughly as he did during the long gestation of *Walden*.

In our survey of Thoreau's career, we do not mean to oversimplify or overschematize. He was a complex thinker and writer, often testing philosophical hypotheses and rhetorical strategies, often rehearsing and debating various perspectives on questions, in different kinds of works that he drafted at the same time. Like other romantics, he did not avoid inconsistency, contradictions, or multiplicity. Sometimes his periods of development overlap (especially as he polished accounts of events many years after they occurred); sometimes he returned nostalgically to earlier periods (as in the late Maine and natural history essays). Yet, as we hope to demonstrate in the following chapters, he did pass through significant and distinct stages in his development as a thinker and writer—stages that are important to the evolving meaning and style of his works.

"We do not learn much from learned books," Thoreau writes in *A Week*, "but from true, sincere, human books, from frank and honest biographies" (W 98). This book—as true and honest as we could make it—is our attempt at that kind of account. It is not a factual biography, such as Walter Harding's *The Days of Henry Thoreau*, or an inner, "spiritual" biography, such as Sherman Paul's *The Shores of America*, or "a life of the mind," such as Robert D. Richardson's *Henry Thoreau*, though it uses (and sometimes suggests modifications of) these excellent works.

Rather, this is a biography of Thoreau's development as a writer by way of being a history of his major works. More, it is a study of the perennial problems for all writers—finding something to talk about, finding a voice, finding an audience—and of the smaller decisions which all must make—organizing, embellishing, and polishing. It sheds light, we hope, on the complex process by which this writer, perhaps any writer, develops initial discoveries into completed texts under a host of informing considerations and pressures.

Guide To Chronological Chart

The chart presents important, concurrent events in Thoreau's most productive years, 1845 to 1854. The histories of individual works are detailed in the Appendix.

Column 1. Biography. Major events with special focus on Thoreau's travels outside Concord.

Column 2. *Walden* manuscripts. The dates when Thoreau was working on the A to G stages, up to publication.

Column 3. Journal 1906. Location of dated passages in the Torrey-Allen Journal. Princeton Journal volume 1 goes up to 1844, volume 2 to 1848.

Column 4. Princeton Journal transcripts. Dates of the manuscript journals in Princeton Journals volumes 1 and 2, and those that will appear in volume 3, with Thoreau's titles or numbers.

Column 5. *A Week*. The dates of the three main versions, up to publication.

Column 6. Lectures, essays. Dates and topics of Thoreau's lectures, based on Harding's Check List and other sources. Dates of magazine articles.

Figure 1: Chronological chart follows

Figure 1: Chronological chart

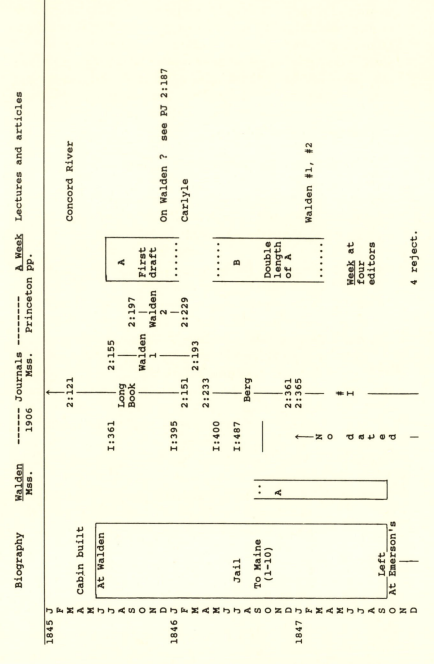

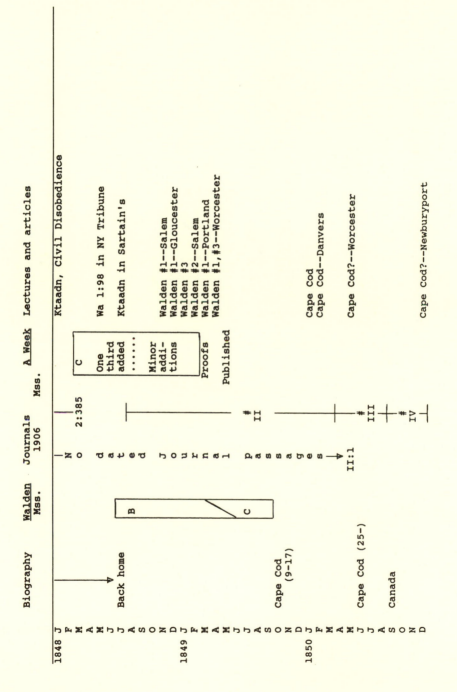

Date	Biography	Walden Mss.	Journals 1906	A Week	Lectures and articles
1851 J			II:134		Cape Cod--Clinton; Walden #1--Medford
F					
M					
A					Wild
M					Walking--Worcester
J					
J	Hull &				
A	Plymouth (25-1 Aug)				
S					
O					
N					
D		..			
1852 J		D	III:172		Canada--Lincoln, Concord
F					Canada--Plymouth
M					Canada
A					Reality--Mech. Inst., Boston
M					Walking or Wild
J					
J					Wa 4:5-13 in Sartain's
A					Wa 4:1-5 in Sartain's
S		E			
O					
N					
D					100 pages of Cape Cod to Putnam's
1853 J		F			
F					
M					
A					
M					
J					
J					
A					
S	Maine (13-28)				
O			IV:436	28: Week	
N				copies	
D		G		returned	Moose Head Lake; Maine article in Putnam's
1854 J			VI:42		
F					
M	First proof -->				
A	Printer's copy				
M	Burns affair				
J					

	Biography	Walden Mss.	Journals 1906	Lectures and articles
1854 J				Slavery in Mass--Framingham
A		Published		Slavery in Mass in Liberator
S				
O				
N				Moonlight--Plymouth
D				Getting a Living--Philadelphia; Moose Hunting--Philadelphia lecture--Providence; Life Without Principle--New Bedford;
1855 J			VII:99	Employment and Higher Life--Worcester \ Getting--Nantucket
F				What Shall if Profit?
M				
A				
M				
J				Cape Cod 1-4
J				in
A				Putnam's
S				
O				
N				
D				
1856 J			VIII:76	
F				
M				
A				
M				
J				
J				
A				
S				Moose Story--Perth Amboy
O				Walking--Perth Amboy
N				Walking--Amherst, NH
D				
1857 J				Walking--Worcester
F				
M				
A				
M				
J	To Maine			
J	(20-8 Aug)			
A				
S				
O				
N				
D				

2
Early Thoreau

WHEN THOREAU LEFT Walden Pond in September 1847, he had assembled draft materials for what would be two books (*A Week* and *Walden*) and the first third of another ("Ktaadn," for *The Maine Woods*). While much of this material was scattered in the Journals and would not be retrieved for years, more of it was in reasonably sustained form: *A Week* in the Long Book, "Ktaadn" in the Berg Journal, and the first version of *Walden*. We will examine closely the fruits of Thoreau's activities from 1845 to 1847, but first we will look at one aspect of his early intellectual development—the germs of his romanticism as shown in his college and early essays and his Journals from the 1830s on.

Many critics speak as though the major works from the late 1840s and 1850s differed from the early works only in Thoreau's skill at shaping and expressing thoughts that he held all along. They assume that, philosophically, he was a full-fledged romantic and Transcendentalist from the start of his career, or at least by the early 1840s.[1] We suggest that this view is somewhat over-

[1] A representative sampling of critics: Norman Foerster: Thoreau "inherited Transcendentalism" ("The Intellectual Heritage of Thoreau," *Texas Review* 2 [1917]:192); Raymond Adams: between 1835 and 1837 "Thoreau had become saturated with transcendentalism" ("Thoreau's Literary Apprenticeship," *Studies in Philology* 29 [1932]:618); Kenneth Walter Cameron: Thoreau's "growing Transcendentalism" is revealed in his Institute library borrowings for 1836–37 (*Thoreau Discovers Emerson: A College Reading Record* [New York: NYPL, 1953], p. 15); Alexander Kern: Thoreau "was a Transcendentalist by 1837 or 1838" ("The Rise of Transcendentalism, 1815–1860," in *Transitions in American Literary History*, ed. Harry Hayden Clark [Durham: Duke Univ. Press, 1954], p. 256); Sherman Paul: Thoreau "did not have to formulate a 'first philosophy' as Emerson had; he found one ready to hand [i.e., Transcendentalism]" (*The Shores of America* (Urbana: Univ. of Illinois Press, 1958], p. 1); Walter Harding: Thoreau "quickly began to look to [Emerson] for guidance and leadership. . . . Emerson in many ways acted as a catalyst for Thoreau" (*DHT* 61); Richard Lebeaux: "In early 1836 [Tho-

simplified—that, although Thoreau demonstrated Transcendental leanings from the first, he also came under other influences and did not adopt a fully romantic vocabulary or concerns until the 1850s. Transcendentalism was, of course, a complex, varied, inconsistent movement, without an exact set of identifying features and doctrines. While there is no precise litmus test to determine Transcendentalist writing, we suggest that Thoreau's early works lack many of the traits which his later writings possess and which historians of Transcendentalism have identified as central to the movement.

Thoreau obviously did grow up in a Transcendental milieu. During his Harvard years (1833–37), he was tutored by Jones Very and Orestes Brownson. He withdrew from the Harvard Institute Library books important to the new philosophy—including Emerson's *Nature*, which he borrowed twice in his senior year and eventually purchased for himself.[2] Returning to Concord, the capital of Transcendentalism, he associated with members of the Hedge Club (fall 1837) and developed a friendship with Emerson (*DHT* 63). From 1841 to 1843 he lived with Emerson, gaining further access to Emerson's library and to the Transcendental sage himself. Cameron, Harding, Lebeaux, and others have clearly established the crucial, profound influence of Emerson on Thoreau.

Some of his contemporaries considered the young Thoreau a

---

reau] . . . absorbed Brownson's brand of Transcendentalism"; by 1841 "Emerson—and the Transcendental 'ideology'—provided Thoreau with the prospect of a new and integrated identity, a romantic self-concept which would help to reduce his ambivalences" (*Young Man Thoreau* [Amherst: Univ. of Massachusetts Press, 1977], pp. 65, 89); Robert Sattelmeyer: Thoreau "had been converted to the 'new views' of Transcendentalism by Emerson's *Nature* while in college" (Historical Introduction, *PJ* 1:593); William Howarth: Thoreau's "formal deficiency" in 1842 "was common to other transcendentalists, for they could not find practical forms that clearly expressed their ideal convictions" (*The Book of Concord* [New York: Viking, 1982], p. 28); Robert D. Richardson, Jr.,: by Fall 1841 Thoreau "clearly now feels he belongs" to the transcendental "movement" (*Henry Thoreau: A Life of the Mind* [Berkeley: Univ. of California Press, 1986], p. 110).

[2] Cameron, *Thoreau Discovers Emerson*, pp. 12–15.

Transcendentalist. In 1842 Hawthorne described him as "somewhat tainted with Transcendentalism"[3] and thought him too exclusive in his poetic tastes, "like all other Transcendentalists, so far as I am acquainted with them."[4] Thoreau's Harvard classmate James Richardson, Jr., listed him among "my mystic brethren" (C 71). In a conversation with Thoreau, Henry James, Sr., "exclaimed, at some careless answer of mine, 'Well, you Transcendentalists are wonderfully consistent'" (C 110).

And yet, at this early period, Thoreau differed with the more orthodox members of the Transcendental Club. For example, Lidian Emerson reports a "Conversation" in which Alcott distinguished Thoreau from Lane and himself because "they went beyond the material object, and were filled with spiritual love and perception (as Mr. T. was not)" (C 92). And, as far as we can tell, Thoreau does not unambiguously refer to himself as a Transcendentalist until much later—1851.[5] From his college days through the 1840s, Thoreau expressed a rich assembly of ideas, which ranged from timeless commentary on the world to thoughts certainly borrowed from and attributed to others, and from eighteenth-century clichés to radical exploration beyond the new orthodoxy of the American version of romanticism—Transcendentalism. The nature of the mixture, when coupled with Thoreau's personal idiosyncracies, fosters our doubts that his thoughts could be labeled exclusively those of any one camp. Our view is buttressed by Thoreau's change in 1851–52 when he explicitly and enthusiastically adopts the vocabulary and accepts the intellectual debts of a "converted" romantic.

[3] Edward C. Sampson, "Three Unpublished Letters by Hawthorne to Epes Sargent," *American Literature* 34 (1962):102–3.

[4] *The American Notebooks*, ed. Claude M. Simpson (Columbus: Ohio State Univ. Press, 1972), p. 354.

[5] In an 1840 letter to his sister Helen, Thoreau does write, "That letter to John, for which you had an opportunity doubtless to substitute a more perfect communication, fell, as was natural, into the hands of his 'transcendental brother,' who is his proxy in such cases" (C 39). The quotation marks here suggest to us that Thoreau acknowledges his reputation as a Transcendentalist but refuses to embrace the label for himself without irony.

Although Professors Kwiat, Raymond Adams, Kern, Harding and others see indications of Transcendentalism in the college essays, especially the later ones, they seem to exaggerate this influence. The essays do show Thoreau's interest in and familiarity with some important romantic and Transcendental tenets and themes. For example, Thoreau begins an essay from his sophomore year by announcing his frequent preference for a painter's sketches over "his most elaborate productions" (*EEM* 8). As a junior he quotes Schlegel on the "sympathy of feeling" between the poet and nature (*EEM* 28–29). And "Being Content with Common Reasons" (*EEM* 101–4), an essay from his senior year, echoes in several places Emerson's *Nature*, which Thoreau had borrowed during the previous month.

But the college essays show as well his social misgivings (he was not a "joiner") and his philosophical distance from the complete ideology and aesthetics of the English romantic movement. We think, too, that Edwin Moser overstates the case when he claims that "all of Thoreau's basic ideas are in the college essays, the seeds are all present, awaiting maturation."[6] We include among Thoreau's basic ideas concern for a sensuous heaven on earth, and for myth as a mode of heightened perception, and for an "extra-vagant," open-ended style of writing—features that we do not find in the early essays. When Thoreau does address in these pieces topics that are central to his later, genuinely romantic thoughts and work, he often approaches them in a neoclassical manner. Thus, imagination for the young Thoreau is not a creative or unifying force that gives access to transcendent reality; it is indistinguishable from what the romantics saw as the fairly banal, mechanical association of memories with current sensory impressions. "Not satisfied with the world around us," he writes in 1836 (his senior year at Harvard), "we delight to revel in an imaginary one of our own creation. The ideas afforded by sensation and reflection are seized upon with avidity by the

---

[6]"Henry David Thoreau: The College Essays" (M.A. thesis, New York University, 1951), p. 62, quoted in Walter Harding and Michael Meyer, *The New Thoreau Handbook* (New York: New York Univ. Press, 1980), p. 33.

imagination, and so combined and arranged as to form new wholes of surpassing beauty, awfulness, or sublimity, as the case may be" (*EEM* 45–46; cf. Addison's *Spectator* 411). In a later essay he quotes the Common Sense philosopher Dugald Stewart on imagination and concludes with a tribute to the pleasures of the imagination, whose products are clearly trivial: the "supreme delight in the building of *cob-houses* and *air castles* out of these fragments of different conceptions" (*EEM* 49; emphasis added).

In his essay on sublimity, too, Thoreau seems neoclassical. Although he rejects Burke's thesis that terror is the source of the sublime, he does not speak, as romantics do, about the sublimity of the quotidian or locate sublimity in the perceiver rather than the object perceived. Instead, he traces the sublime to "an inherent respect, or reverence, which certain objects are fitted to demand" and ultimately to "the Deity" (*EEM* 96). The objects that he lists are conventional eighteenth-century favorites: the ocean, Niagara Falls, thunderstorms, Milton's description of the angelic wars.

Although Thoreau's college essays indicate his reading in Emerson, Schlegel, Wordsworth, and Coleridge, they also show the influence of his reading in Greek and Roman classics, preromantic English poetry, and Enlightenment philosophy. They deal with general, public social topics (as opposed to more personal, introverted themes) in a style characterized by balanced periodic sentences, elaborate parallelism, personification, and other neoclassical devices. They demonstrate that, although Thoreau did encounter Very and did study German with Brownson in 1835–36, he was taught primarily by men grounded in the rational materialistic philosophy that the Transcendentalists were rebelling against.[7]

Edward Tyrrel Channing has long been recognized as Tho-

---

[7] Although Joseph J. Kwiat correctly claims that the Scottish Common Sense philosophers prepared a transition from Lockian materialism to Transcendental idealism ("Thoreau's Philosophical Apprenticeship," *New England Quarterly* 18 [1945]:311–20), the Transcendentalists themselves lumped Locke and the Scots together as the old philosophy to be swept away by the new idealism.

reau's most important teacher at Harvard, and the rhetoric that he taught (primarily from Richard Whately's *Elements of Rhetoric*) pervades Thoreau's college essays. Richard Dillman argues that Channing turned Harvard away from strictly classical rhetoric toward a psychological one that anticipates the romantic insistence on an organic relation between subject and style.[8] Also, Whately's advocacy of "what may be called Suggestive style," which will "suggest to [the reader] more than is actually expressed,"[9] might have contributed to Thoreau's later theory of a "concentrated and nutty" style: "Sentences which suggest far more than they say, which have an atmosphere about them, which do not merely report an old, but make a new, impression" (*J* 2:418).

But Whately's political, religious, and philosophical conservatism permeates the *Elements of Rhetoric*. His main goal is to prepare students to defend the *a priori* truth of Anglican doctrines. Channing, an old school Unitarian and political conservative, is also conservative aesthetically, as his position regarding imagination indicates: "The imagination itself, under the most genuine excitement, may pour forth its real beauties as rapidly and profusely as the false rhetorician can fabricate his trinkets, and with scarcely less injury, unless its exercise is tempered by a well-framed taste. There is no other security against its unreasonable intrusions."[10]

Because wise students write what their professors want to read, perhaps Thoreau's college essays do not reflect his true in-

---

[8]"Thoreau's Harvard Education in Rhetoric and Composition: 1833–37," *Thoreau Journal Quarterly* 13 (1981):47–62, and idem, "The Psychological Rhetoric of *Walden*," *ESQ* 25 (1979):79–81. See also Annette M. Woodlief, "The Influence of Theories of Rhetoric on Thoreau," *Thoreau Journal Quarterly* 7 (1975):13–22.

[9]Richard Whately, *Elements of Rhetoric*, ed. Douglas Ehninger (1828; rpt. Carbondale: Southern Illinois Univ. Press, 1963), p. 309.

[10]Edward Tyrrell Channing, *Lectures Read to the Seniors in Harvard College*, ed. Dorothy I. Anderson and Waldo W. Braden (rpt. Carbondale: Southern Illinois Univ. Press, 1968), p. 258. Cf. *Rassalas*, ch. 44, "The Dangerous Prevalence of Imagination."

tellectual and aesthetic positions. Perhaps the conventional neo-classical style and content of these essays were called forth by the assignments that Channing designed. Channing might better have heeded Whately's warning against exercises that induce "a habit of stringing together empty common-places, and vapid declamations,—of multiplying words and spreading out the matter thin,—of composing in a stiff, artificial, and frigid manner." [11]

If Channing's assignments are to blame for the lack of exploration in Thoreau's early essays, one would expect the writings after graduation to exhibit considerable changes in style and content. As Thoreau commented to his sister Helen a few months after returning from Harvard, "You know we have hardly done our own deeds, thought our own thoughts, or lived our own lives, hitherto" (C 15). His work from 1837 on should reveal, then, Thoreau's own suppressed thoughts if they differ significantly from what he learned in college. If Thoreau's early postcollege works are accurately to be characterized as Transcendental, they should display what scholars have identified as major characteristics of Transcendentalism. Specifically, they should deal with the divine cosmic psyche that animates all, with nature as a consequent symbol of the divine, with the correspondence between man and nature, with imagination as a source of transcendent truth. They should indicate a religious fervor and a reformist attitude in politics. They should be symbolic and use organic metaphors to explore a vital universe in the process of becoming. And when they treat poetry or poets, they should follow the judgments radiating from the criticism of Coleridge and Wordsworth. [12]

[11] Whately, *Elements of Rhetoric*, p. 22.

[12] We draw this simplified list of Transcendentalist characteristics from the following works, which should be consulted for a more thorough account of the movement: Octavius Brooks Frothingham, *Transcendentalism in New England* (New York: Putnam's, 1876); Perry Miller, *The Transcendentalists* (Cambridge: Harvard Univ. Press, 1950); Alexander Kern, "The Rise of Transcendentalism"; George Hochfield, *Selected Writings of the American Transcendentalists* (New York: New American Library, 1966); Brian M. Barbour, *American Transcendentalism: An Anthology of Criticism* (Notre Dame: Univ. of Notre

The essays from 1837 to 1847 do show Thoreau's growing interest in assessing his relation to nature and to his society. He begins to see that nature cannot be approached objectively or rationally, and that he cannot fully perceive it, much less understand it, with himself as a removed observer. In evaluating his view of society, he tended early on to reject the collectivity implied in a phrase such as "common sense," and to prefer a stance of radical individualism, where he would remain apart from both the general culture and from subcultures like the abolitionists and other reformers. These views were clearly compatible with those of Concord neighbors such as Fuller and Emerson, but that compatibility fell short of dedication or embrace.

The first essay that Thoreau wrote after graduation, "The Service" (composed 1840 from Journal entries 1837–40), is his most Transcendental early work. In it, he speaks of "the divinity in man" (*RP* 5), echoes *Nature* ("There is no ill which may not be dissipated like the dark, if you let in a stronger light upon it" [7]), celebrates the correspondence between one's soul and the universe (11), and writes in what Alcott cited as an "orphic" style. Ironically, this Transcendental work was rejected by the Transcendental organ, the *Dial*. Margaret Fuller justly complains of "the grating of tools on the mosaic" (*C* 42); Thoreau has not yet developed his later technique of grounding his insights in a narrative or natural setting. The subsequent early essays lack the idealism and mysticism of "The Service," suggesting perhaps that its disappointing reception discouraged Thoreau for a while from experimenting further with Transcendental themes and form.

In "Natural History of Massachusetts" (composed and published 1842), Thoreau's theory is occasionally Transcendental, but his practice in the essay itself is not. "Nature is mythical and mystical always," he asserts (*Ex* 125); "Let us not underrate the value of a fact; it will one day flower in a truth" (130). Facts will so flower when we approach nature properly, not "by inference

Dame Press, 1973); Lawrence Buell, *Literary Transcendentalism* (Ithaca: Cornell, Univ. Press 1973); Philip F. Gura and Joel Myerson, *Critical Essays on American Transcendentalism* (Boston: G. K. Hall, 1982).

and deduction and the application of mathematics to philosophy, but by direct intercourse and sympathy" (131). But this early essay separates facts and intuitions in a fairly mechanical, eighteenth-century manner; little myth or mysticism is evident; facts have not yet flowered organically in truths. The missing stage, which Thoreau was later to discover and make explicit, involves subjective, personal apprehension of the world. The flowering is not a property of objective facts; to the romantic, it grows from within. In "Natural History," Thoreau seems to be looking forward to some enlightenment in the future rather than celebrating a mode of perception that he experiences in the present. His particular observations of flora and fauna are those of the naturalist. Too, occasional metaphors reveal an essentially Enlightenment scheme of the universe. "Nature will bear the closest inspection," he says; "she invites us to lay our eye level with the smallest leaf, and take an insect view of its plain. She has no interstices; every part is full of life" (107). He conceives of nature as a static chain or structure (without "interstices") to be viewed from the outside, rather than as a living organism perceived most truly through sympathetic, creative imagination. An anecdote from one of his pupils at the Concord Academy shows Thoreau at this period using the stock watchmaker metaphor: "On another occasion [Thoreau] spoke of the certainty of the existence of a wise and friendly power overlooking all. He asked the children: if they should go into a shop and see all the nicely finished wheels, pinions, springs, and frame pieces of a watch lying spread out on a bench and again came to find them put together exactly and working in unison to move the hands on a dial and show the passage of time, whether they could believe that this had come about by chance or rather thought that somebody with thought and plan and power had been there."[13]

"A Walk to Wachusett" (composed 1842, published 1843) and "A Winter Walk" (composed and published 1843) demonstrate Thoreau in greater control of his art, having discovered the "excursion" structure that would inform his major writings.[14] As El-

[13] Edward Emerson, "Notes on Thoreau," quoted in *DHT*, p. 80.

[14] See Joseph J. Moldenhauer, "Images of Circularity in Thoreau's Prose," *Texas Studies in Literature and Language* 1 (1959):245–63.

lery Channing wrote, "Thoreau, unlike some of his neighbors, could not mosaic an essay; but he loved to tell a good story."[15] The "story" that now helps unify and structure his works is that of a circular journey. In these essays Thoreau adapts the excursion form in which the traveler gains insights into himself and the universe as he proceeds on a journey of some kind (literal or metaphorical). But these early essays still separate observation and reflection. They resemble eighteenth-century locodescriptive poetry, since they lack the organic fusion of subject and vehicle described by Abrams and Wasserman.[16]

"A Walk to Wachusett" at first seems a miniature *Week on the Concord and Merrimack Rivers*, and, indeed, Thoreau included portions of this earlier essay (e.g., the poem "With frontier strength ye stand your ground") in the later work. As in *A Week*, the narrator here is a "pilgrim" (*Ex* 138), the goal of whose journey is a mountaintop associated with heaven and gods (134, 143–44). Before ascending the mountain, he consumes a sacramental meal of raspberries and spring water, "thus propitiating the mountain gods by a sacrifice of their own fruits" (142). Once on top of the mountain, though, the pilgrim does not hint at a mystical experience or even a sensuous one but, logocentrically and anticlimactically, reads Virgil and Wordsworth and surveys the geography visible from the summit (143–44). He does not encounter a Spirit that pervades the mountains but instead meditates rather conventionally on "the hand which moulded their opposite slopes, making one to balance the other" (148)—another version of the Enlightenment's rational God. The journey remains in the eighteenth-century tradition, as suggested by the reference to *Rasselas* at the start (135) and by the moral about the elevated life tacked on at the end (151). If this essay is not very romantic, "A Winter Walk" is even less so. Although also

[15] William Ellery Channing, *Thoreau: The Poet-Naturalist*, ed. F. B. Sanborn (Boston: Chas. E. Goodspeed, 1902), p. 272.

[16] M. H. Abrams, "Structure and Style in the Greater Romantic Lyric," in *From Sensibility to Romanticism*, ed. Frederick W. Hilles and Harold Bloom (New York: Oxford Univ. Press, 1965), pp. 527–60; Earl Wasserman, *The Subtler Language* (Baltimore: Johns Hopkins Univ. Press, 1959).

structured as a journey, it draws even more heavily on the loco-descriptive tradition; the facts minutely detailed in it have not flowered in transcendent truths.

"Paradise (To Be) Regained" (1843) follows a familiar New England intellectual line in rejecting external, collective, mechanical reform schemes and in insisting that love "can make a paradise within which will dispense with a paradise without" (*RP* 47). Yet, as with "Natural History," Thoreau's placing individual regeneration ahead of social reform here is (as his title indicates) in the future. His Miltonic title speaks of paradise not in the present (where he locates it in *A Week* and *Walden*) but sometime to be.

Side by side with this radical individualism is evidence of Thoreau's aesthetic conservatism—the continuing influence of his Harvard poetic studies. In "Homer. Ossian. Chaucer." (1843), he might be moving toward a modern aesthetic with his use of the organic metaphor for poetic development ("As naturally as the oak bears an acorn . . ." [*EEM* 154]) and his advocacy of "a fine thought in its natural setting" (a plea for mimesis as opposed to the late neoclassical decay into artifice that so appalled Wordsworth and Coleridge; 170). Most of the essay, however, is devoted to aesthetic concerns straight from the eighteenth century's battle of the books: the primacy of Homer (155), original genius (166), Ossian (whom Thoreau accepts as genuine; 157–62), the ancients preferred to the moderns (159, 162), and the distinction between works of genius and those of taste (171).

When Thoreau turns to a contemporary author—indeed, a major influence on American Transcendentalism—he might be expected to sound more modern or radical. Yet "Thomas Carlyle and His Works" (composed 1845–46, published 1847) pays little attention to "what philosophy and criticism the nineteenth century had to offer" (*EEM* 223). Instead, Thoreau focuses on Carlyle as a stylist and historian, and his judgment of Carlyle as a philosopher is less than enthusiastic: "Carlyle is not a *seer*, but a brave looker-on and *reviewer*" (246); "to sum up our most serious objections, in a few words, we should say that Carlyle indicates a depth,—and we mean not impliedly, but distinctly,—which he neglects to fathom" (257). Even in this essay on a transcendental philosopher, Thoreau does not pay much attention to his transcendental ideas.

This is not to suggest that the early essays are inferior because they are not fully romantic. They do seem less interesting, controlled, rich, and suggestive than *A Week*, *Walden*, "Resistance to Civil Government," or "Walking," but not because more romantic writing is inherently superior. The early essays are apprentice pieces; through writing them, Thoreau learned the craft that he would perfect in his subsequent, better works. While his later conversion to romanticism did provide him with a liberating energy and aesthetic that made his great works possible, our major point here is that Thoreau in the 1840s is not yet the complete Transcendentalist he is often supposed to be.

Like the college and early postcollege essays, the early Journals (beginning October 1837) mention some themes that absorbed his Transcendental neighbors, but Thoreau does not develop or sustain the ideas. The bulk of the material is devoted to practical notetaking on the events around him in nature, his reading, and his communities. His commentary on these events tends to be moral rather than, say, epistemological. He accepts his world as an external reality that needs to be understood; he has not yet begun to worry about the validity of his perceptions (i.e., about innate subjectivity) or about how the perceptions can lead to greater truths about God, ethics, or the self. In the first few years of his journalizing, Thoreau occasionally echoes Emerson (e.g., *PJ* 1:208, 279–86, 460).[17] He treats briefly such topics as consciousness and subjectivity (*PJ* 1:50–51, 236, 340–41, 467–69), self-reform as true reform (*PJ* 1:299), the divinity of man (*PJ* 1:236, 2:175), and the miraculousness of the quotidian as a rival to biblical miracles (*J* 2:33). He also begins an interest in mythology that will later deepen and characterize his major work (*PJ* 1:466, 2:183–86). But he warns us explicitly about making too much of the early entries: "I am startled when I con-

[17]For all of Emerson's early contact with Thoreau—his friendship with the younger man and especially his efforts to get Thoreau writing and published—there remain surprisingly few references, quotations, and allusions from Emerson's work in Thoreau's early writings.

sider how little I am *actually* concerned about the things I write in my journal" (*PJ* 1:131). Thoreau, we suspect, is at this stage experimenting with ideas that will later concern him deeply. He seems in the not uncommon position of young people who grow up in a particular faith that they later either reject or make genuinely their own.

Most of the early Journals are devoted to other concerns. Occasional entries show the continued influence of Thoreau's schooling under men with Enlightenment attitudes and concerns. For example, Thoreau still views the world according to eighteenth-century architectural metaphors ("every chink and cranny of nature is full to overflowing" [*PJ* 1:200]), and he fights the battle of the ancients against the moderns (*PJ* 1:487–89). Some descriptions of nature are colored by eighteenth-century sentiments, as, for example, a sunrise in 1837: "and now the neighboring hilltops telegraph to us poor crawlers of the plain the Monarch's golden ensign in the east—and anon his 'long-levelled rules' fall sector-wise, and humblest cottage windows greet their Lord" (*PJ* 1:19). He alludes to classical myths but does not yet engage in serious mythmaking of his own.

Most of the entries in the early Journals are neither specifically neoclassical nor Transcendental. The majority of books that Thoreau quotes are from before the nineteenth century. His most frequent topics include nature, heroism, classical poetry and philosophy, English poetry, friendship, and music;[18] his treatment of them reveals that, philosophically, he is not yet committed to any one way of viewing the world. As he wrote in an 1841 letter, "For my part if I have any creed it is so to live as to preserve and increase the susceptibleness of my nature to noble impulses—first to observe if any light shine on me, and then faithfully to follow it" (*C* 52). At the start of his Walden period he indicates his openness to, and questioning of, experience: "Life! who

[18] Robert Sattelmeyer argues that from 1841 to 1844 Thoreau worked on a rather un-Transcendental critical anthology of English verse ("Thoreau's Projected Work on the English Poets," *Studies in the American Renaissance, 1980*, ed. Joel Myerson [Boston: Twayne, 1980], pp. 239–57).

knows what it is—what it does? If I am not quite right here I am less wrong than before—and now let us see what they will have" (*PJ* 2:156). Even in the entries that experiment with Transcendental tenets, Thoreau still postulates his enlightenment in the future rather than the present. In April 1843 he rehearses the romantic distinction between modes of knowing: "Reason [i.e., logical, mechanical understanding] will be but a pale cloud like the moon when one ray of divine light comes to illumine the soul" (*PJ* 1:401). He appears to accept some Transcendentalist doctrines but not yet (in Keats's phrase) to have tested them on his own pulses.

Then, in early 1851, Thoreau did begin to experience what before had been to him occasional matters of Transcendental faith. We explore this transition extensively in chapter 9, but it is useful to anticipate that material here. His Journal entries during this period differ significantly from earlier ones. Romantic themes and figures become more important. For example, Thoreau begins to use the romantic metaphor of the aeolian harp to express the action of divine spirit on harmonious earthly receptors (*J* 2:330, 450, 496–97).[19] He begins to theorize more extensively and more seriously about myth as a source of truth (*J* 2:151–52, 169). He reacts now deeply and personally to Wordsworth, especially the "Intimations" Ode (*J* 2:306–7). He wishes for a life of Wordsworthian "natural piety" in a long entry that explores nature for correspondences with man (*J* 2:390–97). In an entry from May 1851, too, facts begin to flower into subjective truths as Thoreau traces "a perfect analogy between the life of the human being and that of the vegetable, both of the body and the mind" (*J* 2:201–5). He discusses the doctrine of correspondences as if it now meant something personal to him.

In the same way, Thoreau treats other Transcendental themes with a new elaborateness and sense of genuine, felt discovery. Although he had before written of the divinity of man, in May

---

[19] See M. H. Abrams, "The Correspondent Breeze: A Romantic Metaphor," *Kenyon Review* 19 (1957):113–30. Many of Thoreau's Journal entries are a playful rendering of the humming telegraph lines as an aeolian harp.

1851 he exclaims about "so divine a creature as man," "it is only within a year that it has occurred to me that there is such a being actually existing on the globe" (J 2:207). The same attitude applies to the divinity of nature, the discovery of which Thoreau now takes as his profession (J 2:472).

At this period, finally, Thoreau explicitly and unambiguously associates himself with the new philosophy. He pictures himself "discoursing Transcendentalism, with only Germany and Greece stretching behind our minds" (J 2:212) and a short while later proclaims, "I begin to be transcendental and show where my heart is. . . . With reference to the near past, we all occupy the region of common sense, but in the prospect of the future we are, by instinct, transcendentalists" (J 2:228–29). In his correspondence, too, he applies the label now to his work; he describes the subject of his lecture "Walden or Life in the Woods" as "Reality rather transcendentally treated" (C 279).

"How hard one must work in order to acquire his language,— words by which to express himself," Thoreau wrote in 1858. He speaks of acquiring new knowledge about a rush when for the first time he learns its name, though he had recognized the plant for twenty years: "With the knowledge of the name comes a distincter recognition and knowledge of the thing. That shore is now more describable, and poetic even. My knowledge was cramped and confined before, and grew rusty because not used,—for it could not be used. My knowledge now becomes communicable and grows by communication" (J 11:137). Similarly, while Thoreau in his early writings shows his familiarity with Transcendental thought, not until the 1850s does he wholeheartedly adopt the vocabulary of the movement—a conversion that spurred completion of his *Walden* project. Before then, his writings show a young thinker still influenced by the Enlightenment philosophy he had grown up with and not yet ready or able to experience fully for himself the Transcendental world that he would enter in 1851.

3

The Early Development
of *A Week*

THE "DRAMA" OF "Sunday" in Thoreau's *A Week on the Concord and Merrimack Rivers* concludes "without regard to any unities which we mortals prize. Whether it might have proved tragedy, or comedy, or tragi-comedy, or pastoral, we cannot tell" (*W* 114). Many readers have shared a like uncertainty about the unity and genre of the *Week* as a whole. James Russell Lowell first scored its "digressions": "they are out of proportion and out of place, and mar our Merrimacking dreadfully. We were bid to a river-party, not to be preached at. They thrust themselves obtrusively out of the narrative, like those quarries of red glass which the Bowery dandies (emulous of Sisyphus) push laboriously before them as breastpins."[1] Following Lowell were, among many others, Henry Seidel Canby, who claimed, "The 'Week' has no structure except as a sequence of days and moods," and Joseph Wood Krutch, who said that "the whole is little more than a notebook."[2] In the late 1950s critical reaction began to shift. Although Walter Harding's 1965 biography of Thoreau echoed Canby in describing the *Week* as a "collection of essays, poems, translations, and quotations, dumped like plums into a pudding" (*DHT* 247) many recent studies have insisted upon the book's unity and coherence.[3]

[1] Review of *A Week on the Concord and Merrimack Rivers*, *Massachusetts Quarterly Review* 3 (1850):47.

[2] Canby, *Thoreau* (Boston: Houghton Mifflin, 1939), p. 52; Krutch, *Henry David Thoreau* (1948; rpt. Westport, Conn.: Greenwood Press, 1973), p. 96.

[3] See, for example, Carl F. Hovde, "Nature into Art: Thoreau's Use of His Journals in *A Week*," *American Literature* 30 (1958):165–84; Paul, *The Shores of America*, pp. 191–233; William Bysshe Stein, "Thoreau's First Book: A Spoor of Yoga," *ESQ* 41 (1965):4–25; Phyllida Anne Kent, "A Study of the Structure of Thoreau's *A Week on the Concord*

The earlier complaints about the *Week* might apply in some degree to the first stages of the work, but even then such criticism is based on questionable assumptions about the genre of Thoreau's book and it ignores Thoreau's experimentation with mixed modes. Yet the later tributes to the unity and coherence of *A Week* perhaps go to the opposite extreme. Often resorting to a vague concept of "organic unity," they seem to gloss over the disruptive, irregular tendencies that rightly bothered earlier readers. In this chapter we examine the initial stages of the *Week*, especially the mixed genres (chiefly travel and Menippean satire) that contribute to the digressive loose-jointedness of the revised, published version (1849). A study of the work's development provides a way of measuring Thoreau's movement toward romanticism. The 1849 *Week* retains neoclassical elements from its early stages while incorporating some of Thoreau's new interest in romance and myth.

Thoreau and his brother John traveled up the Concord and Merrimack rivers and explored the White Mountains from 31 August to 13 September 1839.[4] The following June, Thoreau transcribed notes from his log of the trip and drafted passages

------

and Merrimack Rivers," M.A. Thesis, Carleton (Ottawa), 1967; Joyce M. Holland, "Pattern and Meaning in Thoreau's *A Week*," *ESQ* 50 (1968):48–55; Gail Baker, "The Organic Unity of Henry David Thoreau's *A Week on the Concord and Merrimack Rivers*," Ph.D. Diss., New Mexico, 1970; Mary Suzanne Carroll, "Symbolic Patterns in Henry David Thoreau's *A Week on the Concord and Merrimack Rivers*," Ph.D. Diss., Indiana, 1975; Paul David Johnson, "Thoreau's Redemptive Week," *American Literature* 49 (1977):22–33; Frederick Garber, "A Space for Saddleback: Thoreau's *A Week on the Concord and Merrimack Rivers*," *Centennial Review* 24 (1980):322–37; David B. Suchoff, "'A More Conscious Silence': Friendship and Language in Thoreau's *Week*," *ELH* 49 (1982):673–88; John Carlos Rowe, "'The Being of Language: The Language of Being' in Thoreau's *A Week on the Concord and Merrimack Rivers*," *Through the Custom-House* (Baltimore: Johns Hopkins, 1982), pp. 28–51.

[4]For a detailed chronology of *A Week*, see Linck C. Johnson, Historical Introduction, W 433–500, and idem, *Thoreau's Complex Weave: The Writing of A Week on the Concord and Merrimack Rivers with the Text of the First Draft* (Charlottesville: Univ. Press of Virginia, 1986).

about it into his Journal (*PJ* 1:124–32), probably intending a lecture or essay entitled "Memoirs of a Tour—A Chit-chat with Nature," later retitled "Merrimack and Musketaquid." After John's death from tetanus in January 1842, Thoreau decided to turn the account of the voyage into a tribute to his brother and to friendship. He worked on the project at odd moments, entering into his Journal passages that would ultimately appear in the first draft of *A Week*. In fall 1842 he began to reconstruct his excursion in the "Long Book" and added unrelated Journal entries from 1833–44 as a major step toward drafting a book.[5] He retired to Walden Pond in 1845 to work on it; by fall he completed the first draft.

From its start the book was more than Lowell's "river-party" or a straightforward account of travel. In both his Journal for 1840 and the Long Book, Thoreau intersperses among narrative passages a variety of other material: poems, catalogs of flowers and fish, quotations from Oriental scriptures and local historians, and short essays on heroism, friendship, music, beauty, English literature, etc. These meditations appear, often in different order, in the first draft as well as the 1849 version. They have bothered readers from the start,[6] but as Lawrence Buell insists, they should not.

Buell is one of the first critics to view *A Week* in its literary context. He sees the book as an example of "literary excursion," a potentially encyclopedic form that grew out of conventional travel writing. Buell attributes the digressiveness of the *Week* to its romantic inclination toward "poetic" or imaginative excur-

[5] "Long Book" is the name Thoreau gave to a notebook that he used from 1842 to 1846 (Pierpont Morgan MA 1303). It is reproduced in *PJ* 2:1–152.

[6] Emerson in a letter offering *A Week* to Duyckinck: "The narrative of the little voyage, though faithful, is a very slender thread for such big beads & ingots as are strung on it" (*L* 3:384). Neither Rusk nor the *JMN* indicates that Emerson ever read the complete *Week*. In a letter of 16 July 1846, Emerson wrote that Thoreau "read me some of it under an oak on the river bank the other afternoon, and invigorated me" (*L* 3:338—this would have been the first version). We could find no indication that he read the book after returning from Europe.

sion, which features "interplay between the sequence of actual observations and the interests of a subjectively imposed mood or design." The book was not popular, he claims, because it was too radically Transcendental—too seriously prophetic for readers accustomed to "a convention of levity, a tacit assumption that the prevailing atmosphere is going to be bucolic reverie or musing."[7]

Perhaps, however, *A Week* (especially in its early stages) is in many ways preromantic. Perhaps it was not popular because, as travel writing, it was outdated. It shares much in common with the digressive, didactic neoclassical travel books analyzed by Charles L. Batten, Jr.[8] Like eighteenth-century excursions and the locodescriptive poetry that influenced them, the *Week* often separates observation and didactic reflection; it offers little particular, detailed description of natural scenery; and it does not present the narrating persona as a real, multidimensional individual on a voyage that reveals his personality, or at least his character.

At one point in her *Observations and Reflections* (1789), Hester Lynch Piozzi admonishes herself, "But we must cease reflections and begin describing again."[9] This split between objective and subjective, typical of eighteenth-century travel writing, is evident throughout *A Week*. While Thoreau revised his book to bring it closer to the "interplay" that Buell identifies as being romantic, much of the *Week* still separates and alternates observation and reflection in the manner suggested by Piozzi's title.

The early stages of *A Week* are most clearly neoclassical, as the history of the first chapter reveals. When he drafted in the Long Book his lecture "Concord River," which eventually grew into the first chapter, Thoreau concentrated on physical and historical description of the river (*PJ* 2:103–112). Revising the lecture for the first draft, he added more descriptive material and a section

[7] *Literary Transcendentalism*, pp. 198, 204.

[8] *Pleasurable Instruction: Form and Convention in Eighteenth-Century Travel Literature* (Berkeley: Univ. of California Press, 1978).

[9] *Observations and Reflections Made in the Course of a Journey Through Rome, Italy, and Germany*, ed. Herbert Barrows (Ann Arbor: Univ. of Michigan Press, 1967), p. 332.

of philosophical musings on rivers as journeying atoms, guides to the interior, and emblems of all progress. The chapter splits neatly in two: the first five paragraphs detail the geography and history of the Concord River (*FD* 1–2), while the second five contain reflections that are loosely associated with, but do not grow out of, what has come before (2–3).[10] Like the eighteenth-century poetry that Abrams and Wasserman analyze, the first draft suggests that preexisting private thoughts have been joined somewhat mechanically by laws of association to an apposite and available body of description.[11]

When he revised the first chapter, Thoreau moved it closer to a literature of process in which reflections seem to grow naturally and inevitably out of observations. He begins with geographical and historical notations (*W* 5–6) which then suggest reflections on the freshness of nature (7–8) and prepare for the "mythic center" of this overture (8–9, the third paragraph of the chapter).[12] He points to "flitting perspectives, and demi-experiences of the life that is in nature" and celebrates "the respectable folks." He then returns to the same pattern: physical and historical description (9–11), leading into mythical and philosophical application (11–13). While successful integration of observation and reflection is evident especially in the first three chapters of the 1849 version, the *Week* more often juxtaposes description and thought in the neoclassical manner. Although Thoreau praises writing that offers "a fine thought in its natural setting" (*W* 374), too often preexisting (even previously published) thoughts appear without much regard for smooth transitions

[10] First draft page references are to Johnson, *Thoreau's Complex Weave*.

[11] See Abrams, "Structure and Style in the Greater Romantic Lyric," pp. 527–60, and Wasserman, *The Subtler Language*.

[12] Carl F. Strauch defines the "mythic center" of a work as the point at which the writer "tries to capture the 'germ' of his thought in symbol and fable. . . . the most richly developed expression of the rare moment of aesthetic insight" (Introduction: "Ralph Waldo Emerson," in *American Literary Masters*, 2 vols. [New York: Holt, Rinehart and Winston, 1965] 1:473).

from or close links to the voyage that is supposed to be their
setting. An example is the mechanical, perfunctory transition to
the essay on Anacreon (225).

A Week, particularly in its early drafts, is also neoclassical in
its approach to nature. "Picturesque" travel was fashionable in
America when Thoreau wrote his first book (The Home Book of
the Picturesque appeared in 1852), and Thoreau indicates familiarity with its conventions:

> It [a crystalline day] was like the landscape seen
> through the bottom of a tumbler, clothed in a mild quiet
> light, in which the barns & fences chequer and parti-
> tion it with new regularity, and rough and uneven fields
> stretch away with lawn-like smoothness to the horizon.
> The clouds (in such a case) are finely distinct and pic-
> turesque—The light blue of the sky contrasting with
> their feathery whiteness.—They are a light etherial Per-
> sian draperry [sic]—fit to hang over the Persia of our
> imaginations—
> (PJ 2:12; this passage appears, with minor modifica-
> tions, in FD 20, and the published Week, W 46).

The mixture of roughness and smoothness, evenness and irreg-
ularity, is one hallmark of the style that prepared for romanticism by undermining neoclassical assumptions about order and
beauty.[13] A Week, however, contains little of the conventionally
picturesque. Thoreau rarely describes particular landscapes
from an artistic perspective. He provides little detailed natural
description at all, except of isolated components such as fish,
flowers, trees, and birds. Most specific places appear in quick
sketches—for example: "When we were opposite to the middle
of Billerica, the fields on either hand had occasionally a soft and
cultivated English aspect—whether owing to the quality of the
atmosphere or some peculiarity in the scenery—the village spire
being seen over the copses which skirted the river—and occa-

[13] See Martin Price, "The Picturesque Moment," in From Sensibility
to Romanticism, pp. 259–92.

sional orchard sweeping down to the waterside. It seemed as if one could lead a quiet and civil life there" (*FD* 23; slightly revised in *W* 53–54). More often Thoreau describes not particular places but landscapes universalized in the eighteenth-century manner (e.g., *FD* 84; *W* 194–95). These generalized landscapes provide the setting or background for the foregrounded parts of the book, the meditations which Lowell and others mistake for digressions but which are part of the travel-writing tradition out of which the *Week* grew.

The *Week* remains neoclassical, and un-Byronic, too, in its lack of detailed focus on the traveler traveling. An anonymous reviewer for *Putnam's* formulated the shift in emphasis from place to person: "It is not the things seen, nor the difficulty surmounted, but the man and the hero who sees and surmounts, that interests us."[14] Although Thoreau himself calls for "frank and honest biographies" (*W* 98), he offers little of the biographical information that characterizes much romantic work, especially travel writing. In the Long Book he indicates that he was born on the banks of the Concord (*PJ* 2:5) and that he once sailed on the river with an (unnamed) young maiden (12). To the First Draft he adds that he keeps a melon patch (*FD* 4) and was a fisherman in earliest youth (8). In the published *Week* he finally identifies his fellow traveler as his (unnamed) brother (*W* 15) and reveals that he himself works as "a pencil-maker on the earth" (140), that he has visited Staten Island (239), and that he is dissatisfied by his relationship with an anonymous "woman who possesses a restless and intelligent mind" (279). These few personal details seem quite meager for close to four hundred pages of first-person narrative.

In contrast, Goethe's *Italian Travels*, which Thoreau praises in *A Week* (326–30), reveals much autobiographical information. Details about his personal history, social position, government duties, writings, and specific acquaintances establish Goethe as an actual, complex individual who exists apart from the narrative of his trip through Italy. Margaret Fuller's *Summer on the Lakes* (1844), another possible influence on the *Week*, also resembles

[14]"American Travelers," *Putnam's Monthly Magazine* 5 (1855):568.

the more modern travel writing in its wealth of autobiographical information. Thoreau's *Week*, with its didacticism, its associational juxtaposition of description and observation, its generalized approach to landscape, and its minimal autobiography, follows more closely the conventions of the early eighteenth-century travel books than those of contemporary romantic works.

A Week is rooted, too, in another neoclassical genre—Menippean satire. Northrop Frye defines that genre as "a loose-jointed narrative form" that "relies on the free play of intellectual fancy" and tends to "expand into an encyclopaedic farrago."[15] No one would deny that, from its earliest stages, the *Week* is disjointed. Its underlying travel narrative, like the "story and fabulous portion" of the *Hitopades*, "winds loosely from sentence to sentence as barrows and oases in a desert—It is as indistinct as a camel track between Mourzuk to Darfour" (*PJ* 2:40; revised slightly for *W* 147). Freely moving away from and returning to this narrative spine, Thoreau subjects to the play of his intellectual fancy a wide variety of topics: local history and geography, botany, ichthyology, world scriptures and religions, Greek, British and German literature, ecology, aesthetics, reform movements, friendship, astronomy. Like the Concord River itself, the *Week* becomes a meandering conduit for "a huge volume of matter" (*W* 11). With the learned catalogs of flowers and fish and the quotations drawn from a variety of often obscure poets, naturalists, historians, and other authorities, Thoreau displays the Menippean satirist's delight in "piling up an enormous mass of erudition about his theme."[16] This intellectual genre provides him with the perfect vehicle for didactic meditations in which he can test ideas.

[15] *Anatomy of Criticism* (Princeton: Princeton Univ. Press, 1957), pp. 309–11. For more extended discussion of the genre, see F. Anne Payne, *Chaucer and Menippean Satire* (Madison: Univ. of Wisconsin Press, 1981) and M. M. Bakhtin, *The Problems of Dostoevsky's Poetics*, trans. R. W. Rotsel (Ann Arbor: Univ. of Michigan, 1973). Among the Menippean satirists whom Thoreau knew are Varro, Seneca, Boethius, Chaucer, Walton, Swift, and Goethe.

[16] Frye, *Anatomy*, p. 311.

Also typical of Menippean satire is the variety of literary forms within the *Week*. In addition to travel narrative, it contained from its earliest stages examples of formal and familiar essays, epic catalogs, aphorisms, mock-epic satire, dithyramb or rhapsody, and pastoral elegy. The early stages also abounded with examples of what Lowell calls Thoreau's "worsification," the incidental verses characteristic of many Menippean satires. Besides the pieces printed as verse, Thoreau occasionally experiments with rhymed prose—for example: "Then away it goes with a limping *flight* uncertain where it will *alight*, until a rod of clear sand amid the alders *invites* its *feet*. But now our steady approach compels it to seek a new *retreat*" (FD 64; slightly modified for W 235; italics added). In the revised version he also develops passages of more subtle prose poetry, using assonance and alliteration rather than rhyme for poetic heightening of language: "With our heads so low in the grass, we heard the river whirling and sucking, and lapsing downward, kissing the shore as it went, sometimes rippling louder than usual, and again its mighty current making only a slight limpid trickling sound, as if our water-pail had sprung a leak, and the water were flowing into the grass by our side" (W 332).

Finally, the *Week* shares with other Menippean satires criticism of institutions and ideas, and characterization that is "stylized rather than naturalistic"; the work "deals less with people as such than with mental attitudes."[17] Were Thoreau writing autobiography, we could legitimately demand much more personal information about himself and his brother. Were he writing a standard travel narrative, we could expect the detailed accounts of catching and preparing food and of "blistered hands and sore bottoms" that, according to Denham Sutcliffe, belong to the "conventional story of a camping trip."[18] But as Menippean satire, the *Week* can be expected to offer a somewhat disembodied, or at least depersonalized, intellect more often "voyaging

[17] Ibid., p. 309.

[18] Foreword to *A Week on the Concord and Merrimack Rivers* (New York: New American Library, 1961), p. ix.

through strange seas of Thought," as Wordsworth puts it, than sailing on actual Concord and Merrimack rivers.

If genre helps explain the "digressions" of *A Week*, so also do Thoreau's method of composition and the aesthetic theory that he was exploring in the 1840s. Throughout his career Thoreau composed his lectures, essays, and books by piecing together observations from his Journal and quotations from his reading. In a workbook from the Walden period, he acknowledges the dangers of this method:

> From all points of the compass from the earth beneath
> and the heavens above have come these inspirations
> and been entered duly in such order as they came in
> the Journal. Thereafter when the time arrived they
> were winnowed into Lectures—and again in due time
> from Lectures into Essays—And at last they stand like
> the cubes of Pythagoras firmly on either basis—like
> statues on their pedestals—but the statues rarely take
> hold of hands—There is only such connexion and se
> ries as is attainable in the galleries. And this affects
> their immediate practical & popular influence.
> (*PJ* 2:205–6).

Even earlier, Margaret Fuller had pointed to problems of unity and flow in Thoreau's work when she rejected "The Service" for the *Dial*: "I never once feel myself in a stream of thought, but seem to hear the grating of tools on the mosaic" (*C* 42). Perhaps reacting to Fuller's criticism, Thoreau took up in his Journal for the following month the topic of fluidity in writing. He mocks the demand for smooth flow and argues for "modern books of genius" whose "flow of thought is more like a tidal wave than a prone river, and is the effect of a celestial influence"; intellectual waves from such irregular books "rise from the page like an exhalation—and wash away the brains of most like burr-mill-stones" (*PJ* 1:225–26); in March 1844 Thoreau copied this entry in the Long Book (*PJ* 2:119); although it did not appear in the *FD*, he did include it in the published *Week* (*W* 102–3). He may simply have been defensive about his own out-of-control works at the time, but he may also have been working toward an aesthetic that does not prize conventional, artificial writing and smooth-flowing prose. In his Journal for 6 February 1841 he returns to the problem inherent in his method of composition (making "but a partial heap" of thoughts artificially abstracted from his Journal) and recommends a more natural kind of writing: thoughts should appear within the context that inspired them (*PJ* 1:253; see also 385). This meditation prefigures the kind of writing Thoreau was moving toward, and, indeed, he weaves the passage into a reflexive section of the published book concerning "a fine thought in its natural setting" (*W* 374).[19]

Thoreau's reading in Oriental literature also moved him further toward an aesthetic that justifies, and even values, the loose-jointed writing that he himself was producing. In a meditation on the "Veeshnoo Sarma" (24 March 1842), he defends a deep unity behind an apparent randomness:

> The great thoughts of a wise man seem to the vulgar who do not generalize to stand far apart like isolated mounts—but Science knows that the mountains which rise so solitary in our midst are parts of a great mountain chain—dividing the earth—And the eye that looks into the horizon—toward the blue sierra melting away in the distance may detect their flow of thought . . . The book should be found where the sentence is—and its connexion be as inartificial—It is the inspiration of a day and not of a moment—The links should be gold also—Better that the good be not united than that a bad man be admitted into their society. When men can select they will—if there be any stone in the quarry better than the rest—they will forsake the rest because—of it. Only the good will be quarried.
> In these fables the story goes unregarded—while the

---

[19] That parts of *A Week* are reflexive Thoreau hints when he insists, "This pledge of sanity cannot be spared in a book, that it sometimes pleasantly reflect upon itself" (*W* 147; the sentence first appeared in the Journal [*PJ* 1:388] and was later transcribed in the Long Book, *PJ* 2:40).

reader leaps from sentence to sentence—As the traveller leaps from stone to stone—
(*PJ* 1:389–90; see also 392, 395)

Thoreau included parts of this entry in the *Week* (*W* 147), where,
again, they seem reflexive; he suggests that the comments apply
to the *Week* itself as much as to the Vishnu Sarma. The peaks
are perhaps the meditations which, while they first appear separate, are all part of the underlying spiritual quest that unifies and
structures the seemingly digressive, miscellaneous work.

Though it contains drafts of many parts of the published *Week*,
the Long Book does not indicate what structure the book would
ultimately assume (beyond the trip's chronology) and does not
contain some material crucial to the final version. At the very
start of the Long Book, Thoreau wrote the invocation that would
appear as the first epigraph of the 1849 *Week*:

> Where'er thou sail'st who sailed with me,
> Though now thou climbest loftier mounts
> And fairer rivers dost ascend
> Be thou my muse, my Brother.
>
> (*PJ* 2:3; the epigraph does not appear in the *FD*. When
> he included it in the published *Week*, Thoreau placed a
> dash after "Brother" [*W* 3])

The epigraph suggests the importance of John Thoreau to the
early stages of the *Week*, as do many passages on friendship in
the Long Book, especially in the first half. These passages
confirm that the book began as an elegy to John and a tribute to
friendship. The many early passages on heroism and poetry suggest, too, that the book was part of Thoreau's search for a vocation.

In the published version, the epigraph outlines the basic plot:
a spiritual quest symbolized by ascending rivers and climbing
mountains. Thoreau hints at the spiritual-metaphorical significance of his journey in the Long Book—as when he calls rivers
"the constant lure, where they flow by our door, to distant adventure and exploration. . . . an apt emblem of all progress" (*PJ* 2:5).
Throughout the Long Book, however, there is little emphasis on

the spiritual side of the adventure and little effort to connect the physical trip with its spiritual analogue.

The Long Book does contain scattered segments of what in the published version would be the climactic essay on "natural life" (*PJ* 2:32–33, 51, 55, 73; these passages expand the original Journal entries: *PJ* 1:458, 481), but they hardly add up to the crucial discovery they later became—the core of the *Week*, to which the entire spiritual quest leads. And while the Long Book contains the germ of *A Week*'s physical climax, the ascent of the mountain, this episode is barely recognizable: "We continued up along the banks on foot—until from Merrimack it became the Pemmigewasset that leaped by our side—and after we had passed its fountain head—the wild ammonusuck became our guide to its source amid the mountains" (*PJ* 2:80). This statement, which does not even mention Agiocochook, suggests that Thoreau had not yet seen in his journey up the mountain the significance it would later have. His earlier Journal reveals even less about the event that would become so crucial for the published *Week*. In an entry for 21 June 1840 he transcribes the bare statement from his field notes: "Sept 10th [1839] ascended the mountain and rode to Conway" (*PJ* 1:137).

Scattered manuscripts from the early stages of the *Week* reveal Thoreau adding to his Journal accounts of the trip and polishing his style as he prepared lectures and his longer narrative (e.g., Pierpont Morgan Library MA 608; Houghton Library MS AM 278.5; Huntington Library HM 926, HM 956, HM 13195). These scraps do not, however, indicate what overall shape the book would take or the relations among its parts. When he wrote the first draft, Thoreau arranged passages from the Long Book and the additional drafted pieces into chapters based on days of the week. He later moved the vision of universal flow from "Monday" (*FD* 39) to "Thursday" (*W* 331), shifted the poem "Salmon Brook" from "Monday" (*FD* 45) to "Friday" (*W* 351–52), rearranged passages in the essay on friendship, and changed the order of minor pieces, but the chapters and their materials generally appear in the same order from the first to final draft.

The first draft does not contain all of the Long Book passages that eventually became part of *A Week*. One conspicuous omission is the material on Oriental literature which, as we have

seen, has aesthetic implications for the final text. Aesthetic theorizing in the first draft tends to be neoclassical, as in the discussion of mimetic painting and the laws of perspective (*FD* 20–22).
Thoreau did not include in the first draft the reflexive passages
from the Long Book that would later move the *Week* closer toward a romantic aesthetic of gaps, fragments, and disruptive epiphanies.

Thoreau did add to the first draft passages that hint of an
underlying spiritual quest. He characterized Concord as "a port
of entry and departure for human souls" (*FD* 1), indicated that
the "heavens" are the source of rivers (2), and identified his goal
at the end as "the south west horizon" (the direction of the Indian's heaven [101]). The nature of this quest remains unclear,
however, and there is as yet little connection between the voyage
and the meditations that would in the final version chart his spiritual progress. The climax of the first draft is the essay on friendship. Although that draft contains in embryo the essay on natural
life (which would become the climax of the 1849 version), Thoreau does not indicate any special significance for this essay or
its position in "Friday."

Finally, Thoreau added to the first draft the account of Agiocochook that he had drafted in his Journal (*PJ* 1:476):

> And in fair days as well as foul we walked up the
> country—until from Merrimack it became the Pemige-
> wasset that leaped by our side—and when we had
> passed its fountain-head the wild Amonoosuck whose
> puny channel we crossed at a stride guiding us to its
> distant source among the mountains until without its
> guidance we reached the summit of agiocochook.
>
> But why should we take the reader who may have
> been tenderly nurtured—through that rude country—
> where the crags are steep and the inns none of the
> best, and many a rude blast would have to be encoun-
> tered on the mountain side. (*FD* 82–83)

Though he now names the mountain, he still conveys little of
the importance this episode would have in the final version.

Almost one year after completing the first draft, Thoreau worked out in a different notebook (the Berg Journal, late August 1846) an expanded version of his walking trip to the White Mountains. He now provided some details about the hostelries and inns available to travelers, thereby reducing his earlier emphasis on the rudeness of the country and making it appear more settled and domestic. He also added references to religion and romance:

> We wandered on (by the side and over
> the brows of hoar hills and mountains —
> & through notches which the stream had
>   ~~with awe~~
> made—looking down˄one sunday morn-
> ing over Bethlehem amid the bleating
> of sheep, and hearing as we walked
> the loud spoken prayers of the inhabi-
>   ~~where every house seemd to us a holy sepulchre~~
> tants — like crusaders strolled out from
> ~~Richards as if we were~~
> the camp in Palestine—(T 74)[20]

The allusions to the birth of Christ and the crusades suggest that Thoreau was beginning to add allegorical significance to his mountain trip. The journey was beginning to take on meaning long after Thoreau completed it.

At the end of the Berg passage, Thoreau describes the view from Agiocochook:

> ~~(Like the Pilgims)~~   ~~Our way~~
>   (We) Shuddered˄through that Fran-
>   ⟨ing⟩
> conia where the thermometer is spliced

[20]Quotations from the New York Public Library Berg manuscript are taken from transcriptions made for *Journal 2: 1842–1848*, ed. Robert Sattelmeyer, of the Princeton edition of Thoreau's Writings. We have reprinted the transcribed lines because they show Thoreau's revisions, unlike *PJ* 2, which reproduces only the first level of the text. Words between ⟨ ⟩ marks were inserted in pencil, and words printed thus ~~thus~~ were lined through.

for winter use, saw the blue earth
heaved into mountain waves from Agiocochook, and where the Umbagog Ossipee
and Squam gleamed like dewy cobwebs
in the sun—And like bright ribbons the
streamlets of Connecticut Saco & adros-
coggin "take up their mountain march—
                    ~~(not knowing what to say)~~
  Went on our way, silent & humble
              ~~(at)(vast)~~   ~~(the nick of time)~~
through the Notch,—heard the lambs
bleat in Bartlett on the mountains
              ~~holding unequal parley with the wolves & bears~~
late at night—looked back on
Conway peak—threaded the woods of
Norway pine—and saw the Great
      ~~(once more)~~
Spirit smile,in Winnipiseogee (T 76–77)

Again, Thoreau suggests that the trip to the mountain is a religious journey (a pilgrimage) and that the mountain itself is a
holy place (haunt of the Great Spirit). He still does not describe
in detail his experience on the mountain, but he no longer offers
as an excuse the possibility that his readers may be too "tenderly
nurtured" to be taken along. Rather, he remains "silent and
humble" apparently because his experience on Agiocochook has
approached the ineffable ("not knowing what to say").

In September 1846, a month after the Berg passage on Agi-
ochook, Thoreau climbed Mount Katahdin. The ascent of this
smaller but wilder mountain prompted him to reevaluate once
again his 1839 trip to the White Mountains. Coming to terms
with his experience on Katahdin and writing the first of his
Maine essays spurred the evolution of *A Week*. Thoreau developed a new sense of how myth and romance could unify and
structure the meditations that, he feared, stood in *A Week* on
separate pedestals rather than taking hold of hands.

4

Early Stages Of *Walden*

WHEN THOREAU returned from Walden Pond, how much *Walden* did he bring back? The bibliographer's answer is easily found in J. Lyndon Shanley's *The Making of Walden*—all or part of a draft which covers 117 manuscript sheets (100 pages printed). This first version, or "A" stage, contains materials that eventually wound up in all chapters but the last, and, by and large, in the final order. (Thoreau did not divide the manuscript into chapters until the E stage of 1852–53.) The seasonal drift of A is clear— "Pond in Winter" is followed by "Spring," thus giving A the temporal structure common to books about nature. However, because most of the A material is concentrated in what became the first seven chapters, the sections that went into chapters 8–18 seem largely an appendix to the first half. This stage, then, suggests that the book is concerned mainly with social criticism—it offers Thoreau's program for social and spiritual reform based on leaving town for subsistence farming in nature.

Not by any standards is the first version of *Walden* a unified text. The manuscript is actually in two sections. Thoreau most likely used the first part (about half) as his lecture text—his response to his townsmen's requests that he describe his experiences (*PJ* 1:147, 149–50; see also *Wa* 3, 1:2, A,C).[1] The simplest evidence, Thoreau's numbering system for the leaves, has two starting places. The draft of what became the first chapter,

---

[1] The Journal passage may have been written before 13 March 1846; Harding's *CL* gives 10 February 1847 as the date of the first lecture about Walden Pond at Concord. In citing passages from *Walden*, we use the chapter and paragraph number from the final version and we note the draft of the manuscript, A to G. Instead of Shanley's draft numbers, we have used the letter designations from Ronald Earl Clapper's more recent and complete study of the manuscripts, "The Development of *Walden*: A Genetic Text," Ph.D. Diss., UCLA, 1967. For accuracy, we have checked both Shanley's and Clapper's versions against microfilms of the drafts (HM 924) from the Huntington Library.

"Economy," has pages numbered by Thoreau 1–51, with extra sheets that would bring the manuscript up to 65. The proportion of this draft to the rest of A is about the same as that chapter's bulk in the published book (21.7% vs. 23.6%). Presumably the lectures Thoreau gave on "The History of Myself" at the Concord Lyceum on 10 and 17 February 1847 involved a reading of (or from) the draft of "Economy" (*CL*). In the light of Shanley's comments on the first version manuscript (*S* 122–23), the two parts of the lecture may have been divided between paragraphs 59 and 60. This follows the satirical enumeration of food, shelter, and clothing. Leaf 21r (Thoreau's number 35) was originally half-filled with the fable of Momus, and 21v starts, "Near the end of March 1845 [I borrowed an axe] and went down to the woods." Some time before A, Thoreau rewrote the fable of Momus, talked about our continued ability to live in caves and wear skins, and then ended inspirationally: "With a little more wit we might use these materials so as to become richer than the richest now are, and make our civilization a blessing." This conjecture may be wrong, however, since 20v ends, "But to make haste to my own experiment," which sounds more like a transition than an ending.

A new sequence of numbering starts with the draft of "Where I Lived," paragraph 8, and goes to the end of "Spring," which Thoreau numbered page 235. A couple of sentences and two balance sheets from other chapters are in the A draft of "Economy," and material that wound up at the end of "Where I Lived" appears in "Sounds." The part of the first version that least resembles the final order comes after the sketchy draft of "Higher Laws" (ch. 11) and before "Pond in Winter" (ch. 19); the sequence is:

Ch.	12	12	17	17	15	(1)	12	12	(5)	15	15	15
Para.	?	10?	25	9	13		11	16		2	3	4

Ch.	15	17	15	(1)	15	15	(3)	14	14	14	14	14
Para.	5	12	6		14	14		10	12	13	14	15

Parentheses indicate the number of leaves whose absence is inferred from Thoreau's numbering.

The break at Shanley's page 137 probably marks the end of the text for the two lectures and the beginning of a more or less sustained narrative. Also, signs occur often on the first few leaves that Thoreau was lecturing to an audience addressed in the second person, but then these signs appear rarely until the very end (199).

The lecture material is organized and presented in what must have been familiar ways to Thoreau's Lyceum audiences, if we take Emerson's lectures as a standard. Thus, despite the claims that his would be an unusual presentation (*Wa* 105–6, 112), Thoreau's survey of the basic necessities is essentially abstract and orderly, with key-word signals to the main sections. This is not to discount Thoreau's special way of presenting the material—with humor, and with an occasional concrete reference to pin his generalizations upon. Furthermore, if we look for evidence of traditional Christian and Cynic thought in *Walden*, surely these pages give us plenty. The central idea of giving up one's possessions to leave time for contemplation is clear. But this version offers little to indicate that Thoreau's goal is a spiritual life, or a mystical vision, or any of the other themes which, for example, make "The Ponds" in the published version such a remarkable chapter. The main point explicit in Thoreau's text is that getting rid of material burdens gives him time—he does not say at length what he (or the student-reader) should do with the temporal profits.

The first section (105–10) begins with the speaker introducing himself to his audience, and then continues with a little sermon about their inadequate living. The sermon ends with a plea for faith, not the "work we do," as the preferred basis for our life. Following the rhetorical transition ("Let us consider") Thoreau lists and elaborates upon the "gross necessaries of life," or, more humorously later in the paragraph, "grossest groceries." The sections appear much as they do in the published text—food is the most elaborately told, whereas clothing and shelter give rise to more aphorisms, one-liners, and brief anecdotes. The fable of Momus (122) ends the series, and it may have been the capstone on the first lecture. In the A version, Momus gets a full paragraph, but it is mostly quoted material, so that this first sustained piece of mythological material is decorative and derivative.

"But to make haste to my own experiment" (123), an obvious transition, leads to a narrative about how the cabin was built—it includes several balance sheets and is informative, almost like a settler's account of establishing camp along one of the western trails. The tale ends with the general principle which this section illustrates (that it is possible to get more leisure), and a disclaimer that others need not adopt Thoreau's "mode of living" (133). This part of the first version concludes with an essay on being good versus doing good (a traditional Christian as well as an Emersonian theme), and finally a piece of quoted Persian mythology that Shanley guesses might be appropriately placed here (136, n. 29).

The new series of Thoreau's page numbers begins "When I first went to the pond" (137) and goes through to the end. The style and language seem to change subtly. Where the lectures, like the final version of "Economy," are reasonably straight social criticism with a bit of irony, the later material includes more frequent metaphors and purple patches, as in the elegant description of the house which starts this section—with its balanced phrases and adjectives carefully chosen for their rhythm as much as their content (137–38). The narrator's response to the social ills outlined before is to renounce his inherited time and place for a savored cottage life. This poetic passage includes some now famous lines ("I went down to the pond because I wished to live deliberately" and "Simplicity—Simplicity—Simplicity," [141]). It ends with the final paragraph from what became chapter 2 ("Time is but the stream I go a fishing in"), which celebrates a search for eternity, and then a poem, not in the final text, which celebrates the present (143–45). The shift is striking from such general topics as food, shelter, and clothing to this personal essay with no obvious social dimension.

The next part of the manuscript is a series of brief essays—on books (145–54), on reality (154–57), on sounds (157–63), on solitude (163–76). These pages, as Shanley notes, are clear prototypes for chapters 3 to 5, but they are considerably shorter and seem to be anecdotal and fragmented. It is difficult to believe that they were used for a lecture; instead they resemble Thoreau's more sustained Journal entries.

"Meanwhile my beans," the first sentence of chapter 7, picks

up the now slender thread of the narrative. "What was the meaning of this so steady and self respecting ["this small Herculean,"
in the final version] labor I knew not" reflects a plausible bewil-
derment on Thoreau's part and probably on the reader's as well.
The prototype of "The Bean-Field" (177–84) involves a stylistic
return to the lecture text, and presumably was the core of Thoreau's third Walden lecture, "White Beans and Walden Pond,"
first delivered in 1848–49.

The narrative of bean farming (177–82) begins as a rather
straightforward account of the busy work. It is marked, explicitly,
as a summer experience (181), and thus sets up the seasonal
structure of the final third of this version. Farming is valuable
first for its rhetorical dimension—"some must work in fields if
only for the sake of topics & expressions—to serve a parable-
maker—one day" (181). At the end of this section Thoreau
quotes and amplifies classical texts on agriculture, but the mer-
est paraphrase of those passages remains in the final version of
this chapter. Later drafts of this passage illustrate how "hus-
bandry was once a sacred art" (165, 7:16, E), but the 1846 version of *Walden* does not yet expropriate the old myths.

The passages later included in "Ponds" (186–88) represent
but a small part of that chapter, even when four missing leaves
are taken into account. As we will show in our later chapter on
Walden, and as Anderson has argued persuasively,[2] "The Ponds"
is the central presentation of Thoreau's mystical vision. Here, the
passages continue the account of Thoreau's typical and habitual
practices, as indicated by the paragraphs which begin with time
markers, "Sometimes," "Occasionally."

A transition, interlined after A, leads to a series of animal anecdotes that dominate the end of this draft. An inner voice provides the link: "my Genius said—grow wild according to thy
nature" (189). This passage, later to appear in "Baker Farm," is
one of two or so places in *Walden* where Thoreau uses the intimate second-person pronoun to heighten the language.[3] In this

---

[2] Charles Anderson, *The Magic Circle of Walden* (New York: Holt,
Rinehart and Winston, 1968).

[3] See also "Solitude" (*Wa* 138, 5:17, A), in the poetic paragraph about
"The indescribable innocence & beneficence of nature." Other uses of

draft, the pronoun is used but twice, while the final version has eleven instances in the narrator's extended exhortation to himself.

As noted, the animals mark the seasons: fall (193), frost (198), through the melting ice and "tender signs of the infant year" (203). After many pages, we finally get a specific time marker, "On the 13th of March [1847]." The whole of this section of the first version is a naturalist's elegant account of the New England seasons. It has no well-defined theme beyond the traditional one of nature's renewal. It has no obvious connections with the social criticism in the lecture texts or the drafts for what would become chapters 3 to 8, where animals concern the narrator only when they became pests to dog his farming enterprise.

The narrator concludes that "village life would stagnate . . . if it were not for the unexplored forests and meadows which surround it" (207). Nature is presented as having "inexhaustible vigor, vast features and titanic," and it clearly shows us our limits—shipwrecks, decaying trees, three-week rain storms, the dead horse in his path, and toads run over by wagons. This grim series, illustrative of "universal innocence," finally ends with a brief paragraph, placed in early May, when the trees bud and the birds return—"the seasons went rolling on into summer as one rambles into higher & higher grass—" (207–08), and so the first year in the woods is completed.

In addition to the structural problem of a manuscript on quite different topics, the first version does not yet have the semantic networks that turned occasional ideas into developed, sustained themes.[4] It is clear from a study of revisions and of the many passages Thoreau added that thematic unity and development came later in the growth of the manuscript.

After the first stage Thoreau seems to have laid the manuscript aside. In September 1847 he returned from his two years at the Walden outpost to live in domestic tranquility with Mrs. Emer-

---

"thee," "thy," and "thou" are in quoted passages, except for Thoreau's "Icarian bird" poem.

[4]Donald Ross, "The Style of Thoreau's *Walden*," Ph.D. Diss., Michigan, 1967, esp. ch. 2.

son. His second draft of *A Week* was circulating among publishers; the fourth rejection notice arrived in November. While at the Emersons', he seems to have worked little on *Walden*; few interlined passages appear in the A stage. Presumably, helping Mrs. Emerson run a household that must have seemed infinitely busier than the cabin took much of Thoreau's time, and he was occupied by other projects. At the start of his stay he worked up materials from his Maine trip into the "Ktaadn" lecture, and he entered into the political debates about the election of 1848 with the speech "Resistance to Civil Government." Both lectures were given in January 1848. He then further revised *A Week*, essentially completing it a couple of months after leaving the Emersons in July 1848, though he continued to add to it Journal entries during that fall and winter.

When he did return to the *Walden* manuscript, Thoreau did not attempt a radical revision. The next two stages help fill out the early chapters, but they do not significantly alter the direction of the first stage. Possibly Thoreau began the B stage of *Walden* to organize materials for the 1848–49 winter lecture season, especially to add "White Beans and Walden Pond" to his repertoire. The amount of transcribing from A into B (with stylistic improvements) and the special clarity of the handwriting in B suggest that B started out as a fair copy. Because most of the changes from "lecture" and "hearers" to "book" and "readers" do not appear until they were interlined in B and C, the copy was presumably for Thoreau's personal convenience as a lecturer. He talked on "Student Life in New England, its Economy" at Salem (22 November 1848) and Gloucester (20 December, also a Wednesday); he returned to Salem on 28 February 1849 for a sequel called "Life in the Woods," which he also gave in Portland, Maine, in March 1849; at Concord he delivered "White Beans and Walden Pond" on 3 January 1849; and Worcester may have received the "full treatment" in April—"Life in the Woods" on the twentieth, the same or a sequel on the twenty-seventh, and "Beans" also in April.[5]

[5]*CL* 81–82; Philip Van Doren Stern, *The Annotated Walden* (New York: Clarkson N. Potter, 1970), p. 78; Hubert H. Hoeltje, "Thoreau as Lecturer," *New England Quarterly* 19 (1946):485–90; *DHT* 242.

Figure 2: Stages in the growth of Walden

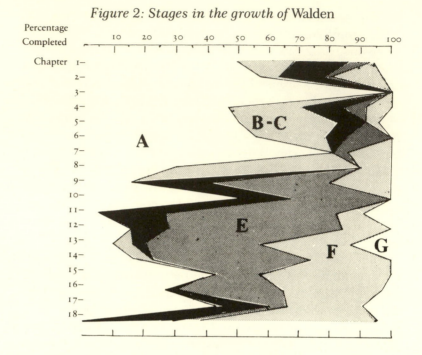

Figure 2 shows graphically how each of the stages added to the shape of the book:

The figure's vertical axis shows the eighteen chapters, and the horizontal axis gives the percentage of material present at each stage of the manuscript.

Quite understandably, Thoreau lost interest in making a complete fair copy of A, and may have picked sheets for legibility; obviously he copied some so that transcribed passages would end up at the same place on a page. While no physical evidence exists, we assume that he kept a pile of manuscript pages which represented the current "stage" of *Walden*. We conjecture that he took only the appropriate sheets when he lectured out of them, since the working pile must have been one hundred fifty leaves long. As he recopied and revised for style, he must have put the superseded pages aside in another pile; it seems unlikely that he would have added to the confusion by keeping new material and rejects together. One curiosity in the writing process

is why Thoreau did not throw pages away once they were transcribed (Shanley and Clapper catalogue relatively few missing
leaves). We know of colleagues who do exactly as Thoreau did;
they keep copies of all drafts of an article, at least until it is published. As Elizabeth Witherell points out, "The process of construction must have involved much shifting of papers as well as
recopying. In fact, pinholes and cuts throughout the manuscript
indicate that leaves now assigned to separate versions must have
been combined at earlier stages of the work."[6] Identifying a passage as having been in one of the seven stages tells us when it
appears in a working draft, even though we may never be able to
reconstruct fully what that draft contained at any particular
time.

Also, we cannot know for sure what Thoreau discarded or
what has been lost. In tracing the evolution of *Walden*, we must
use the available evidence while remaining aware of its short-
comings. Theoretically, it is possible that Thoreau drafted nearly
all of the complete *Walden* soon after he began work on it—that
crucial leaves from the second half of the book existed from the
start but are now lost. However, the surviving evidence suggests
that such was not the case. Instead, as we argue in chapter 10,
Walden changed significantly over the eight years of its writing,
with most of the important changes occurring after 1852. First,
much of the *Walden* manuscript does appear to have survived.
From Thoreau's own pagination we can tell where gaps occur
and roughly how many leaves are missing. As Shanley argues,
"Thoreau may have destroyed or discarded some of them as they
became useless because of revisions; the greatest losses occur at
points where he revised his work most radically. . . . Only in the
last half of *Walden* in II and III is there any remarkable lack of
manuscript, and I think this is owing primarily not to a loss of
manuscript leaves but to the fact that Thoreau probably did not
do much revision there" (S 14). Second, many of the crucial additions derive from Thoreau's Journals from 1852 to 1854. No
other possibly earlier source for this material has come to light.

One way to measure how Thoreau's book grew is to note how

[6]Personal communication, 1 June 1980.

Table 1:   Ratios of New to Copied Passages

Version	All Chapters		"Economy" Removed	
	No. of passages	Ratio of first draft copied	No. of passages	Ratio of first draft copied
B	185	.38 to 1	93	.58 to 1
C	89	.35	20	.18
D	139	1.98	61	2.81
E	205	1.38	180	1.40
F	186	.84	183	.83
G	78	.44	57	.27

much of each stage is new material and how much was recopied. For example, the D version in surviving sheets had 119 paragraphs or significantly long parts of paragraphs. Of these 40 were copied, while the rest appear for the first time in the *Walden* manuscript (even though they may have been drafted first in the Journals). The ratios of first drafts to transcribed passages for each stage after A (all first draft, naturally) appear in table 1. Since the ratios change significantly when material from "Economy" is removed, those data are also shown.

The table indicates that the B and C stages have the smallest proportion of new material, although the amount of transcription for "Economy" into B is pronounced. Shanley remarks that these stages "almost seem one piece; . . . the pagination of the two versions runs in one series" (*S* 28). Thoreau worked on them from summer 1848 until (presumably) his trip to Cape Cod in October 1849. *A Week* was published in June 1849,[7] which may mark the point when Thoreau stopped the relatively neat copying of B and started C.

The B and C stages do add new paragraphs and pieces that advance several of the early chapters toward completion. As shown in figure 2, these stages add significantly to chapters 1, 4, 5, 6, and 8, which were all about three-quarters complete by

[7]Thoreau planned to release *Walden* soon after, as indicated by the notice at the end of *A Week* that *Walden* would "soon be published" (James Playstead Wood, "Mr. Thoreau Writes a Book," *New Colophon* 1 [1948]:376).

the 1849 Cape Cod trip. We conclude that the C stage fulfilled the original premise of *Walden*: namely, that Thoreau would justify his leaving "civilized life" (*Wa* 3, 1:1, C) in the mock-serious economic terms of "Economy," and then that he would give enough information about his life at the pond for a moderately tolerant reader to see that his experiment in deliberate living had succeeded.

Thoreau's revisions in these stages are important because they show that he stopped thinking of his manuscript as a text for lectures and began to call it a book. Among other changes, he canceled references to "hearers" and "audience," and interlined mention of "readers," "book," and "pages" in 1:2, 1:3, 1:7, 1:22, 1:25, and 1:80; in 1:76 and 2:22 he canceled references to Salem, Portland, and Worcester that he had included for lectures at those places. He also adjusted his narrative to gave it a past perspective. For example, 1:96 in A and B starts, "*At present* I *maintain* myself solely by the labor of my hands" (emphasis added). In C, the time marker is definite past, and verb tense shifts: "*For more than five years* I *maintained* myself solely by the labor" (emphasis added).[8] Not only did Thoreau consider *Walden* a book by this stage, but he started to prepare it for publication. Instances of his penciled instructions to a printer appear in B and C. For example, on the last leaf in folder C of HM 924, Thoreau requests "2 white lines" after the draft of one paragraph.

At the end of fragmentary Journal "I" (winter 1846–47 to spring 1848), we find an interesting confluence of Thoreau's first three books (*PJ* 2:379–85). The leaves present, nearly intact, the dialogue between the Hermit and Poet from *Walden*, chapter 12 (paragraphs 2 to 7). Aside from several changes in phrasing, only two sentences are not in this draft. The dialogue first appeared in the E version of *Walden*.[9] Immediately following is part of an essay on friendship and on the need to sustain that state through

---

[8] Clapper, p. 224. The exact time of the shifts is indeterminate, since both A and B have "i.e., when this was written" interlined after "At present." The changes to the past tense are interlined in B. We cannot guess which five years Thoreau means.

[9] Clapper has 12:2 and 12:3 in E; 12:4 and 12:5 as not being in the MS; 12:5b, and 12:6 and 12:7 in E. The pieces missing from E were

silence—passages later added to the "Wednesday" chapter of *A Week* (*W* 289). The next section is a piece from *A Week* on the relation between ancient history and biography and what we call mythology, with the notion that contemporary tales can also become myths by long retelling (*W* 60); it ends, "The most comprehensive most pithy & significant book is the mythology" (no punctuation). This is followed directly by a long description of the melting bankside, which eventually wound up in "Spring" of *Walden*. Thoreau, even in 1847 or 1848, takes the physical details to their full metaphorical and fanciful extremes—the rivulets of sand are like lava or like vines, "obeying half way the law of currents & half way the law of vegetation . . . some mythological vegetation," and so on. The conclusion, while not so dramatic as "There is nothing inorganic," does stress the analogies ("So the stream is but a leaf") and it ends with the bizarre link between the formation of human fingers and the melting bankside. The final part of the passage is from "Ktaadn" (paragraph 46; not in the Maine section of the Berg Journal)—this time we get the bulk of the paragraph and the lead line from paragraph 47. (The lead appears in Berg 591 [*PJ* 2:321] with the full paragraph.) The *Walden* passage and *The Maine Woods* paragraph are totally interlined with each other. In Thoreau's manuscript the *Walden* lines are crossed out.

Journal "I" shows Thoreau working simultaneously on all three books; this is quite conscious for the "Ktaadn" paragraph where the pointer to the rest of the draft is clear. Sentences from the notebook were added to the essay on friendship already in the first draft of *A Week*; the section on mythology became part of the crucial revisions of the first draft that gave *A Week* new direction and meaning (see our ch. 6). The *Walden* passages did not get into the working draft of that book until the E version for the dialogue and the F version for the bankside.[10]

---

probably present when Thoreau transcribed the whole section from his Journal in 1852.

[10] See *S* 204, where Shanley says "Compare 6." The passage in the A version, only a few sentences, is probably an early version, since it merely sketches out the argument and the imagery. It is not clear that

In chapter 10 we will explore the implications of these crucial stages. Briefly, we maintain that the *Walden* project remained fallow for over two years. Then Thoreau's conversion to romanticism in 1851–52 provided the emotional impetus, sharper focus, and program of aesthetic experimentation that prompted him to complete the work. He clarified what were to become the related concerns of the book and evolved a narrative that would better shape it. In the first half, his narrative persona leaves society to seek an authentic life; imagination provides the direct apprehension of nature's divine essence that climaxes this initial quest. In the second half, which Thoreau revised most radically, the narrator assumes the role of poet and mythmaker recommitted to the world and seeking unity and order behind the apparent chaos of experience—a quest that leads to his discovery of organicism. Thoreau's experiments with a romantic aesthetic of suggestiveness and multisignificance would finally give the completed *Walden* its rich complexity.

Thoreau wrote one as a second draft of the other—they might be independent treatments of the same topic.

5

"Ktaadn": "The Main Astonishment at Last"

THOREAU TOOK a vacation from his life at Walden (itself a serious kind of vacation) with a trip to Maine in early September 1846. The first record of that trip (in the Berg Journal) consists of brief field notes or transcriptions of field notes. Thoreau simply outlines his journey, jotting down names and places under the appropriate dates; for example: "to base of high peak. burnt land poplars ~~moo~~ blueberries   thick woods moose dung bear dung rabbits dung—moose tracks browsing" (T 85 for 7 Sept).[1] The outline ends with a brief list of dates for other expeditions to Katahdin. Next come six pages of draft passages that would later appear in various sections of the completed essay. The drafting at first is fairly smooth, fluid, and confident, with few insertions and cancellations. But then the manuscript gives way to many interlinings and false starts. The special care Thoreau gave to this particular section suggests its importance to him and to "Ktaadn." The new section begins:

> It is difficult to conceive
> ~~region~~
> of an country uninhabited by man
> ~~habitually presume his   exaggerate his influence~~
> we naturally suppose them on

[1] Quotations from Thoreau's contemporaneous account of his first trip to Maine are taken from transcriptions made for *Journal 2: 1842–1848,* ed. Robert Sattelmeyer, of the Princeton edition of Thoreau's *Writings.* The passages are from a Journal in the Berg Library; we have reprinted the lines as they appear in the transcripts, rather than *PJ* 2, to show the changes Thoreau made. Words between ⟨ ⟩ marks were inserted in pencil, and words printed thus ~~thus~~ were lined through. No intervening stages of "Ktaadn" survive between the Berg Journal draft and the essay that appeared serially in *Sartain's Union Magazine* (1848).

~~presence &~~
the horizon everywhere—And yet
pure
we have not seen‸nature unless
we have once seen her thus vast
whether in the wilderness or
and grim and drear—~~for to be~~
~~vast though~~ in the midst of
⟨but⟩
cities—for to be Vast is how near
to being waste.
  Coming down the Mt perhaps
I first ~~most~~ fully realized that
⟨untamed primeval⟩
that this was unhanselled and ancient
~~or whater else men call it~~
Demonic Nature, *natura*,~~or~~
⟨name man has best applied⟩ ~~while coming~~
⟨s⟩   ~~down the Mt.~~
whatever man has named it.
⟨Titanic⟩
 The nature primitive—powerful
⟨yet⟩
gigantic aweful and‸beautiful,
Untamed forever. We were passing
~~burnt by lightning perchance~~
over burnt lands‸with occasional
strips of timber crossing it. (T 89–90)

The reader who is familiar with the "Ktaadn" essay will recognize this outburst, in a slightly tamer version, as the passage on the "Burnt Lands," which follows Thoreau's solitary climb to the peak of the mountain (*MW* 69–71). In its final place, the segment picks up a major theme of the essay—the disjunction of man from nature. For the first two thirds of the narrative we see Thoreau's typical posture of regretting that nature is gradually being taken over by human institutions. After his traumatic climb to the summit, Thoreau's narrative persona realizes with a shock that nature may well have the ultimate control, but that such control is not comforting and benign—it is frightening. The Berg Journal passage ends, "The main astonishment at last is that man has brought so little change—And yet man so overtops nature in his estimation" (T 91).

 Did Thoreau ever recover from his ascent of Ktaadn?

Leo Stoller argues that after Thoreau's experience on the mountain, "the universe pantheistically informed with a benign godhead had suddenly dissociated into its parts. For the rest of his life he was to strive in vain to reunite them."[2] In the context of his entire career, however, the mountain excursion seems not to have affected Thoreau so radically or permanently. His experience of alien, hostile nature on Mount Katahdin did not prevent him from making subsequent mountain excursions or from expressing diverse and sometimes contradictory views of nature. During and after composition of "Ktaadn" (completed autumn 1847), he also worked on *A Week* and *Walden*, which portray a nature more benign and closer to man. Ahead of him, especially, lay his intense personal commitment to a Transcendental worldview in 1851–52 (a spiritual rebirth that gave new significance to attitudes Thoreau had long been familiar with) and his celebration (in the expanded "Ponds" section of *Walden*) of the divine essence of nature and man's ability to live close to nature.

The experience on Katahdin apparently did, however, prompt Thoreau to reevaluate his position—to test his inherited assumptions against his own experience. And his attempt to recreate that experience in writing led him to experiment with what he calls in the Berg Journal "the truth of mythology" (*PJ* 2:279) and with the role myth can play in shaping narrative. He also moves closer to the romantic travel writing that dramatizes a narrative persona's discovering meaning in the process of a journey.

[2] *After Walden* (Stanford: Stanford Univ. Press, 1957), p. 47. We find more convincing the treatment of "Ktaadn" by Jonathan Fairbanks, "Thoreau: Speaker for Wildness," *South Atlantic Quarterly* 70 (1971):487–506; James McIntosh, *Thoreau as Romantic Naturalist: His Shifting Stance toward Nature* (Ithaca: Cornell Univ. Press, 1974), pp. 179–215; and Frederick Garber, *Thoreau's Redemptive Imagination* (New York: New York Univ. Press, 1977), pp. 75–101. Other important criticism includes Paul, *The Shores of America*, pp. 358–62; Lewis Leary, "Beyond the Brink of Fear: Thoreau's Wilderness," *Studies in the Literary Imagination* 7 (1974):67–76; Robert F. Sayre, *Thoreau and the American Indian* (Princeton: Princeton Univ. Press, 1977), pp. 159–66; Howarth, *The Book of Concord*, pp. 44–46; and Richard Lebeaux, *Thoreau's Seasons* (Amherst: Univ. of Massachusetts Press, 1984), pp. 49–58.

While it seems simplistic and misleading, then, to assume that Thoreau never recovered from his trip to Katahdin, what about recovery within the "Ktaadn" essay itself? McIntosh, Garber, and Howarth claim that by the end of the essay Thoreau regains his equilibrium after his alienating confrontation with intractable matter.[3] But their accounts ignore what seems an important change after the narrative of the ascent (*MW* 56–65) and the major passage on the Burnt Lands (69–71). *Before* climbing Katahdin, Thoreau stresses evidence of civilization in the wilderness and looks forward to a time when all of Maine (and by extension, all of America) will be cleared and settled by man. After his encounter with "hard matter" (71), however, he looks backward in time and emphasizes wildness. Though his journey is circular, he neither returns spiritually to his starting point nor recovers the state of mind with which he began. Rather, we hope to show that, within "Ktaadn," Thoreau's confrontation with alien nature changes his perceptions of man's relation to the wilderness: nature suddenly assumes and maintains mastery. New approaches to mythology and to fire signal this reversal at the center of the excursion.

From the first paragraph of "Ktaadn," and periodically thereafter, Thoreau reminds us that he is traveling to a "primitive forest" (*MW* 4), "unnamed and unincorporated wilderness" (8). Yet up to the Burnt Lands passage, he focuses on the evidence of man's civilizing drive into the wild, particularly on the lumbering operations that, he foresees, will eventually level the Maine woods. The first sentence of "Ktaadn" calls attention to "the lumber trade" (3) and references to sawmills frame the essay. Thoreau's narrative starts with mills "by which the Maine woods are converted into lumber" (4) and concludes with reference to "the

---

[3] McIntosh suggests that Thoreau regains his balance by "forgetting" his encounter with nature as impersonal chaos and returning to nature as growth (pp. 207–15). After noting the unfortunate passage on "blissful, innocent Nature," Garber insists that "in the following paragraphs, however, Thoreau recovers completely. . . . At the end of the essay the accustomed modes of organization show that they can indeed work with complete success" (p. 94). Howarth claims that "moving downstream, [Thoreau's] party gradually regains its confidence" (p. 46).

confused din and clink of a hundred saws which never rest" (79). On the way to Katahdin, he dwells frequently on other aspects of lumbering: supply stores, camping grounds, areas culled of white pines, portages marked by lumbermen's spikes, techniques for hauling equipment into the woods and lumber out. All this attention emphasizes the considerable human energy and ingenuity pitted against woods destined to fall: "the mission of men there seems to be, like so many busy demons, to drive the forest all out of the country, from every solitary beaver swamp, and mountain side, as soon as possible" (5).

Thoreau and his companions went from the large mill towns to the woods that feed them. Constantly he reminds us of the evidence of man in the landscape. After Bangor he passes through Stillwater and Oldtown (4) to Lincoln, "quite a village" (9), and finds a spacious public house at Molunkus (12). Before leaving the road, he visits a small store (13) and a clearing being burned (14). Even though off the road, Thoreau has not yet left civilization behind. He passes, among other settlements, Mattaseunk's mill with it wooden railroad (17), the extensive clearings of Waite and McCauslin (21), Thomas Fowler's cabin (27), and Old Fowler's, the last inhabited house, although Gibson's clearing still lies above (29).

He playfully sets up a series by which each presumably last sign of humanity is followed shortly by another last sign. Thus, even beyond the settlements, civilization persists. Quakish Lake shows "no traces of man but some low boom in a distant cove, reserved for spring use" (33), a sentence that emphasizes by its structure the one significant trace of man found there. The loggers' camp at the dam above Quakish "was the last habitation of any kind in this direction" (35), but the white pines had already been culled out around North Twin Lake and "the lake lay open to the light with even a civilized aspect, as if expecting trade and commerce, and towns and villas" (36). Thoreau still keeps coming upon further evidence of logging: camping grounds (39, 45), "'fencing stuff' . . . for spring use" (41–42), "a whole brick" (45),[4] a pork barrel (46), paths cut through the woods (47), "a large

---

[4] The Berg prototype adds that it would be "rather cumbersome in climbing mountains" if they lugged a brick along as "simple evidence of

flaming Oak Hall hand-bill" (50), rocks "covered with the dents made by the spikes in the lumberers' boots." (51), logs marked with their owners' symbols (52), and fishing poles on the shore a dozen miles from the summit of Katahdin (53).

Garber argues that "as they went on he and his companions looked nervously for instances of the human or the domesticated, dwelling on them and turning them over and around as though reluctant to let them go by."[5] But perhaps Thoreau emphasizes the human presence because it is, indeed, inescapable. He finds considerable evidence of man's advance north and anticipates (before encountering the Burnt Lands) the inevitable progress of civilization.

Even when he ascends Mount Katahdin without "the slightest trace of man to guide us further in this direction," he remains conscious of "our predecessors" on the climb (56), and he speaks of numerous moose "being driven into this wilderness from all sides by the settlements" (57). Here, finally, is a last refuge. He is struck by the wildness of the country to the west and south: "No clearing, no house. It did not look as if a solitary traveller had cut so much as a walking-stick there." And yet he frames this observation with assurances that even this area will eventually be civilized: "When the country is settled and roads are made, these cranberries will perhaps become an article of commerce," he says, and "it was a large farm for somebody, when cleared" (66).

However, the ascent of Katahdin does mark a shift in Thoreau's perception of man in nature—a shift registered by his changing treatment of myth. Earlier he used myth decoratively, as with his casual allusion to "the Argo . . . passing through the Symplegades" (32), or humorously, as when he asked Louis Neptune "if he thought Pomola would let us go up" Katahdin (10),[6]

---

civilization." The Journal passage ends, "Go where you will somebody has been there before you" (*PJ* 2:320).

[5] Garber, 78.

[6] "Neptune" calls to mind Western rather than Indian myth and first hints that this Indian will not be the noble savage that Thoreau hoped would guide him through the wild. No "child of nature," Neptune turns out to represent the "degraded savage" (*MW* 78).

or, ironically, as when he alludes to Orpheus in a passage celebrating beer "which would acclimate and naturalize a man at
once" (28—cf. Thoreau's alienation from nature on the mountain). The light, superficial treatment of myth suits the fairly
conventional travel piece that "Ktaadn" has been up to this point.
At the start Thoreau places his essay in the tradition of works
written by men who "have made the excursion and told their
stories" (4). Twice he singles out a specialized audience for his
account—people "who may have occasion to travel this way"
(18) and "future tourists" (46). With the ascent of the mountain,
conventional travel gives way to a Promethian quest for the secrets of nature, and Thoreau mythologizes more extensively and
seriously. The mythic elements transform his individual adventures into something significant and universal—as he suggests
shortly before his account of the climb: "all history, indeed, put
to a terrestrial use, is mere history; but put to a celestial, is mythology always" (54).

He signals the change in his narrative by providing a sacramental frame for the episode; it starts with a kind of communion,
"a wafer of hard bread, and a dipper of condensed cloud or water-
spout" (62), and ends with "the continual bathing of our bodies
in mountain water" which miraculously leaves their clothes soon
dry (68). The travelers are baptized into a new world. As in *A
Week* and *Walden*, Thoreau turns himself into a mythic hero. He
now sets himself apart from the others of the "invalid party" (47)
as a superior mountaineer—the best judge of distances and the
leader by reason of his experience as "the oldest mountain-
climber" (56). On both their days in the mountains, he leaves
the others behind, traveling up two peaks alone when his companions weary (60), get "on the sick list" (62), or pick berries (66).

Tapping Milton's adaptation of Christian myth, he compares
himself with Satan struggling through Chaos (60; cf. 64 and
70—Satan appears here not as Milton's villain but as the archetypal rebel and adventurer that the romantics pictured). He engages in some mythmaking of his own when he ironically
metamorphoses rocks into "flocks and herds that pastured,
chewing a rocky cud at sunset" (61), a passage that emphasizes

the distance between the nature in pastoral fantasy and the nature he discovers on the barren mountain. The terrain reminds him "of the creations of the old epic and dramatic poets," especially of Aeschylus' setting for *Prometheus Bound*: "It was vast, Titanic, and such as man never inhabits" (64).[7] Thoreau himself becomes a kind of Prometheus, isolated from his mortal traveling companions, rebellious, defiant, struggling against a hostile environment. As Aeschylus' Prometheus is the champion of man and the archetypal civilizer, Thoreau on the mountain is quite explicit in representing himself as a special being amid alien nature—"Such was Caucasus and the rock where Prometheus was bound" (64). The setting seems vastly different from the forests that he previously saw as being threatened by civilization. Now "inhuman Nature" takes control and singles Thoreau out for mountaintop revelations, couched in archaic, biblical syntax: "I have never made this soil for thy feet, this air for thy breathing, these rocks for thy neighbors. . . . Shouldst thou freeze or starve, or shudder thy life away, here is no shrine, nor altar, nor any access to my ear" (64). Thoreau alludes again to Indian myth, this time more seriously, when he includes himself among the "daring and insolent men" who alone trespass on sacred mountains: "Pomola is always angry with those who climb to the summit of Ktaadn." Finally, the defiant, overreaching Thoreau is "compelled to descend" (65). He finds his companions gathering berries in a province of nature where domestication is possible.

Not until he arrives at the Burnt Lands is Thoreau completely awed by "a region uninhabited by man . . . vast, and drear, and inhuman" (70, a reworking of the draft passage quoted earlier). The impression alienates him from his own body, which he refers

[7] Thoreau's translation of *Prometheus Bound* appeared in the January 1843 *Dial.* He was probably familiar with other versions of the Prometheus myth, too, from works such as Lempriére's *Classical Dictionary* and Alexander Ross's *Mystagogus Poeticus, or The Muses Interpreter*; see Ethel Seybold, *Thoreau: The Quest and the Classics* (New Haven: Yale Univ. Press, 1951), pp. 26, 59. For a different treatment of mythology in "Ktaadn," see Robert D. Richardson, Jr., *Myth and Literature in the American Renaissance* (Bloomington: Indiana Univ. Press, 1978), pp. 105–17.

to as a "Titan," thus linking it with the "Titanic" mountaintop (64). Mystified by "our life in nature," he puzzles over the split between spirit and matter and he desperately questions human identity: "*Contact! Contact! Who* are we? *where* are we?" (71). The Burnt Lands challenge his earlier belief that civilization would prevail. After this climactic section Thoreau eliminates most references to human mastery of nature and concentrates instead on savagery and awe, vastness and terror (70). He reports a clearing a mile farther up the river, but it contains only "a deserted log hut" and his party's supplies are dangerously low (72). On the return journey, he no longer points to signs of man. He even violates the chronology of the trip to emphasize evidence of civilization on the way up and suppress it on the way down the river. Before his account of ascending Katahdin, he mentions an incident from the trip back: "I remember that I was strangely affected when we were returning, by the sight of a ring-bolt well drilled into a rock, and fastened with lead, at the head of this solitary Ambejijis Lake" (42). His sense of time shifts, too. On the mountain he saw rocks as "raw materials of a planet dropped from an unseen quarry, which the vast chemistry of nature would anon work up, or work down, into the smiling and verdant plains and valleys of earth" (63). Yet coming through the Burnt Lands, he admits, "I most fully realized that this was primeval, untamed, and forever untameable *Nature*" (69). And where before he looked to the future civilizing of the Maine woods, now he sees in those woods "the primitive age of the world . . . three thousand years deep into time." Imaginatively he travels "further back into history than this" to glimpse "the red face of man" (79).

Our examination of the Berg manuscript bears out Robert C. Cosbey's conclusion that Thoreau revised "Ktaadn" to emphasize wildness.[8] Thoreau dropped from his notes for the piece many passages concerning more civilized parts of Maine (e.g., those about the voyage to Portland and the Canadian's "fandango" swing), and he added numerous descriptive phrases that empha-

[8] "Thoreau at Work: The Writing of 'Ktaadn,'" *Bulletin of the New York Public Library* 65 (1961):21–30.

sized the wildness of the Maine woods. Howarth sees an opposite movement in the published version. He cites the passage about taming the waters as evidence of Thoreau's regaining his confidence,[9] but this paragraph suggests to us a different reading. "*After* such a voyage," Thoreau writes, "the troubled and angry waters, which once had seemed terrible and not to be trifled with, appeared tamed and subdued" (77; emphasis added). His point here may well be that people tend to distort their experience when looking back on it from a safer position, especially when that experience is unpleasant or unflattering to them (which seems to be Stephen Crane's message, also, at the end of "The Open Boat"). Thoreau's rapid change of perspective seems comic and intentionally ironic; in one paragraph he pictures his boat as "a bait bobbing for some river monster amid the eddies" (76), and in the next he speaks of those eddies with exaggerated contempt: "they had been bearded and worried in their channels, pricked and whipped into submission with the spike-pole and paddle, gone through and through with impunity, and all their spirit and their danger taken out of them, and the most swollen and impetuous rivers seemed but playthings henceforth" (77). He seems here to be self-consciously cheering himself up.

Thoreau's changing attitude toward man and wild nature is also evident in the important fire imagery throughout "Ktaadn." At first, fire betokens human civilization, particularly the clearing of the Maine woods. Thoreau contemplates white pines "sold, perchance to the New England Friction Match Company" (5). He details how wooded areas are repeatedly burned to make clearings (14) and he foresees that "the whole of that solid and interminable forest is doomed to be gradually devoured thus by fire" (17). He notes fires at the various settlements, including "huge fires" at the logging camps (19) and frequent forest blazes caused by lumberers, who "rarely trouble themselves to put out their fires" (41). Thoreau feels ambivalent about fire. A campfire provides "cheerfulness" and "the main comfort of a camp," but it burns the party's tent (39) and creates "grotesque and fiendlike forms and motions" when one stirs it up at midnight (40). Fire

[9] Howarth, p. 46.

is a "good citizen of the world," and yet when it ignites a fir tree, one of the group "sprang up, with a cry, from his bed, thinking the world on fire, and drew the whole camp after him" (62). These images of fiends and apocalyptic destruction revive the opening vision of men as "busy demons" driving the forests out of the country (5).

At the top of Mount Katahdin actual fires are replaced by metaphoric ones. Thoreau observes, "It was like sitting in a chimney and waiting for the smoke to blow away" (63–64), yet the smoke is really cloud vapor;[10] the barren mountain offers no combustible material to keep men warm. Leaving the cheery campfire behind, Thoreau has climbed toward "solid cold" (61). The rocky mountaintop reminds him "of Atlas, Vulcan, the Cyclops, and Prometheus" (64)—mythical figures associated with both mountains and fire. Again, Prometheus, the civilizer, is the most important. The rebel, who, according to one version of the myth, animated the first man and woman with fire he stole from heaven contrasts with "inhuman Nature" on Katahdin, which catches man alone "and pilfers him of some of his divine faculty" (64). Nature takes back some of the spark that Prometheus gave (perhaps Thoreau is playing on Pro-metheus—"forethought"— when he notes his own loss "of substantial thought and fair understanding" [64]). Thoreau does not thereafter mention seeing campfires or intentionally burned clearings. Instead he encounters the Burnt Lands, much more extensive than the clearings made by man. This territory was devastated by a natural force, lightning—"man was not to be associated with it."[11] Fire now changes from being an instrument of man to another sign of "vast, and drear, and inhuman" nature (70).

[10] The "smoke" prevents Thoreau from ever seeing clearly or completely the top of Katahdin (21, 33, 63, 65, 67). The mountain remains, then, at least partially a theoretical construct, a projection of Thoreau's own obsessions and fears.

[11] When he suggests that this area was "burnt by lightning, perchance" (70), Thoreau might again be alluding to the Prometheus myth. In *Prometheus Bound*, Zeus threatens to destroy Prometheus with lightning.

The six-paragraph peroration of "Ktaadn" best indicates Thoreau's changed vision. On the trip up the river he emphasized the clearings and evidence of human activity; back in Massachusetts he remembers most "the continuousness of the forest" (80). At first he spoke of "the Indian's history" as "the history of his extinction" with the advance of white civilization (6); he insists at the end that "the aborigines have never been dispossessed, nor nature disforested" (80) and that "the Indian still hunts" (82). He earlier saw the lumber and milling operations as a gigantic "steel riddle" through which the Maine forest is "relentlessly sifted, till it comes out boards, clapboards, laths, and shingles" (5); now he maintains that "only a few axe-men have gone 'up-river' into the howling wilderness which feeds it" (83).

Having encountered on Katahdin the smallness of man and failure of his imagination to create a human space there, Thoreau no longer anticipates a future in which civilization turns the wilderness into lumber. Instead, three centuries collapse for him and he sees the wilderness, both Maine and the West (82), swallow civilization: "America is still unsettled and unexplored" (81)—it looks "like a desolate island, and No-man's Land" (82). His subsequent trips to Maine (1853, 1857) would again change his perspective, but in "Ktaadn" itself the wilderness takes over. Above Orono "the country is virtually unmapped and unexplored," the essay concludes, "and there still waves the virgin forest of the New World" (83).

Thoreau would never again let himself be isolated in a natural setting as threatening as the wastelands of Katahdin's summit. His own clearing work was apparently a much more modest challenge: "Near the end of March, 1845, I borrowed an axe and went down to the woods by Walden Pond" (Wa 40).

6

The Later *Week*

IN THE SUMMER of 1846 Emerson indicated that *A Week* (the first draft) was ready for publication (*L* 3:338), but Thoreau kept the manuscript for revisions before submitting it to a publisher. Quite likely his Mount Katahdin trip caused him to rethink his earlier excursion on the Concord and Merrimack rivers. As he worked on the first draft (A) of *Walden* during the winter of 1846–47, he also added to *A Week*. He transferred to it recent Journal entries and inserted essays previously published in the *Dial* ("Anacreon," "Dark Ages," and "Homer. Ossian. Chaucer."). By March 1847 the second draft of *A Week* had grown to nearly twice the length of the first draft, and, although Emerson again pronounced it "quite ready" for publication (*L* 3:384), Thoreau continued to revise and expand the manuscript. He submitted the book to Duyckinck (of Wiley and Putnam) in May, recalled it for further revisions in June, and resubmitted it in July (*C* 181, 184). When Wiley and Putnam failed to act, he sent it to James Munroe and then refused their terms for publishing it at his own expense. Thoreau described the book at this stage as being "about the size of one vol of Emerson's essays" (*C* 185), indicating that the manuscript had expanded by roughly another 20,000 words since the previous March.

Surviving manuscripts from 1847–48 show Thoreau adding pieces to all of the chapters. For example, HM 13195 contains material on music and Dunstable history that went into "Monday"; HM 13182 adds sections on traveling for "Thursday" and on autumn for "Friday." AM 278.5 contains scattered sections that were included in "Monday" (folder 10, the trip to Wachusett), "Tuesday" (folder 15, on mountains and commerce), and other chapters. Thoreau also drafted materials that were apparently intended for *A Week* but were ultimately left out of the book (e.g., folder 11, notes on Nathaniel Rogers).

In November 1847 Thoreau recorded rejections by four pub-

lishers and in the same letter admitted that "for the last month
or two I have forgotten it, but shall certainly remember it again"
(*C* 191). He apparently left the manuscript untouched as he
worked on the lectures "Ktaadn" and "Resistance to Civil Government." He resumed work in March 1848 and reported in May
that "my book is swelling again under my hands" (*C* 225). Continuing to add recent Journal entries, he also expanded and rearranged the essay on friendship (in "Wednesday") and added the
Dial article "Aulus Persius Flaccus" and critiques of orthodox
Christianity and Hinduism. After working on the manuscript
through the fall and winter, in February 1849 he finally arranged
for publication with Munroe, worked on proofsheets in March
and April, and published the book in May.

As a Menippean satire and loose-jointed, meditative travel
book, the first draft of *A Week* could easily accommodate additions without changing its character, and many of the additions
suit its essentially neoclassical nature—for example, the concern with original genius that pervades the added sections on
Homer, Ossian, and Chaucer. But Thoreau also introduced material that signals fundamental changes in his conception of the
book. Perhaps most important, the additions show a new sense
of myth as a mode of perceiving and knowing, and as a method
for structuring his narrative beyond merely recording the week's
events. With these significant additions, Thoreau turned the narrative into his own quest myth, his search for a goal that he identified as God and heaven. Tapping traditional romance, he plotted
more clearly and carefully the spiritual quest that he had only
hinted at in the Long Book and the first draft. The romance provides a narrative spine that helps structure and unify the various
digressions and meditations that would disturb Lowell and others. Thoreau also added reflexive sections of literary theorizing
which help to explain the book's rhetorical strategy and which
show him moving closer to an aesthetic of fluidity and process.
Finally, additions to *A Week* increased the importance of the two
mountain passages (the ascents of Saddleback and Agiocochook)
and the meditation on natural life, which became the book's thematic climax. Almost a decade after his excursion on the rivers,
Thoreau at last discovered and revealed the full significance of
his journey.

Theories of Myths

In the first draft of *A Week*, as in the first part of "Ktaadn," Thoreau uses myth primarily for decoration and historical analogue. For example, he alludes to "flowers which Proserpine might have dropped" (*FD* 6), talks casually of "river gods" (*FD* 52), and likens the annual cattle show to "the Corybantes and Bachannals—the rude primitive tragedians with their procession and goat song and the whole paraphanalia of the Panathenaea" (*FD* 91–92—also in *W* 337–38).

In revising the *Week*, he increases the number of classical allusions, but he also reveals a new seriousness toward myth through theoretical statements and by introducing his own invented myths. Thoreau's Journal for 1845 also records the renewed interest in charting a role for both traditional and constructed myths (e.g., *PJ* 1:183–86); many of those passages were added to *A Week*.[1] Theoretical meditations on myth also appear in the Berg notebook narrative of "Ktaadn," among them passages that went into *A Week* (another indication that the experience on that mountain and writing about that trip significantly affected the later stages of *A Week*). For example, between sections on the initial ascent of Katahdin (*PJ* 2:334), in a passage later transferred to *A Week* (59), he talks about how posterity adds to myth. Another page of the Berg notebook concerns "one memorable addition" to the old mythology, the "Christian fable," and it identifies Christ as "The New Prometheus" (*PJ* 2:353). This passage, with its links to the Promethean myth in "Ktaadn," was transferred to the revised *Week* (66).

Much of the new theorizing about myth went into the meditation on fables, a significant addition to final book (57–61). Here Thoreau argues that myth is more than decoration. It is the collective creation of all mankind, "an approach to that universal language which men have sought in vain" (59), and it "contains only enduring and essential truth" (60). Thoreau stresses partic-

[1] For Thoreau's important earlier reading in mythology, see Louise Cristan Kertez, "A Study of Thoreau as Myth Theorist and Myth Maker," Ph.D. diss., Illinois, 1970.

ularly the multiple significance of myths, "the readiness with which they may be made to express a variety of truths," and the access that fables give to a higher "poetical" truth: "In the mythus a superhuman intelligence uses the unconscious thoughts and dreams of men as its hieroglyphics to address men unborn" (61).

Besides theorizing about myth, Thoreau also added to *A Week* examples of his own mythmaking, such as the passage on "the respectable folks" that forms the mythic center of "Concord River" (8–9). Especially he works toward a new American mythology. He begins by associating "our muddy and much abused Concord River" with the famous rivers of Greek mythology (12), but he quickly and repeatedly moves beyond mere association to proclaim his preference for the American rivers so important to his own mythological landscape:

> Such waters do the gods distil,
> And pour down every hill
>   For their New England men;
> A draught of this wild nectar bring,
> And I'll not taste the spring
>   Of Helicon again. (84)

Somewhat defensively, he insists on the superiority of American to classical materials for myth:

> In vain I search a foreign land,
>   To find our Bunker Hill,
> And Lexington and Concord stand
> By no Laconian rill. (18)

By creating a new mythology from American history and biography, Thoreau assumes the role of poet as bard, as definer of the nation. He thus answers Emerson's call for a poet who recognizes "the value of our incomparable materials" (*CW* 3:21), and he anticipates Whitman's taking on the same role. Thoreau defines the identity and ideals of the nation chiefly by recording "the deeds of heroes" (part of the "profession of the bard" [346]) and by creating a new pantheon of American mythic figures such as the adventurous Sudbury farmers (8), the Tyne fisherman "almost grown to be the sun's familiar" (24), the "demigod" Franklin, and the legendary race of American fishermen who pulled in "miraculous draughts of fishes" (34).

In developing his own treatment of myth, Thoreau thus recapitulates the course of interest in myth from the early eighteenth century through the romantic period. As we have seen, he first used myth as decorative literary allusion—ornamentation that displayed his classical learning but would have no truth value for his enlightened, rational readers (the early essays, the first part of "Ktaadn," the early stages of A Week). Gradually taking myth more seriously as a way of organizing perceptions, he adapted and embellished classical myths, playing off previous treatments of archetypal stories to universalize his own experience. For example, he taps the Prometheus story at the climax of "Ktaadn" to explore the significance of his ascent of the mountain (MW 63–65). Just as nationalism helped to deepen interest in myth throughout the eighteenth century (important texts include the Ossianic materials and collections such as those by the brothers Grimm), Thoreau's own brand of patriotism increased his interest in Native American tales and prompted his heightened treatment of American historical figures.

Going beyond this stage, Thoreau allied himself with the radical romantics in the debate over the viability of creating myth in the modern era. Preromantic writers such as Vico and Herder, while taking myth seriously as the expression of a culture's identity, worldview, and aspirations, insisted that mythmaking was essentially primitive and collective—a mode of perception limited to the early period of a society. Thoreau eventually sided with Frederich von Schlegel's camp in believing that individual (modern) poets could and should revitalize those early myths of a culture by adding to them.[2] Thus, in A Week Thoreau turns into mythic heroes not only historical Americans but also his own

[2] For an overview of this controversy, see Burton Feldman and Robert D. Richardson, The Rise of Modern Mythology: 1680–1860 (Bloomington: Univ. of Indiana Press, 1972). The debate was still open during

contemporaries (e.g., Hawthorne [19], the canal-boatmen [201, 211]). More important, as we shall see, he casts himself as a heroic quester in the romance myth that helps him to create his own coherent, meaningful cosmos out of the chaos of experience and to unify and structure the revised *Week*. Like others in his era, he sets out to make himself his own mythic hero.

The allusion to Luke (5:1–11) in Thoreau's reference to "miraculous draughts of fishes" (34) points to another role Thoreau assumes as poet and mythmaker—that of writing new scriptures. He sees the poet not only as the creator of a national identity but also as a religious leader ("in his era we hear of no other priest than he" [i.e., Ossian, 343]) and as the writer of sacred codes, which always need refreshing.

The Mythic Quest

Myth is more important to the revised *Week* because it provides a structuring narrative that holds the various meditations together. Thoreau creates his own myth, with himself as the hero bound on what become symbolic adventures. He adapts the archetypal romance mythos that Northrop Frye identifies as central to romanticism: a narrative "with the poet for hero" and with the theme of attaining "an expanded consciousness, the sense of identity with God and nature."[3] Thoreau's revision of the Saddleback episode indicates the outline of this controlling myth.

In the first draft the episode is a brief (200-word) reminiscence prompted by a foggy Tuesday morning (*FD* 49–50). Thoreau recalled his vision of a picturesque sunrise seen from the mountaintop while clouds veiled the landscape below. In the revised *Week* he expanded the episode to eleven pages (*W* 180–90) and changed its nature almost entirely. The passage begins as a realistic account of the 1844 excursion, but it gradually takes

---

Thoreau's apprenticeship, with Margaret Fuller siding with the conservatives and Emerson with the radicals; see Caroline Healey Dall, *Margaret and Her Friends* (Boston: Roberts Bros., 1895), pp. 37, 50 ff.

[3] *A Study of English Romanticism* (New York: Random House, 1968), p. 37.

on suggestions of allegory and romance. Rhetorically, Thoreau transforms the actual vacation trip into a symbolic journey, a quest for paradise.

Pursuing "a road for the pilgrim to enter upon who would climb to the gates of heaven," he finds himself in a region fit for "the most singular and heavenly-minded man" (181, 182). On his way up the steep and narrow path, he reaches a house where the path diverges from the summit. Charles Anderson takes the woman he meets there to be a kind of benevolent "goddess" looking down with interest on the human world.[4] However, phrases in the passage ("in a dishabille," "long black hair") create an echo from traditional romances to suggest that she is what Frye calls the "lady of pleasure," the dark siren or beautiful witch who vies with the fair-haired "lady of duty" in testing the knight.[5] Her "interest in that lower world" hints that she is the temptress who might block the heaven-bound quester. She reminds him of "a cousin," implying perhaps that she symbolizes some earthly part of himself. But Thoreau, of course, resists the temptation that she represents and continues alone, directly to the top of the mountain, but by a path different from that of the "pretty wild set of fellows" with whom the woman is familiar.

His route takes him through a *selva oscura* where "the trees began to have a scraggy and infernal look, as if contending with frost goblins" (184). At the summit his major concern is water, which is first supplied by pools that "stood in the tracks of the horses which had carried travelers up" (184). Anderson perceptively points out the allusion: "It was when the winged horse Pegasus struck Mt. Helicon with his hoof that the Hippocrene fountain, sacred to the Muses, gushed forth. So the poet on Saddleback found his spring of inspiration."[6] We might push Anderson's analysis further. Because this spring proves insufficient, Thoreau must create his own. Remembering a moist spot he no-

---

[4] *Thoreau's Vision* (Englewood Cliffs, N.J.: Prentice-Hall, 1973), p. 22.

[5] *Anatomy*, p. 196.

[6] *Thoreau's Vision*, p. 22.

ticed on the way up, he returns to it "and here, with sharp stones and my hands, in the twilight, I made a well about two feet deep, which was soon filled with pure cold water, and the birds too came and drank at it" (184–85). This episode illustrates "the mysterious rapport with nature that so often marks the central figure of romance."[7] It also merges with the theme, recurrent in the revised *Week*, of the need for an authentic, independent American literature, fed by American sources. The "spring of inspiration" associated with the Greek Hippocrene cannot sustain the American poet. Tapping his intimate knowledge of his own land, he digs his own well. This account of obtaining water functions, then, as a kind of parable to support Thoreau's earlier apologia for an American literature, in the course of which he had quoted Denham's "Coopers Hill" on providing one's own inspiration:

> Sure there are poets which did never dream
> Upon Parnassus, nor did taste the stream
> Of Helicon; we therefore may suppose
> Those made not poets, but the poets those. (12)

On Saddleback the poet-quester literally makes his own fountain, and a thoroughly democratic one, associated with neither gods nor aristocrats.

After a sacramental "supper of rice" (185),[8] Thoreau undertakes another stage of the ritual that will prepare him for the next morning's epiphany—a symbolic death and burial. "I at length encased myself completely in boards," he says, "managing even to put a board on top of me, with a large stone on it" (186). That this resting place is meant to suggest a coffin and headstone is clear from the slightly earlier discussion of graveyards: "It is remarkable that the dead lie everywhere under stones" (169). Thoreau's arrangement for the night becomes the equivalent of what

---

[7] *Anatomy*, p. 197.

[8] Thoreau associates rice with holy living, and particularly with Hinduism (see *Wa* 61); later in *A Week* he eats a rice dinner to help purify himself after the "crime" of slaughtering squirrels (224).

Jessie L. Weston calls the romance hero's "test for the primary initiation, that into the sources of physical life," a test that "would probably consist in a contact with the horrors of physical death."[9]

So far the account of the night on Saddleback exemplifies the stages of the romance mythos outlined by Frye,[10] even though Thoreau undercuts or at least tempers his adventures by reminding us that this quest is also a pleasant summer outing. The *agon*, or conflict, includes resisting the temptation represented by the dark-haired woman, working his way through the "scraggy and infernal" woods, and overcoming thirst by digging his own well. The *pathos*, or death struggle, is represented by his separation from the lower world in reaching the mountaintop and by the symbolic "death" of sleep. The third stage, the disappearance of the hero (*sparagmos*), is symbolized by his enclosure in the coffinlike boards. But these boards remind him that Irish children use a "door to put over them in winter nights" (186), and his own symbolic coffin becomes the "door" to the final stage of romance, the rebirth and revelation, or *anagnorisis*, that takes place the next morning.

Having undergone the preparatory stages and rituals, Thoreau finally rises to attain a glimpse of the "new world," the dream "paradise" that is the goal of his romance quest (188). "Here," he reports, "I saw the gracious god" (189). On the mountaintop, the place on earth closest to heaven, he experiences what Frye calls a romance's epiphany, the "symbolic presentation of the point at which the undisputed apocalyptic world and the cyclical world of nature come into alignment."[11] The experience is as brief as it is intense. Echoing, perhaps, the speaker of Keats's "Ode to a Nightingale," and like most other romantic questers, he sinks "down again into that 'forlorn world,' from which the celestial Sun had hid his visage" (190). But Thoreau insists that his quest goes on. He finds himself in the position of the major romance

---

[9] *From Ritual to Romance* (1920; rpt. Garden City, N.Y.: Doubleday Anchor Books, 1957), p. 182.

[10] *Anatomy*, pp. 187–92.

[11] Ibid., p. 203.

heroes alluded to throughout *A Week*—Redcrosse Knight in *The Faerie Queene*, who glimpses the New Jerusalem from the Mount of Contemplation (1:10), and Christian in *The Pilgrim's Progress*, who sees the Celestial City from the top of hill Clear in the Delectable Mountains. Thoreau sets off for "the summits of new and yet higher mountains . . . by which I might hope to climb to heaven again" (190). We recall that the ascent of Saddleback took place in the past; the subsequent journey recounted in the *Week* continues his romance quest for those higher mountains. He thus asks us to read the Saddleback episode as a prelude to the ascent of Agiocochook in "Thursday," where its full significance will be revealed.

Allusions to romance pervade not only the Saddleback episode but the whole of the revised *Week*. For example, in the second paragraph of "Concord River" Thoreau takes us upstream to see "Sudbury, that is Southborough men . . . keeping their castles" (7–8), and through the fluid time of the *Week*, he keeps returning to the age of romance: "we imagined that the river flowed through an extensive manor, and that the few inhabitants were retainers to a lord, and a feudal state of things prevailed" (195). In the mock-heroic poem that he added to "Monday," he pictures himself as a cosmic knight jousting to become the "champion new" of Heaven (177–78). And in "Wednesday" he pictures friends as modern knights: "Their relation implies such qualities as the warrior prizes; for it takes a valor to open the hearts of men as well as the gates of castles" (274). In the first draft, this last phrase read "gates of cities" (*FD* 78)—Thoreau revised it to bring it into line with the other allusions to romance.

The new references to romance thus help to unify the *Week* by joining its diverse parts in a dominant mood and a network of traditional characters and motifs. Even more important for the structure of the book, romance provides an underlying narrative skeleton. Although Emerson recognized from the first that the *Week* is more than a miscellaneous collection of essays, the metaphor he used to describe it conveys some doubt about its unity: "The narrative of the little voyage, though faithful, is a very slender thread for such big beads & ingots as are strung on it" (*L* 3:384). We might consider the *Week* in the light of a different image, the typically romantic, organic metaphor that Thoreau uses in a later Journal meditation on literary structure: "Find out as soon as possible what are the best things in your composition, and then shape the rest to fit them. The former will be the midrib and veins of the leaf" (J 12:39; the image looks back on the passage in *Walden* concerning the Ur-leaf, 308). According to Thoreau's metaphor, the meditations in *A Week* on such topics as literature, history, religion, and science—usually considered digressions from the main narrative—become the leafy tissue growing from and fed by the quest that forms the midrib and veins. In a sense, these meditations are the adventures (*agones*) encountered along the way and parts of the "treasure" that becomes one goal of the quest.

The first three epigraphs that Thoreau added to the *Week* establish the atmosphere of romance and outline the basic plot. The first, an invocation of the muse, introduces the motif of the poet as quester. It insists on the symbolic nature of the voyage, inviting us to consider it as his version of the imaginative "excursion," and it presents the two most structurally important symbolic actions: ascending rivers and climbing mountains. The basic unifying narrative will involve tracing the Merrimack to its source on the summit of Agiocochook.

In the revised first chapter Thoreau says of mountains, "The heavens are not yet drained over their sources" (12). According to the cosmology of the *Week*, rain falls from the heavens onto the mountaintops and then flows down to the rivers and eventually to the sea. To trace the river to its source, then, is to travel to the verge of heaven. This association becomes explicit in important sections of the text. In his celebration of Wachusett, for example, Thoreau says of the mountain, that "distant nursery of rills,"

> I fancy even
> Through your defiles windeth the way to heaven;
> And yonder still, in spite of history's page,
> Linger the golden and the silver age. (164)

The Wachusett passage prepares us for the two crucial episodes of mountain climbing. At the temporal center of the *Week* (Tuesday in a week that begins on Saturday) comes the ascent of Saddleback. As we have seen, Thoreau travels up that mountain by a path that leads "to the gates of heaven" (181) and enjoys at the top an enraptured vision of "the gracious god" (189). After his inevitable descent, he intends "to climb to heaven again" by way of the higher mountains in the distance (190). This epiphany at the temporal center thus prepares us for an even more spectacular revelation at the spatial midpoint of the trip (the spot farthest from Concord, the port of departure and return), when Thoreau climbs a higher mountain, Agiocochook.

The second epigraph introduces the motive of questing for treasure. It also sketches a romance landscape of distant shores and lonely isles. Especially important is the reference to "the barren sands of a desolate creek," since the wasteland motif recurs throughout the book and is, as Weston points out, a standard element of the traditional romance.

Some varieties of the symbolic treasure are introduced in the third epigraph: "I sailed up a river with a pleasant wind,/New lands, new people, and new thoughts to find." Throughout *A Week* Thoreau emphasizes freshness. The brothers work their way up the river "gradually adjusting our thoughts to novelties, beholding from its placid bosom a new nature and new works of men, . . . not following any beaten path, but the windings of the river, as ever the nearest way for us" (109–10). Thoreau insists on exploring new worlds both within and without himself. Novelty of perception, crucial for the various revelations along the way, also bears on the theme of personal renewal, since their journey becomes a search for rebirth. Yet the quest can never be fully completed because the ultimate goal—which Thoreau does not name but only addresses with the respectful "THOU"—remains "the cape never rounded, nor wandered o'er."[12]

In the third epigraph Thoreau anticipates "many dangers"—

---

[12] Some time after *A Week* was published in 1849, Thoreau added a fourth epigraph (first printed in the 1868 Ticknor and Fields edition) which supplements the awe and mystery and suggestion of divinity surrounding the "THOU" of the third. The antecedent of "he" in the quotation from Ovid is "whichever of the gods he was" (quisquis fuit ille deorum, *Metamorphoses*, 1:32).

the series of *agones* or adventures—that he must survive before the climactic struggle, disappearance, and rebirth. Dragons appear, but in the context of the nineteenth century. For example, Thoreau fears "that some monster institution would at length embrace and crush its free members in its scaly folds," and he recalls a past encounter with "Massachusetts, that huge she Briareus, Argus, and Colchian Dragon conjoined, set to watch the Heifer of the Constitution and the Golden Fleece" (130–31).

Thoreau frequently encounters another kind of danger in the factories and their dams, which suggest the destructive potential inherent in any institution and which, like some malevolent enchanter, transform the river into "a mere *waste water*" (87). They have already flooded "thousands of acres" with stagnant water (6), destroyed valuable hay, abraded the banks of the river (86), prevented lamprey eels from going upstream, and ended the migration of salmon, shad, and alewives (33–34). In romance terms, the "Corporation with its dam" (is Thoreau playing on "the Devil and his dam"?) proves too strong a foe for the knightly fish "still wandering the sea in thy scaly armor to inquire humbly at the mouths of rivers if man has perchance left them free for thee to enter." Braving the dangers, Thoreau offers to become the fishes' paladin, armed not with a lance but a crowbar (37).

Threats to the natural environment also take on symbolic significance, especially in light of the *Week*'s seasonal imagery. In Sudbury, Thoreau discovers "alders, and birches, and oaks, and maples full of glee and sap, holding in their buds until the waters subside" (7). But dams prevent the waters from subsiding—in effect preventing the spring's renewal. Figuratively, in the terms of romance, the dragon of winter, which also represents death and the sea, retains its hold over the wasteland.[13] As the romance quester, Thoreau must slay the dragon to restore the land to fertility.

"A man's life should be constantly as fresh as this river," he insists; "it should be the same channel, but a new water every instant" (132). Dams represent anything that hinders this re-

[13]*Anatomy*, pp. 191–92.

freshing flow or stops the migration of Thoreau's symbolic fish—
the thoughts and insights so important to the treasure motif.[14]
Church and state are two of the figurative dams in *A Week*. Playing on the etymology of religion, Thoreau pictures the church as
a "ligature" (64), a preventer of movement. Like the actual dams,
American churches "deform the landscape" (76), and they
impede the quest for the divine by throwing up "a fixture, that
old Jewish scheme," between man and heaven (70). Oriental religions are condemned, too, for being "infinitely stagnant" (136).
Quite appropriately, then, Thoreau's major dissection of religion
is followed by reference to the destructive "influence of the Paw-
tucket Dam" (86). As we have seen, the state is another "monster
institution" that threatens the quester with the stasis of impris-
onment. Consisting of "institutions of the dead," it poses "*outward* obstacles" to the flow of true life (130).

But not all dams or obstacles are outward; many internal problems also prevent the flow of new life. Even too great an interest
in eliminating the abuses of church and state can be harmful.
Satirists like Persius and Juvenal remain relatively underdevel-
oped as artists because they are "concerned rather about the
monster which they have escaped, than the fair prospect before
them" (308). Hence, too, Thoreau's low regard for those mis-
guided knights, the fanatic reformers. He insists that outward
reform must begin within: "still every where the relentless op-
ponents of reform bear a strange resemblance to ourselves"
(126). A major threat to reform is "the old routine" (124). As a
vacation the brothers' river excursion is one method of breaking
through their old routine, of exploring the "new lands, new
people, and new thoughts" required for self-renewal (3). Al-

---

[14] Throughout the book Thoreau links fish with both treasure ("silver
or golden fish" [26], "a brilliant coin . . . a perfect jewel of the river" [28],
"pull up twopence, sixpence, and twelvepence, as fast as you can haul
and veer a line" [89]) and with thought, insight, epiphany. He celebrates
fishing as "a contemplative man's recreation" and insists that "the fruit
of the naturalist's observations is not in new genera or species, but in
new contemplations still" (25). Metaphorically, to catch a fish, "this fabulous inhabitant of another element" (30), is to contact a new world, to
deepen one's consciousness.

though "all men are partially buried in the grave of custom" (132), a kind of resurrection awaits the questers who challenge the customs and institutions they observe along the way from the constantly new perspectives their floating observatory affords.

Faulty perception, though, remains an internal obstacle on the quest for renewal. Thoreau treats this theme humorously in "Sunday" when the brothers pursue "what seemed a sturgeon or larger fish" and the "halibut-skinned monster" turns suddenly into "a huge imprisoned spar, placed there as a buoy, to warn sailors of sunken rocks" (114). Playing the wicked enchanter on their own, they lead themselves into danger by allowing their preconceptions ("we remembered that this was the Sturgeon River") to obscure their vision.

The open-ended nature of this quest is emphasized in the final stages of A Week with the image of the "two herons . . . travelling high over our heads" (390), emblems of the brothers themselves as their mental excursion continues even while this particular trip comes to an end. Their quest is never really completed. They return home not to rest or resume the old routine but to "find some autumnal work to do, and help on the revolution of the seasons" (388–89).

But their sense of confidence and possibility is tempered by the backward-looking tendency of all romance as well as by ironies that arise from the complex shifts in the book's scheme of time. Thus, at the start of the narrative that ends so hopefully, Thoreau reminds us that

> since we sailed
> Some things have failed,
> And many a dream
> Gone down the stream. (18)

The idyllic voyage in the past is recalled at a time when, among other things, the narrator's brother and companion has been dead for years, and Massachusetts, a leader in the 1775 war of liberation, is engaged "in holding slaves" and "in conquering Mexico" (130). With its abrupt shift to autumnal imagery in "Friday" and recurrent ubi sunt meditations on past heroes recalled in "these degenerate days" (334), the *Week* includes the detached and contemplative strain characteristic of what Frye calls the sixth, or *penseroso*, phase of romance.

A predominantly hopeful and forward-looking mood is still possible in the autumnal section of *A Week*, however, because, again according to Frye, built into the sixth phase is a sense of history not only as a linear sequence of events but "as a cycle of which the audience is the end, and, as the last page indicates, the beginning as well."[15] Cyclical seasonal imagery pervades the book, and the stress on autumn in the last chapter is balanced by the emphasis on spring in the first and by references to "spring freshets" that frame the work (6, 393). If one seasonal cycle is over, another is about to begin. Having completed this particular voyage, Thoreau turns his book and the quest itself over to his audience in the final meditation on silence.

An Aesthetic of Silences

Romance thus provides an underlying narrative skeleton for the revised *Week*. It is a centripetal force that helps unify the book and make it more coherent than the first draft. But even in its revised form the book is not so symmetrical and unified as some recent critics suggest (see ch. 3, n. 4). The centrifugal, digressive, fragmentary tendencies that bothered Lowell and others remain, but Thoreau now attempts to provide an aesthetic justification for them.

The romance elements that help structure the book themselves prepare the reader for a loose, meandering flow. As Eugene Vinaver points out, romance is unified, but unified according to other than Aristotelian standards. It developed historically as "an art which surrenders the 'restful' kind of symmetry for the play of fancy in which both movement and depth are achieved by structural richness and infinite multiplicity."[16] In ro-

---

[15] *Anatomy*, p. 203.

[16] *The Rise of Romance* (New York: Oxford, 1971), p. 78.

mance, theme and plot often do not progress straightforwardly, but various strands of the story are interlaced. A strand is introduced, then interrupted by a different one, then picked up again later in the narrative, as in the prose *Lancelot* of the Arthurian cycle, or, indeed, the leitmotivs of Wagner's operas. Interweaving the ideas throughout *A Week*, Thoreau gives each a new shading and even coloration every time it reappears by setting it next to separate but often related themes. The work is not "closed," then, because themes or problems are never finally resolved. Instead, the book offers the "pattern of unresolved stresses" typical of the romance.[17]

Even before he revised *A Week* in the direction of romance, however, Thoreau was working toward an experimental aesthetic that valued openness. In his Journal for 23 June 1840, two days after he transcribed his log for the previous summer's excursion on the Concord and Merrimack, Thoreau wrote, "Yes and No are lies—A true answer will not aim to establish anything, but rather to set all well afloat" (*PJ* 1:139). His theory and practice in the revised *Week* take him closer toward a romantic aesthetic of process rather than product, and power rather than knowledge. He attempts to set things afloat chiefly by dramatizing the process of his thought and by involving the reader in the experience or performance of the work.

Appropriately for such a self-reflexive book, the rivers he explores furnish Thoreau with metaphors for the *Week* and offer hints about his aesthetic of floating possibilities. Like the Merrimack and Concord, the *Week* meanders; it digresses, twists, and turns, reaches its destination by indirection. Also like the rivers, the *Week* remains fresh because it constantly flows. Thoreau emphasizes fluidity throughout, associating with it the process of creative thinking. "There are fishes wherever there is a fluid medium," he insists (26). Since he frequently equates fish and thoughts, he suggests that the *Week* itself is a fluid in which move a variety of meditations and insights. Hence, again, the symbolic importance of dams, which Thoreau links with insti-

---

[17] Ibid., p. 47n. See *FD* for Linck C. Johnson's discussion of the "complex weave" involved in Thoreau's writing of *A Week*.

tutions of church and state, and which he threatens with a crowbar (37). By clearing out dogmas and routine perceptions, those dams to "the flow of thought" (102), Thoreau encourages what Carl Hovde calls "the major concern of the whole work—the mind's proper fluidity."[18] Physical and psychological fluidity converge at the moment in "Thursday" when "all things seemed with us to flow." After an ecstatic vision of flowing cliffs, trees, stars, and rocks, Thoreau concludes with a pun: "our thoughts flowed and circulated, and this portion of time was but the current hour" (331). In revising *A Week*, Thoreau moved this passage from "Monday" (*FD* 39) to "Thursday," where it follows the climactic ascent of Agiocochook.

Rivers are also significant for his aesthetic theory because their twisting course leads to new territories and fresh perspectives. He makes explicit the analogy: "The current of our thoughts made as sudden bends as the river, which was continually opening new prospects" (339). Thoreau incorporates this recurrent metaphor into his aesthetic of momentary insights, glimpses, and epiphanies—of "flitting perspectives, and demi-experiences of the life that is in nature" (8). His stress on transience stems from his movement toward romantic epistemology, his sense that truth is grasped only in moments of intense imaginative vision or in the "brief and indeterminate glimpses" that Poe takes to be the object of all art.[19] To reproduce these glimpses, Thoreau implies, a book must resemble not only the river but the sky as well, an image of even greater fluidity and unpredictability: "The wind sets the types on this blue ground, and the inquiring may always read a new truth there" (359).

Recurrent flood imagery in *A Week* also takes on aesthetic significance. Thoreau praises writing that "is more like a tidal wave than a prone river, and is the result of a celestial influence, not any declivity in its channel. . . . if we would appreciate the flow that is in these books, we must expect to feel it rise from the page like an exhalation, and wash away our critical brains like burr

[18]"Literary Materials in Thoreau's *A Week*," *PMLA* 80 (1965):76.

[19]"The Poetic Principle," in *The Complete Works of Edgar Allan Poe*, ed. James A. Harrison (New York: George D. Sproul, 1902), 14:274.

millstones, flowing to higher levels above and behind ourselves"
(102–3). These tidal waves are epiphanies, intense visions that
transcend rational understanding and transform the world: "I
stop my habitual thinking, as if the plow had suddenly run
deeper in its furrow through the crust of the world. How can I
go on, who have just stepped over such a bottomless skylight in
the bog of my life" (173). In a book these "moments that we
stand/Astonished on the Olympian land!" (382) disrupt the flow
of the text, as dams fall to the writer's metaphorical crowbar.
They represent shifts "from a comparatively narrow and partial,
what is called common sense view of things, to an infinitely expanding and liberating one" (386). Among the major epiphanies
that disrupt *A Week* are the revelation on Monday night, when
"suddenly old Time winked at me,—Ah you know me, you
rogue,—and news had come that IT was well" (173), the vision
of "the gracious god" from the top of Saddleback (189), and the
message of the Muse in "Friday" (378–79).

Both to recreate and inspire epiphanic moments, Thoreau in-
terrupts the flow of *A Week* by incorporating in it fragments, surprising juxtapositions, contradictions, suggestive indistinctness,
and gaps or silences.

Great works, he says, seem made to be fragmented: "A work
of genius is rough-hewn from the first, because it anticipates the
lapse of time, and has an ingrained polish, which still appears
when fragments are broken off, an essential quality of its sub-
stance" (376–77). From other writers he borrows pieces, giving
them new meaning in their new context. Also, as Hovde argues,
Thoreau occasionally "seems to assume the reader's knowledge
of the original text; it is as though he hoped the reader would
remember the work, and enjoy his variations on the author's
theme."[20] He also appeals to our imagination to complete texts
that are fragmented because they are unfinished. For instance,
he approaches Alexander Henry's *Travels and Adventures in
Canada and the Indian Territories* as a "rough sketching"—as
"the argument to a great poem on the primitive state of the country and its inhabitants, and the *reader imagines* what in each

---

[20] Hovde, p. 77.

case with the invocation of the Muse might be sung" (218–19, emphasis added). Thoreau also presents himself as a reader who uses lines abstracted from others' works as springboards for his own imagination. The essay "Aulus Persius Flaccus" ("Thursday") is devoted not so much to the Roman poet as to free meditations on themes suggested by fragments from Persius' satires (307–13).

Beside the borrowed fragments, sudden and unusual juxtapositions provide another way to disrupt the flow of ordinary thought and to inspire epiphanies. For example, in "Monday" Thoreau places together major essays on social reform, Eastern religion, and history, leaving the reader to work out the relations among them. The theme of action versus contemplation clearly unites the first two. Through juxtaposition we are invited to trace that theme in the third meditation, and to apply our new perspective to history. Our focus shifts away from actions in the past to the observer (or contemplator) in the present: "the researcher is more memorable than the researched . . . the *past* cannot be *presented*; we cannot know what we are not" (154–55).

Thoreau later claimed to have developed many of his insights through chance arrival of material in his Journal: "Thoughts accidentally thrown together become a frame in which more may be developed and exhibited. . . . Having by chance recorded a few disconnected thoughts and then brought them into juxtaposition, they suggest a whole new field in which it was possible to labor and to think. Thought begat thought" (J 3:217). A similar strategy for inspiration underlies the *Week*, but the thoughts here are not "accidentally thrown together," though they may at first so seem. Instead, Thoreau places ideas side by side to suggest whole new fields for the readers, who are challenged to labor and think for themselves, and thus generate insights of their own.

Contradictions, too, challenge the reader throughout *A Week*. Thoreau gives contradictory evaluations of such topics as truth in narrative (325, compared with 303), the direction of human development (34 vs. 127), and the value of commerce (177 vs. 212–13), in order to stress the relativity of truth ("Yes and No are lies"), and to inspire insights through a paradoxical logic that transcends the rational understanding. The *Week* resembles, then, that magical stretch of the Concord in which the brothers "were uncertain whether the water floated the land, or the land held the water in its bosom" (45). The important response is not choosing one of the alternatives but floating the possibilities. That the uncertainties and contradictions are not simply careless mistakes Thoreau implies by celebrating "places where one may have thoughts and not decide any thing" (351). His book itself becomes one of those places.

This concern for openness is a function of Thoreau's belief in the multiple significance of things. He finds "manifold visions in the direction of every object" (48), and he complains, therefore, of "one-idea'd" writing (185) that cannot hope to suggest the complexity of experience. He values fables, we remember, especially because of "the readiness with which they may be made to express a variety of truths" (61). To increase the suggestiveness of his own writing—its potential for multiple significance—Thoreau prevents the outlines of *A Week* from becoming too fixed or solid. Hence the importance to the book not only of flowing water but of fog, mist, haze, clouds, and smoke—constantly changing substances without definite bounds. The mystery, latency, and resistance to definition implied by these recurrent images pervade his discussions of such major topics as Oriental religion (152–53), history (154), and friendship (261). In his discussion of aesthetics, especially, Thoreau returns often to his favorite images of indistinctness. For him the best writing is the result of stimulation "by an *aura* which never even colors the afternoons of common men" (342); it has a "halo" or "haze" about it; it offers "the hue and fragrance of the thought" (103). Poetry is important mainly for "the atmosphere which surrounds it. . . . true verses come toward us indistinctly, as the very breath of all friendliness, and envelope us in their spirit and fragrance" (374).

Perhaps the most radical way that Thoreau disrupts the *Week*, inspires moments of insight, and compels the reader's involvement is by including in it gaps or silences. Sometimes he indicates these overtly in the text, as when he ends the first epigraph with an open dash (3), or traces the history of Hudson ("once it was Nottingham,—once—   " [154, where a line and a half are left blank]), or writes that the *Bhagavad-Gita* is "said to have

been written by Kreeshna Dwypayen Veias,—known to have
been written by———, more than four thousand years ago"
(142). He suggests other, unidentified gaps in his own tale when
he admits, "Unfortunately many things have been omitted which
should have been recorded in our journal." He blames these
omissions on the fact that the important experience is too ab-
sorbing to write about, "and so indifferent things get recorded,
while that is frequently neglected" (332). But he also suggests
more significant aesthetic and rhetorical reasons for the gaps. In
his discussion of Ralegh, he points out: "There is a natural emphasis in his style, like a man's tread, and a breathing space between the sentences, which the best of modern writing does not
furnish. His chapters are like English parks, or say rather like a
western forest, where the larger growth keeps down the underwood, and one may ride on horseback through the openings"
(104). These openings are similar to the "intervening spaces"
that render history "atmospheric and roving or free" (154), or the
spaces that roughen the texture of picturesque landscape painting, challenging conventional ideas of beautiful order. These
holes provide opportunities for unusual perceptions, as Thoreau
implies in a digression within his digression on the ascent of
Saddleback: "When walking in the interior there [Staten Island],
in the midst of rural scenery, where there was as little to remind
me of the ocean as amid the New Hampshire hills, I have suddenly, through a gap, a cleft or 'clove road,' as the Dutch settlers
called it, caught sight of a ship under full sail, over a field of corn,
twenty or thirty miles at sea. The effect was similar, since I
had no means of measuring distances, to seeing a painted
ship passed backwards and forwards through a magic lantern"
(181–82).

The most important gap or silence in *A Week*, and the book's
most daring structural experiment, occurs in "Thursday." As a
number of critics have recognized, *A Week* builds to what should
be a climax on top of Mount Agiocochook. At the temporal center
("Tuesday"), Thoreau recalls the epiphany on Mount Saddleback: an encounter with "the gracious god" in a supernatural
setting (189). We expect an even greater revelation—perhaps
the divine "THOU" that is the spiritual goal of Thoreau's quest
(3)—when, at the spatial midpoint of the journey, he reaches his

physical destination by tracing the Merrimack to its source and ascending the highest mountain in New England. Instead, we get a gap, an empty space, silence. He tells us that "at length . . . we were enabled to reach the summit AGIOCOCHOOK"; then he separates this section from the next with a large space and begins the narrative of his return journey from Hookset a week later (314).

But what happened on the mountaintop? We are naturally bothered by the same questions that Thoreau put to H. G. O. Blake in 1857: "If you have been to the top of Mount Washington, let me ask, what did you find there? . . . What did the mountain say? What did the mountain do?" (C 498). Did Thoreau again encounter the "gracious god"? Did he encounter anything at all? Why has his journey led up to this moment if he is going to remain silent about it?

Using hints he has given in chapters that frame the climactic silence, we can explore some of its possible implications. First, as some critics argue, the silence can be interpreted as something positive—as the only reaction possible to an encounter with the ineffable. The epiphany on the mountaintop is so overwhelming that it cannot be expressed by words; it can only be suggested by a profound silence. Thoreau prepares for such a positive interpretation of his reaction on Agiocochook when he characterizes the revelation on Saddleback as "a favor for which to be forever silent to be shown this vision" (188). Indeed, references to the positive mystical nature of silence pervade the *Week.* In his discussion of religion, for example, Thoreau asks, "Can you put mysteries into words? Do you presume to fable of the ineffable?" (70). And he says of friendship, "Our finest relations are not simply kept silent about, but buried under a positive depth of silence, never to be revealed" (278). These references culminate in the essay on silence, which concludes the book. Here Thoreau defines silence as "when we hear inwardly" and he celebrates it as "earnestly to be sought after. . . . Truth's speaking trumpet, the sole oracle, the true Delphi and Dodona" (391–92). Because silence is the source of intuitive, imaginative insight, perhaps he does actually provide, then—however indirectly—the epiphany he has led us to expect.

Thoreau also suggests a positive interpretation of the silence at the climax by printing AGIOCOCHOOK in capital letters. Other words so treated in the text provide a pattern of clues to his intention: "THOU seemest the only permanent shore,/The cape never rounded, nor wandered o'er" (3). "Suddenly old Time winked at me,—Ah you know me, you rogue,—and news had come that IT was well" (173). "Let him build himself a log-house with the bark on where he is, *fronting* IT" (304). "I am not without hope that we may, even here and now, obtain some accurate information concerning that OTHER WORLD which the instinct of mankind has so long predicted" (385). Each of the words in capital letters suggests some ultimate reality that Thoreau hints is divine but never names. We recollect that in his discussion of religion, he referred to the Supreme Being as "the Unnamed" (136).

That the ascent of the mountain represents an encounter with God he suggests, too, by giving instead of the modern patriotic name of the peak (Mount Washington) only the Indian name, which has been translated as "The Place of the Great Spirit of the Forest" and as "at the place of the concealed one."[21] From Belknap and Fox, whom he quotes in the *Week*, Thoreau must have learned that "the Indians . . . had a superstitious veneration for the summit [of Agiocochook], as the habitation of invisible beings,"[22] and that "the Indian was a child of Nature, and gazed upon her charms with filial admiration. With a true sense of the sublime, to him 'the mountains were God's altars,' and he looked up to their cloud-capped summits with deep awe, as the dwelling place of 'the Great Spirit.'"[23]

The silence atop the mountain can thus be interpreted as an encounter with God, and the gap at the heart of the *Week* can be

[21] See Allen Beecher Hovey, *The Hidden Thoreau* (Beiruit: Hovey, 1966), pp. 76–78, and John C. Huden, *Indian Place Names of New England* (New York: Heye Foundation, 1962), p. 19.

[22] Jeremy Belknap, *The History of New Hampshire*, 2 vols. (Dover ed. of 1812; rpt. New York: Johnson Reprints, 1970), 2:31.

[23] Charles James Fox, *History of the Old Township of Dunstable* (Nashua, N.H.: C. J. Gill, 1846), p. 22.

seen as the equivalent of the blinding core of light at the heart of nineteenth-century luminist paintings—a paradoxically full void, a luminous emptiness that indicates the presence of the divine.

But a different interpretation is possible. Perhaps the silence represents a negative void—a revelation not of God but of nothingness. Such a possibility suggests a reassessment of the earlier Saddleback episode, which would appear to have established the presence of a transcendent deity whom Thoreau briefly encountered. The episode is troubling, though, because of the images of artificiality and insubstantiality throughout it. Once on the mountaintop, for example, Thoreau's response is different from the one he had on Katahdin or would have on Agiocochook. After his dinner he spends the evening reading newspapers, studying even the price lists and ads—in these texts he finds "poetic" and "suggestive" names of commodities. Here, it seems, we find Thoreau at his most "logocentric"—in the face of nature, the night when he will put himself into his own coffin to keep out the elements, he reads, and he sees a world, not defined by nature, but rather by urban man's texts (185–87). He enjoys the fact that this mountain is quite well known to humans—it has on it the observatory building for Williamstown College. At the top of this mountain, he still wants to give names to parts of the world. The mist has obscured the states (the places), so he labels it July (a time). The earth is now veiled, but he is not yet away from it.

At dawn he characterizes the "new world into which I had risen in the night, the new terra-firma perchance of my future life" as a "cloudland" (188); this terra is hardly firm. Finally, the style of the passage is highly artificial. Thoreau emphasizes how completely cut off from earth he is in the tower on Saddleback, and he loads the episode with allusions and quotations from pastoral poetry, Homer, Shakespeare, Giles Fletcher, and Plato. He finds himself "drifting amid the saffron-colored clouds, and playing with the rosy fingers of the Dawn, in the very path of the Sun's chariot, and sprinkled with its dewy dust, enjoying the benignant smile, and near at hand the far-darting glances of the god" (189). This hackneyed imagery represents the overblown and insincere literary ornamentation and trivial, extraneous citations of classical myths that the romantics rejected. Perhaps

Thoreau is suggesting that the failure of this vision is owing not "to some unworthiness in myself" (189) but to the illusory nature of the whole experience, its source in the mechanical and artificial poetic language that Wordsworth denounces in his "Appendix to the Preface" (1802). On the subsequent ascent of Agiocochook, Thoreau no longer projects poetic gods, but confronts the absence of any transcendent deity. He prepares for such a reading when he talks about hesitating to visit distant, idealized mountains because of "misgivings that thereafter no visible fairyland would exist for us" (165).

Thoreau's account of his disturbing ascent of Mount Katahdin supports an anti-Transcendental reading of the climactic episode. In "Ktaadn," we remember, he tells of feeling alienated from his own body and all matter on the mountain. He encounters there, not God, but "vast, Titanic, inhuman Nature," which catches man at a disadvantage and "pilfers him of some of his divine faculty" (*MW* 64). He climbed Katahdin in September 1846, between composing the first and second drafts of *A Week*, and his experience there most likely prompted him to reinterpret the significance of his earlier mountain excursion. In the first draft he politely explained away his failure to comment on what he found when he "reached the summit of Agiocochook": "But why should we take the reader who may have been tenderly nurtured—through that rude country—where the crags are steep and the inns none of the best, and many a rude blast would have to be encountered on the mountain side" (*FD* 83). Only after his experience of alienation on Katahdin did Thoreau capitalize "AGIOCOCHOOK" and drop the apologetic paragraph, leaving the reverberating silence at the heart of *A Week*.[24]

A negative interpretation of "Thursday's" silence is supported by undercurrents throughout the other chapters. In "Sunday" Thoreau claims, "What man believes, God believes" (66), implying that man creates God in his own image. He makes the point

---

[24] That he came to link Katahdin and Agiocochook Thoreau indicates in a letter to Blake, where he speaks of climbing Mount Washington "to learn your relation to matter, and so to your own body, for *it* is at home there, though *you* are not" (*C* 497)—which is the lesson he learned on Katahdin.

explicitly in the passage on Jehovah as "the almighty mortal, hardly as yet apotheosized" and on the genesis of gods from "the overwhelming authority and respectability of mankind combined" (65). Also, in contrast to the recurrent theme of progressive ascent by man, which is emphasized at the end of the Saddleback episode, he speaks of life as a disease (36) and looks forward to the time when man will disappear from the earth (37–38). Perhaps the nothingness that he finds on Agiocochook is part of the very texture and process of life.

If, indeed, Thoreau confronts on the mountain a negative silence, the absence of a transcendent deity, he does not respond with nihilism or despair. He does not give up his quest for God and heaven simply because he has not found them where they are conventionally sought, above the earth. Rather, in the following chapter he relocates God and heaven on earth. In the essay on "*natural* life" ("Friday"), Thoreau presents the thematic core of the book, his discovery of heaven as the "*purely* sensuous life" (382). Finding no heaven when earth is left behind, he declares, "Here or nowhere is our heaven" (380). Discovering no transcendent God beyond nature, he asks, "Is not Nature, rightly read, that of which she is commonly taken to be the symbol merely?" (382)—that is, of God. And since no preexistent value comes down from above, he creates his own value (as man creates God) on earth.

The many metaphors of flowing in the *Week* imply a corollary interpretation of the silence on the mountaintop. His prolonged exposure to flow and to meandering and shifting scenery and thoughts has undercut the presumed value of the rocky pinnacle that suggests timeless absolutes. The repeated emphasis on relativity, perspectivism, and change has prepared for the absence of a culminating supernatural revelation that can be brought down from Agiocochook.

But Thoreau does not choose between conflicting possible interpretations; he leaves the silence ambiguous. By doing so, he remains consistent in his refusal to dogmatize. "Silence keeps things 'open,'" as Susan Sontag writes.[25] Silence also invites the

[25]"The Aesthetics of Silence," in *Styles of Radical Will* (New York: Farrar, Straus & Giroux, 1969), p. 20.

reader's participation in the play of possible meanings suggested by the *Week*. Behind this strategy lies the romantic insistence on the subjectivity of all perception—the active nature of encounters between any subject and object, including a reader and a text. "Each man can interpret another's experience only by his own" (365), Thoreau maintains, aware of the implications for his readers. Emphasis keeps shifting from the text to the reader, a part of Thoreau's general theme of the relation of art to life—"the researcher is more memorable than the researched" (154).

When Thoreau tells his audience to read "only great poems, and when they failed, read them again, or perchance write more" (95–96), he places himself in another romantic tradition: he insists that the proper response to art is the creation of more art. Thus, Thoreau expects his reader to continue the imaginative work of the *Week*: "A good book is the plectrum with which our else silent lyres are struck. We not infrequently refer the interest which belongs to our own unwritten sequel, to the written and comparatively lifeless body of the work. Of all books this sequel is the most indispensable part" (392–93). Like all creation, the *Week* is the "visible frame-work" of silence (391). The silence at its climax and the equally important silence that follows the last page are meant to challenge our own creativity—to involve us radically in the process of the book. A poem early in the *Week* praises a soul "by whom the work which God begun/Is finished, and not undone" (75). In the same way Thoreau leaves his book unfinished, with blank spaces at its climax and conclusion, for us to complete as we can.[26]

A *Week*, in its final version, still reveals its origins in Menippean satire and neoclassical travel writing. But the revised book also shows how far Thoreau has moved toward reevaluating mythology and using the structure of the journey not so much for recording a past vacation as for starting readers along on their own imaginative excursions.

---

[26]A *Week*, like *Walden* after it, can be characterized in Roland Barthes's terms as "writerly" ("scriptible"), since the writer makes the reader the ultimate producer of the text's meaning (S/Z).

7

"An Excursion to Canada"

THE THOREAU of *A Week* mentions that Massachusetts imprisoned him for refusing to pay a tax, but he insists that "to one who habitually endeavors to contemplate the true state of things, the political state can hardly be said to have any existence whatever" (*W* 129). As we will see in chapter 12, the Thoreau of "Resistance to Civil Government" (also published in 1849) treats the same incident at greater length, still insisting that he remains essentially unaffected by politics and the state. The Thoreau of "An Excursion to Canada" is not so fortunate. This piece anticipates the antislavery essays in which social-political concerns interfere with his perception of and communion with nature. "An Excursion" also shows Thoreau experimenting further with ways of organizing travel narrative beyond simple chronology and with efforts to involve the reader actively in the "performance" of a work.

One year after publication of *A Week* and "Resistance to Civil Government," Thoreau left Concord on another travel adventure. With Ellery Channing and 1,500 other Yankees, he visited Canada from 25 September to 3 October 1850 on a "cheap excursion" offered by the railroad (*Ex* 100).[1] Upon his return he began reading about Canada and eventually filled 139 pages of what is known as his Canadian notebook.[2] By summer 1851 he was preparing lectures on Canada: "I found last winter that it was expected by my townsmen that I would give some account of Canada because I had *visited* it, and because many of them had,

---

[1] Eighty-four pages of his Journal for this period are missing—"doubtless the Canada journal" (*J* 2:74).

[2] Lawrence Willson argues that this notebook (Morgan MA 595), which contains material on the cartography and history not only of Canada but of the eastern U.S., is the first volume of the Indian notebooks ("Thoreau's Canada Notebook," *Huntington Library Quarterly* 22 [1959]:180).

and so felt interested in the subject" (*J* 2:417). His Journal for July and August contains drafts for the lectures and notes that eventually made their way into his essay "An Excursion to Canada." Thoreau worked on the piece as his *Walden* project lay fallow and completed "An Excursion" early in 1852, probably before he resumed *Walden* at the D stage.

Howarth dates the earliest surviving manuscript (HM 949, 194 sides of an early lecture draft) before 7 January 1852 (*LMHDT* 229). The materials, emphases, and structure here are quite similar to the finished "Excursion." Although Thoreau added substantially to the piece, he supplemented what was already in the first version rather than changing its nature radically. He also dropped some materials, apparently to improve the narrative flow—for example, sections on the steamer trip out of Burlington (5–6), an American surgeon who attended the wounded in an 1814 naval battle (6v–6), Champlain's notes on Indian warfare (11–14v), and the scenery around St. Anne (56v–62). Thoreau probably read portions of this version at Concord on 7 January 1852 and perhaps the previous evening in Lincoln, Massachusetts (*CL* 82–83).

Before he next lectured about Canada, on 17 March to the Concord Lyceum, he revised and rearranged the first part of the narrative. For this version (HM 950), he pared down the material that he was later to eliminate from the "Excursion." For example, he reduced the section on Champlain's Indian wars from eight pages to one paragraph. Also in March he sent a manuscript of his Canada essay to Horace Greeley, who acted as his literary agent. Greeley complained that "your longer account of a canadian tour . . . looks unmanageable"; he recommended that Thoreau cut material from it and divide it into sections (*C* 277). Apparently Thoreau took back the manuscript and followed Greeley's advice at least as far as dividing the tale into segments. Huntington HM 953, which dates from this period, begins with a clean version of the first two chapters, almost identical to the published work. Chapter titles and numbers are penciled into the rest of the manuscript, which is messier, heavily revised, and incomplete. Greeley wrote on 20 April, "Your Quebeck notes don't reach me yet," but then on 26 May he acknowledged re-

ceipt of a package that presumably contained the latest manuscript (*C* 281). Greeley sent "An Excursion" to the *American
Whig Review* and other journals before he finally succeeded in
placing it with *Putnam's Monthly Magazine*.

Putnam's published most of the first three chapters in its January, February, and March issues for 1853 (volume 1). Thoreau
was angered, however, when George William Curtis removed
from the first chapter some acerbic comments about religion: "I
am not sure but this Catholic religion would be an admirable one
if the priest were quite omitted. I think that I might go to church
myself some Monday, if I lived in a city where there was such a
one to go to" (*Ex* 14). Thoreau withdrew the rest of the manuscript, as he reported to Blake, "because the editor Curtis requires the liberty to omit the heresies without consulting me—a
privilege California is not rich enough to bid for" (*C* 299). Some
time later Thoreau added to the first three chapters a second
epigraph, two footnotes, and some sentences from his continued
reading notes on Canada (*Ex* 2, 22, 49, 58–59), but he appears
not to have changed "An Excursion to Canada" extensively. The
work dates mainly from late 1850–51, although it was not published in full until 1866 when it appeared in *A Yankee in Canada,
with Anti-Slavery and Reform Papers*.

The lack of a long evolution and extensive revisions suggests
that Thoreau did not consider "An Excursion" a major work. His
own comments on the piece support this supposition. He called
it "insignificant" (*C* 294) and wrote to Blake, "I do not wonder
that you do not like my Canada story. It concerns me but little,
and probably is not worth the time it took to tell it" (*C* 299). Readers since then have generally accepted Thoreau's remarks at face
value and ignored the book. What little attention it has received
is mostly unfavorable. Critics usually dismiss it as a perfunctory
account of a rather uninteresting tour ("It is one of Thoreau's
least inspired 'excursions,'" according to Walter Harding), and
they especially deplore its lack of coherence (Edward G. Berry
characterizes it as "simply some stray notes roughly put together
into a brief diary of a journey").[3]

[3] Harding and Meyer, *The New Thoreau Handbook*, p. 47; Berry,
"Thoreau in Canada," *Dalhousie Review* 23 (1943):74.

The rest of Thoreau's comments to Blake suggest, however, some reason for taking another look at "An Excursion:" "Yet I had absolutely no design whatever in my mind, but simply to report what I saw. I have inserted all of myself that was implicated or made the excursion" (C 299). Why did Thoreau, so remarkable for his powers of observation, leave Canada "not having seen much" (Ex 3)? Why was he not completely "implicated" in the excursion? Financial considerations aside, the question arises of why, if there were so little to report, he even bothered trying? Perhaps it is more profitable to approach "An Excursion" not as an uninteresting story of a package tour but as Thoreau's account of a failure of vision and his exploration of the social forces behind that failure. If this was Thoreau's interest, perhaps, also, he employs a deliberate rhetorical strategy that makes the book more coherent than it might at first appear.

Thoreau hints at the aesthetic behind "An Excursion" in a Journal entry about writing that follows a trial version of the book's first paragraph. This proximity suggests that he was thinking of his own forthcoming work, and when he dissects the "fault of some excellent writers," he points specifically to "De Quincey's first impressions on seeing London," a subject obviously related to his own first impressions on seeing Canada. These writers are at fault, Thoreau insists, because "they express themselves with too great fullness and detail":

> They do not affect us by an ineffectual earnestness and
> a reserve of meaning, like a stutterer; they say all they
> mean. Their sentences are not concentrated and nutty.
> Sentences which suggest far more than they say, which
> have an atmosphere about them, which do not merely
> report an old, but make a new impression, . . . which
> contain the seed of other sentences, not mere repeti-
> tion, but creation; which a man might sell his grounds
> and castles to build. If De Quincey had suggested each
> of his pages in a sentence and passed on, it would have
> been far more excellent writing. (J 2:418–19)

Perhaps, then, what Harding calls the "atypical, staccato" sentence structure in "An Excursion" might not be "pedestrian journalese"[4] but Thoreau's attempt at the spare, concentrated, suggestive writing that he calls for in his Journal—writing that is "kinked and knotted up into something hard and significant" (J 2:419).

This "concentrated and nutty" writing places a considerable burden on the reader, who must pick up and develop the suggestions, cultivate the "seeds," and search for what Thoreau means but does not explicitly say. Thoreau returns here to the experiment he had begun in A Week of involving the reader actively in the process of a work. The danger with this strategy is, of course, that the reader may refuse the burden. Confronted with images, impressions, and observations that are not unified in a traditional sense or connected by transitions or shaped according to a clear plan, the reader may simply dismiss "An Excursion," as many have done, as a generally incoherent book with a few worthwhile passages. For the cooperative reader, however, the work can approach the aesthetic goal that Thoreau implies when he praises the inscription on the Wolfe-Montcalm monument: "saying much in little, and that to the purpose" (73).

In the second paragraph of "An Excursion," Thoreau confronts the reader with the abrupt, apparently digressive kind of writing to be found throughout. He jumps from the red woodbine garlanding dead trees and "suggesting bloodshed, or at least a military life," to views of Monadnock and the landscape around Troy, New Hampshire, to anecdotes about Keene Street, to advice about laying plans widely in youth, to the scenery of mountain towns (3–5). Thoreau not only evokes here the sensation of being "whirled rapidly along" as various sights flash by the window of the railroad car and inspire kaleidoscopic thoughts, but he also plants "seeds" or suggestions of important themes. The red woodbine, for example, introduces a color motif that pervades the book. The glorious red of the New England autumn contrasts with the inglorious red of the useless Commonwealth soldiers ("a military life") whom Thoreau encounters in Canada and with the "*bonnets rouges* like fools' caps" (45) worn by the French Canadian "peasants" whom Thoreau finds contemptible

[4] *Handbook*, p. 47.

for their feudal ways. Thoreau also characterizes the autumnal tints as "an Indian warfare . . . waged through the forest" (3), preparing for the later contrast that he implies between the past, when heroic bands of Indians roved about Canada (7–8), and the present, when "a few squalid Indians" try to sell baskets at the railroad depot in Montreal, the "stone-built city of white men" (99). The apparent digression on Keene Street also reverberates through "An Excursion." The eight-rod-wide New England street, which Thoreau associates with progress, growth, clarity of vision, and foresightedness, contrasts—again implicitly—with the dark, narrow, zigzagging streets of the feudal fortress that is Quebec and with the muddy, little-traveled road to St. Anne, a road that characterizes the French Canadians as static and backward-looking. Keene Street also helps to frame "An Excursion"; the book opens with a celebration of this road and concludes with reference to the "*Iter Canadense*" by which Thoreau proposes one day "to make a longer excursion on foot through the wilder parts of Canada" (101).

What might at first seem random, disjointed tourist notes become, then, the "seeds" of later image patterns and repeated themes that develop into a network of associations and help to unify and suggest the underlying significance of "An Excursion to Canada." We will concentrate here on two of those major structural and thematic patterns: one concerned with seeing and with barriers to vision, and the other with motion and stasis or, metaphorically, the river and the wall.

"Not Having Seen Much"

The narrative spine of "An Excursion" is Thoreau's circular journey from Concord to Canada, where he voyages down the St. Lawrence to Montreal and Quebec and visits a series of spectacular waterfalls:

I.   "Concord to Montreal" (3–19), travel through countryside by train and boat
II.   "Quebec and Montmorenci" (20–39), city scenes; excursion to Falls of Montmorenci

III. "St. Anne" (40–68), walking tour to Falls of St. Anne, fur-
      thest point on trip, through the least developed country
IV.   "The Walls of Quebec" (69–84), excursion to Falls of the
      Chaudière; city scenes
V.   "The Scenery of Quebec; and the River St. Lawrence" (85–
      101), travel through countryside by boat and train

Thoreau's week in Canada bears some resemblance to his earlier
Week on the Concord and Merrimack Rivers. Both are circular
journeys with a climax occurring at the farthest point from Concord. Both involve travel in time as well as space. In *A Week* Thoreau frequently returns us, through epigraphs and allusions, to
the heroic Middle Ages; for example, in "Monday": "we imagined
that the river flowed through an extensive manor, and that the
few inhabitants were retainers to a lord, and a feudal state of
things prevailed" (*W* 195). That feudal state pervades "An Excursion to Canada." Quebec's Prescott Gate "was such a reminiscence of the Middle Ages as Scott's novels" (23); the whole of
Canada East "realized much that I had heard of Europe and the
Middle Ages. . . . I began to dream of Provence and the Troubadours" (57); the omnipresent Canadian fortifications "carry us
back to the Middle Ages, the siege of Jerusalem, and St. Jean
d'Acre, and the days of the Bucaniers" (77). These transports
also resemble the psychological escape from the Concord jail at
the center of "Resistance to Civil Government" (*RP* 82).

The feudal settings in *A Week* allowed Thoreau to assume the
role of heroic knight so important to the quest myth that helps
structure the book (see ch. 6). In "An Excursion," too, Thoreau
becomes an odd kind of Yankee knight in a feudal setting, anticipating Mark Twain's later fantasy along similar lines. From the
start Thoreau pictures himself and his fellow travelers as an in-
vasion force. While the Yankees watched the British soldiers
being drilled, Thoreau reports, "I heard some of our party dis-
cussing the possibility of their driving these troops off the field
with their umbrellas" (10). He returns to this theme when he
scouts the medieval fortifications of Quebec: "I thought that, if
seven champions were enough against the latter [the gates of
Thebes], one would be enough against Quebec, though he bore
for all armor and device only an umbrella and a bundle" (74).

Thoreau refers here to his identification of himself and his companion as "the Knights of the Umbrella and the Bundle" (33).

As in *A Week*, however, Thoreau's knightly role is not so much that of a warrior as a quester. His goal in "An Excursion" is not as ambitious as it was in *A Week*, where he sought out God and heaven, but it is fundamentally serious. "Well," he says to himself as he starts down the St. Lawrence, "here I am in a foreign country; let me have my eyes about me, and take it all in" (31). Since "An Excursion" is, like *Cape Cod*, basically a travel piece, his goal of seeing obviously refers to conventional sight-seeing. But as it does so often in Thoreau's writing, the goal of perception involves a kind of heightened seeing, an intuitive grasping of essentials in an act that joins subject and object. Early in the piece he alludes to this special kind of perception: "Inexpressibly beautiful appears the recognition [etymologically, 'to examine,' 'inspect,' 'know again'] by man of the least natural fact, and the allying of his life to it" (20). In the same passage he speaks of the poetry involved in properly naming things and places such as Pointe aux Trembles: "All the world reiterating this slender truth, that aspens once grew there; and the swift inference is that men were there to *see* them" (20, emphasis added). Another inference, as Thoreau sets off on his quest to "take it all in," is that good poetry—and writing in general—depends on the writer's ability to see without hindrance.

The conditions for seeing are apparently ideal in Canada because of the wonderful "purity and transparency of the atmosphere" (34) and the "steel-like and flashing air" (88). Indeed, Thoreau does enjoy a series of "grand views" on his tour. He sees the St. Lawrence with its tributaries and falls, Notre Dame, the sparkling tin roofs of Montreal, the fortifications of Quebec, panoramas of the countryside from Cape Diamond and Mount Royal, colorful soldiers everywhere (including the bare-kneed Highlanders), and many historical sights.

But Thoreau also gives considerable emphasis to what he does not see. In his very first sentence he admits, "I fear that I have not got much to say about Canada, not having seen much" (3), and references to blocked or distorted vision recur throughout the book. Some of these obstacles arise from the nature of the excursion Thoreau takes, radically different from his leisurely trip on the Concord and Merrimack rivers, or the walking tours of Cape Cod, or his visits to the Maine woods. Along with his fellow vacationers, Thoreau joins an organized tour that commits him to a tight, hurried schedule. The limit of one week in Canada East forces him to rush by worthwhile sights and frequently to travel in the dark. Confined to a railroad car, he gets "only a glimpse" of Lake Champlain at Vergennes and reaches Burlington "too late to see the lake" (7). Steaming down the St. Lawrence from Montreal to Quebec, he misses most of the scenery because "the daylight now failed us, and we went below" (20). At Quebec, Thoreau resorts to a caleche under the pressure of time but discovers that "the route which we took to the Chaudière did not afford us those views of Quebec which we had expected" (70). And on the way back to Montreal, he retraces the journey Jacques Cartier called "'full of the most beautiful trees in the world,' which he goes on to describe. But we merely slept and woke again to find that we had passed through all that country which he was eight days in sailing through" (97). Because Thoreau does not have the leisure or liberty for his customary sauntering, he misses the glimpses of wild nature that inspired his most imaginative insights.

Besides his mode of travel, cultural conditions in Canada prevent him from seeing as much as he wants. Thoreau discovers damaging political and intellectual barriers to the freedom and growth of the individual in Canada. For example, at St. John's, his first stop outside the United States, he reports, "We saw but little of the village here, for nobody could tell us when the cars would start; that was kept a profound secret, perhaps for political reasons; and therefore we were tied to our seats" (10). In Quebec he runs into more bureaucratic interference when he must obtain a pass from the Town Major in order to see the citadel (24). At Montmorenci, too, his sight-seeing is frustrated by Canada's archaic and obtrusive social system: "We were disappointed to find that we were in some measure shut out from the west side of the fall by the private grounds and fences of Patterson, who appropriates not only a part of the water for his mill, but a still much larger part of the prospect . . . which should, in every sense, belong to mankind" (37–38).

Ironically, the social realities that hinder vision in Canada are themselves obscured at first by the omnipresent French place-names that create for Thoreau a poetic atmosphere. The names of the squares in Montreal first suggest that "a French Revolution might break out any moment" (15), but he eventually learns that, in truth, the Canadians "are very far from a revolution, have no quarrel with Church or State, but their vice and their virtue is content" (64). In the countryside, too, names such as "*St. Feréol* or *St. Anne*, the *Guardian Angel* or the *Holy Joseph's*" inspire Thoreau "to dream of Provence and the Troubadours," but he soon realizes that such poetic ideals "have no existence on the earth." The quaint names associated with Europe and the Middle Ages "veiled the Indian and the primitive forest," obscuring the wild parts of Canada that for Thoreau remained unrealized on this frustrating tour; "the woods toward Hudson's Bay were only as the forests of France and Germany" (57).

He tires of "these saintly names" (57) also because they remind him of another major impediment to true vision in Canada, the church. He is impressed by Montreal's Notre Dame, but only because he can transform it imaginatively from a man-made religious structure into a natural secular one—a cave: "It was a great cave in the midst of a city; and what were the altars and the tinsel but the sparkling stalactites, into which you entered in a moment, and where the still atmosphere and the sombre light disposed to a serious and profitable thought? . . . where you do your own preaching, where the universe preaches to you and can be heard" (13–14). But Thoreau cannot so easily transform the other ecclesiastical institutions he encounters. He finds the schoolhouse near St. Anne "like a place where the process, not of enlightening, but of obfuscating the mind was going on, and the pupils received only so much light as could penetrate the shadow of the Catholic Church" (46). The same darkness overshadows the Canadian nunneries, which Thoreau learns to distinguish "by the blinds" (74). When he sees some Sisters of Charity outside their convent, they "looked as if they had almost cried their eyes out" and they keep their injured eyes carefully fixed on the ground (15, 16).

Windows recur as a motif throughout "An Excursion," with

obvious relevance to the theme of vision. If blinds shroud the nunneries, the French Canadian houses have "no door nor cheerful window on the road side" (44), and the barracks of the soldiers feature "very narrow windows . . . serving as loop-holes for musketry" (28–29) rather than as sources of light. The entire city of Quebec seems closed in, dark, impenetrable, like a medieval castle. To get anywhere, Thoreau is forced to zigzag through narrow streets and tunnellike gates manned by sentries (25–26). These alleys clearly contrast with "wide, level, straight, and long" Keene Street. Recalling the metaphorical significance of the New England street, which Thoreau associates with men laying plans widely in youth, "for then land is cheap, and it is but too easy to contract our views afterward," one can appreciate the importance of the contracted, narrow passageways of Quebec. And, implicitly contrasting with the New England youth "prepared for the most remotely successful and glorious life" (4), the young soldiers who obstruct the streets of Canada are stripped of their individuality to become "one vast centipede of a man . . . peculiarly destitute of originality and independence" (17, 27).

"The wall was the main thing in Quebec" (74), Thoreau says, and in describing the city he catalogues various kinds of walls obstructing vision and mobility. The oppressive masses of stone around the city and the walls of churches, convents, barracks, and armories embody the oppressive social and political atmosphere in Canada. Both the "huge stone structures" and the institutions of Church and State they represent "rather oppress than liberate the mind" (78). They limit vision for people who can "speculate only within bounds," in contrast to Americans, who "in more than one sense, can *speculate* without bounds" (83; Thoreau italicizes the word to emphasize its etymology and relation to seeing). Thoreau playfully admits some fears for the health of his own vision in this city of walls. "Not wishing to get a black eye," he avoids the artillery barracks which are "so arranged as to give a startling *coup d'oeil* to strangers" (75). And at last he declares, "I went no farther by the wall for fear that I should become wall-eyed" (76).

Underneath the wordplay is a justified concern, for, in a sense, Canada really does damage Thoreau's vision. In a Journal passage that he later tapped for the first paragraph of "An Excursion," Thoreau claimed that he visited Canada "as the bullet visits the wall at which it is fired, and from which it rebounds as quickly, and flattened (somewhat damaged, perchance)!" (J 2:417; Thoreau included this sentence in his early lecture draft [HM 949, 1], but it does not appear in the later drafts [HM 950 or HM 953]). In the essay itself he suggests that his perception has been distorted by the omnipresent "symbolical knickknacks" in Canada: "I could not look at an honest weathercock in this walk without mistrusting that there was some covert reference in it to St. Peter" (45–46). More important, after shunning the obstacles to vision presented by his package tour, the bureaucracy, and feudal land laws, when he does finally observe some spectacular natural scenery, his reactions seem anticlimactic. He appears not to have seen fully what was before him, as if he were distracted. Of Montmorenci Falls he writes, "The most I could say . . . would only have the force of one other testimony to assure the reader that it is there" (38). He displays the same lack of emotional and imaginative engagement at the Falls of the Chaudière: "Though they were the largest which I saw in Canada, I was not proportionately interested by them" (71).

Thoreau's muted response to these natural sights seems particularly unsettling in light of his earlier insistence that "inexpressibly beautiful appears the recognition by man of the least natural fact, and the allying his life to it" (20). He celebrates this fertile relation to nature at length in a Journal passage that appears immediately after a discussion of the debilitating effects of the Canadian political system (later incorporated into "Excursion," ch. 4). The proximity suggests a close connection between the two topics in his mind. Thoreau insists on the active, imaginative mode of seeing, and he praises the faculty "which can paint the most barren landscape and humblest life in glorious colors" (J 2:413). Clearly, this faculty does not operate for him in Canada. If "it is the marriage of the soul with Nature that makes the intellect fruitful, that gives birth to imagination," no such marriage takes place during his tour north.[5] Thoreau claims pri-

[5] Laraine Fergenson points out Thoreau's allusion here to Wordsworth's *The Recluse*: "the discerning intellect of Man/ . . . wedded to this goodly universe/In love and holy passion" ("Prospectus," ll. 805–7)

vately that when we achieve this relation to Nature, "suddenly the sky is all one rainbow" (J 2:413). The passage helps us appreciate the gulf between himself and nature suggested by his reaction to the rainbow at the Falls of the Chaudière. Though it is, he claims, "the most brilliant rainbow that I ever imagined," he displays no imaginative involvement with it: "Evidently a picture painted on mist for the men and animals that come to the falls to look at; but for what special purpose beyond this, I know not" (71). His reaction here contrasts greatly with his reaction to the rainbows that would later frame "Baker Farm" in *Walden*, E version, which he uses to reaffirm his own special election and vocation. The different responses to the rainbows indicate extensive damage to Thoreau's powers of viewing and animating nature.

Early drafts of the passages on both the Montmorenci and Chaudière falls suggest that Thoreau revised them to emphasize disappointment and anticimax. HM 949 contains more—and more upbeat—information about Montmorenci. Thoreau discusses the history of the area and describes the faint rainbows that emerged with the sun. His tone is fairly positive when he speaks of "a very perfect & unique fall—not so wild or even wondrous as some—but simply & wholly grand" (42–v43; not in later surviving drafts). His early passage on the Chaudière, too, is fuller and conveys more excitement as he describes "the most brilliant rainbow that I ever saw or imagined" (73). Not until later did he drop his celebration of "that wonderfully beautiful rainbow trembling before us, formed by the sun's rays on mist which this tremendous fall produced" and add the indication of his disappointment.

Why did his imaginative vision fail in Canada? Thoreau claims that he lost interest in the great waterfalls "probably from satiety" (71), but he was never satiated by the ponds around Concord, the ocean at Cape Cod, or the Maine woods. He does suggest, though, another reason for his disengagement. Immediately after recounting his disappointment with the Falls of the Chau-

---

("Was Thoreau Re-reading Wordsworth in 1851?" *Thoreau Journal Quarterly* 5 [1975]:22–23).

dière and its brilliant rainbow, and in the same paragraph, he remarks, "At the farthest point in this ride, and when most inland, unexpectedly at a turn in the road we descried the frowning citadel of Quebec in the horizon, like the beak of a bird of prey. . . . When we were opposite to Quebec, I was surprised to see that in the Lower Town, under the shadow of the rock, the lamps were lit" (71). The shadow of this fortress, a bird of prey, follows Thoreau throughout Canada. His vision of nature is so affected by the stone walls of the city—and the oppressive institutions they represent—that he never escapes during his week there: "The fortifications of Cape Diamond are omnipresent. They preside, they frown over the river and surrounding country. You travel ten, twenty, thirty miles up or down the river's banks, you ramble fifteen miles amid the hills on either side, and then, when you have long since forgotten them, perchance slept on them by the way, at a turn of the road or of your body, there they are still, with their geometry against the sky" (87–88). The fortifications keep reminding Thoreau of "antiquity and barbarism" (78), and he cannot evade their deadening atmosphere. They interfere with his attempts to view Canada scientifically as well as imaginatively; "even I yielded in some degree to the influence of historical associations, and found it hard to attend to the geology of Cape Diamond or the botany of the Plains of Abraham" (88).

This theme of cities (and all they symbolize) interfering with proper vision is crucial to "An Excursion." Quite understandably, then, Thoreau ignored the advice of Horace Greeley who "suggested that Thoreau . . . omit the sections on Montreal and Quebec, obviously realizing that Thoreau's caustic comments on church and state would alienate both editors and readers, and emphasize the natural history" (*DHT* 282). Thoreau's point is precisely that the cities could not be ignored—that they prevented him from seeing or interacting with nature vitally and imaginatively. The dying man he sees on the wharf after returning from the Falls of the Chaudière might well symbolize his own failing powers of perception (72). In effect, the walls of Quebec bury his poetic faculty: "they are tombs for the souls of men" (78).

On a less melodramatic note, Thoreau treats his damaged vision in terms of a minor health problem caused by the Canadian weather. He finds that it "felt a good deal colder than it had in New England" (31), and a Scotchman tells him that "it was colder there than usual at that season" (76). Like so many other features of Canada, the climate takes on symbolic significance. Canada is "that cold country" (49) metaphorically as well as physically, for it is intellectually barren, hostile to warm and vivifying imagination, and frozen in its allegiance to an archaic social system. Provided only with "my thin hat and sack," Thoreau succumbs to the weather. He claims in the first sentence of the book, "what I got by going to Canada was a cold" (3). He sees everything there through smarting, watery eyes and speaks as if out of the remoteness of a fever and a stuffy head. His cold makes him irritable and unusually curmudgeonly. He is no longer warmed by the "subterranean fire in nature" that he enjoys on his winter walks in Concord.[6]

Thoreau wrestles with failed imaginative vision in another essay, part of which was drafted in the Journals shortly after "An Excursion"—"Slavery in Massachusetts."[7] In both works, political repression by a corrupt state affects Thoreau's perception of and relation to nature. Because of its cooperation with slaveholders, Massachusetts changes in Thoreau's view from a fertile wonderland to part of "the empire of hell": "I walk toward one of

[6]"A Winter Walk" (*Ex* 167). Just as his reactions to the rainbow and other natural phenomena in Canada are uncharacteristic and blunted—and for the same reasons—Thoreau's response to cold in "An Excursion" is atypical. The wintry weather here dulls his perceptions and comes to symbolize stasis. In *Walden*, "A Winter Walk," and the Journal, the cold season more often proves bracing, purifying, revivifying. For a discussion of Thoreau's usual attitude toward winter as the productive "season for intellectual work," see Willard H. Bonner, "The Harvest of Thought in Thoreau's 'Autumnal Tints,'" *ESQ* 22 (1976):81–82.

[7]The Fugitive Slave Act became law on 18 September 1850, seven days before Thoreau went to Canada, and the Simms affair took place in April 1851, a few months before the Journal entries show Thoreau working on his Canada lectures. Thoreau's entries on those political events later went into "Slavery in Massachusetts."

our ponds, but what signifies the beauty of nature when men are base? We walk to lakes to see our serenity reflected in them; when we are not serene, we go not to them" (*RP* 108). In the same way, Canada's "imperfect and tyrannical government" (17) prevents Thoreau from seeing the Canadian landscape with the serenity and the transforming colors of the imagination necessary for the fertile "marriage of the soul with Nature." "An Excursion" thus foreshadows Thoreau's later development, when social-political concerns help move him away from nature and more idealistic aspirations. Because of this emphasis on vision impaired by political circumstance, it seems appropriate that the complete "Excursion to Canada" first appeared with *Anti-Slavery and Reform Papers* (1866) rather than in *Excursions*, where it is placed in the Riverside (1893) and Walden (1906) editions of Thoreau's writings, and where it will appear in the Princeton edition.

Rivers and Walls

Another way to approach the underlying significance of "An Excursion to Canada" is through its structurally and thematically important references to flowing water. Sidney Poger points out that "An Excursion" is organized around the image of the St. Lawrence River, but he claims that Thoreau "never became involved with the river"; as a result, the book "suffers from the lack of focus on a natural object as in his other books."[8] But perhaps, as we have argued, Thoreau intended to explore *why* he did not become involved with the major natural features of Canada, the rivers and their falls. Perhaps the accounts of the generally disappointing views of nature "suggest far more than they say" and are the "seeds" that develop into his deepest concerns in the work.

"An Excursion" is another of Thoreau's water-logged books. The importance of water, particularly flowing water, appears from the start, as Thoreau prefaces the book with two epigraphs

[8]"Thoreau as Yankee in Canada," *American Transcendental Quarterly*, no. 14 (1972):174.

on "the famous River of Canada" (2). Reaching Bellows Falls on the train to Canada, he records his disappointment "in the size of the river here [the Connecticut]; it appeared shrunk to a mere mountain-stream" (5). This comment prepares us for the first glimpse of the St. Lawrence, which "was the main feature in the landscape" (49), and which guides his tour and helps structure his account of that tour. Thoreau follows the St. Lawrence from Montreal to Quebec to St. Anne and then back, stopping to view the falls of rivers that feed the great River of Canada.

Not surprisingly, these masses of flowing water take on symbolic significance. Rivers, streams, freshets, and rain symbolize for Thoreau freshness, energy, growth, spontaneity, and the flow of life. In *A Week on the Concord and Merrimack Rivers*, for example, he insists that "a man's life should be constantly as fresh as this river," and at a climactic point in that journey he experiences an epiphany during which "all things seemed with us to flow. . . . There were rivers of rock on the surface of the earth, and rivers of ore in its bowels, and our thoughts flowed and circulated, and this portion of time was but the current hour" (W 132, 331). At a corresponding point in *Walden* comes the passage on the thawing bank of the Deep Cut whose flowing sands inspire Thoreau's vision of universal flow and renewal (*Wa* 304–9). In "An Excursion," too, the St. Lawrence takes on positive connotations as the only flowing thing in a land of stasis.

The major metaphorical dialectic in the book is between the river and the wall. Opposed to the potential for progress and growth represented by the river is the walled fortress, "a reminiscence of the Middle Ages" (23), removed from the stream of time. Walls symbolize the ossification of Canada, as Thoreau suggests when he speaks of the thickness of Quebec's "parietal bones" (75). This fortified town reminds him of "a man cased in the heavy armor of antiquity, with a horse-load of broadswords and small arms slung to him, endeavoring to go about his business" (78). Soldiers weighed down like this are no match for the "Knights of the Umbrella and the Bundle" (33), who are free to move where they choose. The stasis of any fortified town is its chief drawback: "We shall at length hear that an enemy sailed by it in the night, for it cannot sail itself, and both it and its inhabitants are always benighted" (79). And, again, Quebec's walls and all "huge stone structures" remind Thoreau of the ultimate stasis, death: "They are tombs for the souls of men, as frequently for their bodies also" (78).

The implied opposition between the river, main feature of the countryside, and the wall, main feature of the city, helps to illuminate the structure of "An Excursion." The book is framed by chapters that recount the journey from Concord to Montreal (1) and back again (5), with emphasis on river travel and the countryside. Between these come chapters devoted to Quebec city and its walls, though they also cover short, disappointing excursions just outside Quebec to falls on the Montmorenci (2) and Chaudière (4) rivers. At the structurally emphatic center comes Thoreau's visit to the Falls of St. Anne (3). Earlier, Thoreau had announced his intention to "take one honest walk" in Canada (3), and the walk to St. Anne, which gets him to his farthest point down the St. Lawrence and through the country which has "undergone the least change from the beginning" (41), is the closest he comes to fulfilling that goal. One might expect, then, some sort of climax, just as *A Week* leads to the crucial ascent of Agiocochook. And Thoreau does approach at the Falls of St. Anne the heightened perception and imaginative transformation of nature that highlight the climaxes of his more successful excursions. His description of the falls takes on symbolic significance in relation to the framing chapters. Exploring the series of falls, he comes upon

> the highest perpendicular wall of bare rock that I ever saw. In front of me tumbled in from the summit of the cliff a tributary stream, making a beautiful cascade, which was a remarkable fall in itself, and there was a cleft in this precipice, apparently four or five feet wide, perfectly straight up and down from top to bottom . . . This precipice . . . rises perpendicular, like the *side of a mountain fortress*, and is cracked into vast cubical masses of gray and black rock shining with moisture, as if it were the *ruin of an ancient wall* built by Titans. . . . Take it altogether, it was a most wild and rugged and

stupendous chasm, so deep and narrow, *where a river
had worn itself a passage through a mountain of rock,*
and all around was the comparatively untrodden wilderness. (55; emphasis added)

The passage is significant not only because Thoreau reacts to
the Falls of St. Anne more vividly than he does to the physically
more impressive falls of Montmorenci and the Chaudière but
also because his description becomes a symbolic victory of the
river over the wall. Interacting imaginatively with the natural
scene, Thoreau envisions the possibility that those forces of freedom, fluidity, and growth represented by the river can overcome
the stasis and resistance to change symbolized by the cliff that is
allied to the walls of Quebec.

But the vision of the ideal proves momentary and evanescent.
Thoreau finds himself again in the real world where the poverty
of the French Canadians distracts him from the enjoyment of
nature. The Falls of St. Anne recede from view, and in the rest
of the chapter Thoreau dissects the feudal tenure which keeps
the "peasant" population "very inferior, intellectually and even
physically, to that of New England" (64). Then back at Quebec,
he loses interest in the spectacular Falls of the Chaudière and
can make no poetic use of its glorious rainbow. To paraphrase
Coleridge, he can see, not feel, how beautiful they are. He does
experience one other moment of imaginative elevation when,
looking beyond the fortress, he feels "the citadel under my feet,
and all historical associations, were swept away again by an influence from the wilds and from Nature, . . . an influence which,
like the Great River itself, flowed from the Arctic fastnesses and
Western forests with irresistible force over all" (89). But back in
the city he finds himself once again within the shadows of the
feudal walls, "like a rat looking for a hole" (72).

As in the sections on the Montmorenci and Chaudière, Thoreau revised this part to tone down his original positive responses
and to emphasize disappointment. After the passage on the Falls
of St. Anne, his early lecture draft (HM 949) contains three
sheets describing grand scenery: "From our seat amidst the
aspens we had a glorious view of the St. Lawrence—its [*word*

illegible] and Cape Tourment . . . for the transparency of the atmosphere was incredible" (61–62). Thoreau reduced this material to a few sentences in HM 953 and then omitted it entirely from the published "Excursion," which moves much more quickly to the social criticism that dominates the rest of the chapter. He also increased the amount and the biting tone of that criticism from the early lecture draft to the final version.

The St. Lawrence flows through Canada East as an emblem of potential freedom, but, Thoreau insists, the French Canadians do not use the river. He is scandalized to see "men in the streets sawing logs pit-fashion, and afterward, with a common wood-saw and horse . . . This looked very shiftless, especially in a country abounding in water-power, and reminded me that I was no longer in Yankeeland" (29). Thoreau relates this failure to employ the physical force of the river to the feudal economic structure of Canada: "I found, on inquiry, that the excuse for this was that labor was so cheap; and I thought, with some pain, how cheap men are here!" (29–30). The Canadians do not use the river extensively for commerce, either. Thoreau discovers in Montmorenci County "five Roman Catholic churches, and no others, five cures and five presbyteries . . . and five river crafts, whose tonnage amounted to sixty-nine tons! This, notwithstanding that it has a frontage of more than thirty miles on the river" (62). Thoreau once more hints at the role of the feudal Catholic Church in the failure to develop the valley's potential when he reports that "Emery de Caen, Champlain's contemporary, told the Huguenot sailors that 'Monsigneur the Duke de Ventador (Viceroy) did not wish that they should sing psalms in the Great River'" (52). The Catholic French Canadians will not even use the river as a setting appropriate for prayer.

In regard to transportation, too, Thoreau finds that the Canadians "were no sailors, and made but little use of the river" (56). After missing a trip to the Isle of Orleans because the local pirogues prove unsafe in a wind, Thoreau accuses the Canadians of being "shiftless . . . for not having provided any other conveyance" (70). He sees the people along the St. Lawrence "almost wholly confined to its banks" (62). In effect, they treat the symbol of free passage as if it were a wall or barrier. They travel neither by river nor land. The only route to St. Anne is a muddy lane, and the houses along it "had no door nor cheerful window on the road side" (44). "There were no guide-boards where we walked," Thoreau reports, "because there was but one road; . . . and there were no taverns, because there were no travelers" (50). Of the houses along the way he notes that "every part is for the use of the occupant exclusively, and no part has reference to the traveler or to travel" (59). If the French Canadians are not interested in traditional means of travel, they are not likely to experiment with new ones: "They have no money invested in railroad stocks, and probably never will have" (64).

The physical immobility of the Canadians is obviously a function of their social, political, and intellectual stagnation. Although the St. Lawrence flows through their settlements, an emblem of potential development and renewal, the Canadians have not really recognized this "natural fact" or allied their lives to it (20). "I saw there . . . little evidence of any recent growth" (62). Because of this physical and moral stagnation, Thoreau predicts that the Canadians will eventually be replaced by the more progressive, energetic, and adventurous race of New England "sailors" (67), men who have remained allied to the rivers: "The impression made on me was that the French Canadians were even sharing the fate of the Indians, or at least gradually disappearing in what is called the Saxon *current*" (66; emphasis added).

Thoreau points out, however, that the Canadians have not always opposed themselves to travel, adventure, and improvement. Although the eighteenth-century French Canadians had to be compelled by law to spread out from the riverbanks and cultivate new land, the seventeenth-century explorers "possessed a roving spirit of adventure which carried them further, in exposure to hardship and danger, than even the New England colonist went, and led them, though not to clear and colonize the wilderness, yet to range over it as *coureurs de bois*, or runners of the woods, or, as Hontan prefers to call them, *coureurs de risques*, runners of risks" (43). These explorers are the closest Thoreau comes in "An Excursion" to the mythic figures he features in *A Week*, *Walden*, and *The Maine Woods*. Ironically, they seem more modern than the Canadians of Thoreau's own time, who remind him of Europe and the Middle Ages. Thoreau is disgusted by the filthy and unintelligent "nation of peasants" (82) in modern Canada, but he acknowledges a "sympathy with that spirit of adventure which distinguished the French and Spaniards [of the sixteenth century], and made them especially the explorers of the American continent,—which so early carried the former to the Great Lakes and the Mississippi on the north, and the latter to the same river on the south" (67–68). Not only did they know how to use the river for adventure and travel, but they also perceived it more imaginatively: "The early explorers saw many whales and other sea-monsters far up the St. Lawrence" (91).

Commenting on the many quotations in "An Excursion" from the sixteenth-century explorers, John Aldrich Christie contends that "the later experiences which Thoreau's reading furnished him clouded or even substituted for the firsthand experience that had been his own."[9] The clash that Christie notes between the physical and vicarious travel may not be the result of inadequate "stitching together" but a deliberate strategy. Sherman Paul has suggested that Thoreau juxtaposes the past and present to emphasize and dramatize his disappointment when "his actual trip did not bring him so close as he desired to the Canada of the early explorers, the Jesuits, the Indians, and the fur traders."[10] His use of history thus resembles Eliot's use of myth in poems such as *The Waste Land*.

In the final pages of "An Excursion to Canada," Thoreau presents a great deal of geographical data to support his contention that the St. Lawrence "easily bears off the palm from all the rivers on the globe" (94). "But, unfortunately," he points out, "this noble river is closed by ice from the beginning of December to the middle of April" (95). Again, the cold is symbolic as well as physical; it represents the petrifying atmosphere created by Canada's institutions. Having himself caught cold on his northern tour, Thoreau produced not so much a disappointing travelogue

[9]*Thoreau as World Traveler* (New York: Columbia Univ. Press, 1965), p. 99.

[10]*The Shores of America*, p. 369.

as a suggestive account of the factors that prevent him from seeing much—that is, seeing imaginatively—in Canada.

A few months before his Canada trip, Thoreau wrote: "Man and his affairs,—Church and State and school, trade and commerce and agriculture,—Politics,—for that is the word for them all here to-day,—I am pleased to see how little space it occupies in the landscape" (*J* 2:53). Politics in this sense is exactly what defeated the Knight of the Umbrella and the Bundle on his quest in Canada and what would later in his career diminish Thoreau's ability to perceive even the landscape around Concord with the vision he exercised at the height of his romantic period. But in 1850–51, as he wrote "An Excursion to Canada," that period was still ahead of him. He included the Journal entry above in "Walking" (*Ex* 212–213), parts of which he gave as lectures in 1851 and 1856—after the Canada trip. And when he resumed *Walden* at the D stage, he added to it (particularly to the second half) significant sections on perception and myth that turned it into a romantic celebration of the imaginative seeing that had failed him in Canada.

8
Cape Cod

WHILE WORKING on "An Excursion to Canada," Thoreau was putting together another travel piece, one that has received considerably more attention. The criticism of *Cape Cod* is as varied as Thoreau found the ocean to be at Cohasset. Reading it leaves an impression similar to the one Thoreau got comparing earlier accounts of the Cape with his own experience: how can perceptions of the same thing differ so radically? What Krutch and Harding take to be a sunny holiday travelogue is to Maiden an account of Thoreau's loss of romantic faith and his development of a pessimistic modern existentialist consciousness. What Porte and Paul read as a book of inward exploration and spiritual discovery is to D'Avanzo and Sattelmeyer a dissertation on human culture.[1]

Cape Cod poses problems not only of its genre and theme but also of its place in Thoreau's intellectual development. Many critics see the book, with its opening emphasis on "Death!" (*CC* 5)

[1] Joseph Wood Krutch, Introduction, *Cape Cod* (New York: Heritage Press, 1968); Harding and Meyer, *The New Thoreau Handbook*, pp. 66–69; Emory Virgil Maiden, Jr., "*Cape Cod*: Thoreau's Handling of the Sublime and Picturesque," Ph.D. diss., Virginia, 1972; Joel Porte, "Henry Thoreau and the Reverend Poluphloisboios Thalassa," in *The Chief Glory of Every People*, ed. Matthew J. Bruccoli (Carbondale: Southern Illinois Univ. Press, 1977), pp. 193–210; Paul, *The Shores of America*, pp. 379–88; Mario D'Avanzo, "Fortitude and Nature in Thoreau's *Cape Cod*," *ESQ* 20 (1974):131–38; Robert Sattelmeyer, "Away from Concord: The Travel Writings of Henry Thoreau," Ph.D. diss., New Mexico, 1975. For other recent criticism see Richard Bridgman, *Dark Thoreau* (Lincoln: Univ. of Nebraska Press, 1982), pp. 158–87; Linck C. Johnson, "Into History: Thoreau's Earliest 'Indian Book' and His First Trip to *Cape Cod*," *ESQ* 28 (1982):74–88; John Hildebilde, *Thoreau: A Naturalist's Liberty* (Cambridge: Harvard Univ. Press, 1983), pp. 126–46; Sherman Paul, "From Walden Out," *Thoreau Quarterly* 16 (1984):75–81; and Robert D. Richardson, Jr., *Henry Thoreau: A Life of the Mind* (Berkeley: Univ. of California Press, 1986), pp. 201–04.

and man's alienation from nature, as a repudiation of *Walden* and Thoreau's early idealistic Transcendental faith. We will show that *Cape Cod* is earlier than the complete *Walden*; that it was composed before and during Thoreau's conversion to romanticism, when he was experimenting with various attitudes toward nature; and that it differs from *Walden* mainly because Thoreau intended it as a conventional and popular travel book, albeit more challenging and sophisticated than most.

The publication history of *Cape Cod* contributes to the confusion about it. The first four chapters appeared serially in the summer of 1855; two more chapters came out in 1864, when the complete book was also published. But although it was in print after *Walden* (summer 1854), most of *Cape Cod* was composed earlier.

The basic shape of the book and much of its contents were determined by Thoreau's first trip to the Cape, 9–17 October 1849 (five months after publication of *A Week*). This visit provided the structural trunk onto which Thoreau grafted materials from his subsequent visits. Early in 1850 he lectured four times about the Cape. He revisited it briefly in June and then spoke on it twice more later in the year. Preparing for a lecture that he gave in February 1850, he wrote, "I propose to read this evening as many extracts as the time will permit from a long account of a visit to Cape Cod made last October [1849], particularly those parts relating to Nauset beach."[2] Sections of this long text survive in "A Course of Lectures on Cape Cod" HM 13206), which also contains drafts and revisions for much of the book. This manuscript suggests that Thoreau's account was quite extensive by 1850. He then added materials, chiefly geographical, biological, and botanical, from his visit to Hull and Plymouth in the summer of 1851.

In November 1852 he submitted to *Putnam's Monthly Magazine* the first three chapters and promised the fourth. This packet, he wrote, was "not yet half the whole" (C 288), implying that by this date he had determined fairly well the shape and

---

[2]"A Course of Lectures on Cape Cod," Huntington manuscript HM 13206, leaf numbered 4.

extent of the entire work. Perhaps because of difficulties with George William Curtis over publication of "An Excursion to Canada," the *Cape Cod* material did not appear until 1855, when the first four chapters were published in the June, July, and August issues of *Putnam's*.

Thoreau visited the Cape a third time in July 1855 and soon thereafter wrote Curtis asking "to substitute the accompanying sheets for about ten pages of my MS, in the chapter called 'The Beach Again' [ch. 6]'" (*C* 379). Presumably the new sheets included material from this third visit, which also supplied additions to chapters 7 and 8 (for example, the blackfish section of ch. 7). A note following chapter 4 promised "To be continued," but *Putnam's* published no more of the manuscript. Recent research by Joseph J. Moldenhauer indicates that Curtis, not Thoreau, decided to halt serial publication of *Cape Cod*, probably because Curtis had not anticipated how long the whole manuscript would prove and because he grew tired of what he took to be Thoreau's abrasive tone.[3] Thoreau seems not to have worked extensively on *Cape Cod* after 1855. He added to chapter 6 half a paragraph from his Journal for 7 April 1857 (*J* 9:321), but no subsequent Journal materials appear in the book, even though he visited the Cape again two months later and recorded many lively and appropriate observations (*J* 9:413–55). Thoreau did add quotations from his reading to the manuscript as late as 1860, when he included extracts from David Crantz's *Greenland* (one of the last books he withdrew from Harvard Library),[4] but no evidence exists for substantial additions or alterations after 1855.

[3] Moldenhauer, "The Princeton Edition of *Cape Cod*," 1984 MLA Annual Convention, Washington, D.C.

[4] In "Thoreau's Canadian Notebook," p. 181, Lawrence Willson cautions, "It is dangerous . . . to assume that [Thoreau] first read a book at the time when he drew it from the library." He uses as an example the quotation from Crantz in ch. 4 (*CC* 60–61), a chapter that was published in 1855, five years before Thoreau withdrew Crantz's book from Harvard. But though ch. 4 did appear in *Putnam's*, the paragraph in which Thoreau quotes Crantz did not—suggesting that the quotation was added after 1855 and most likely in 1860 or after.

The chapters that appeared in *Putnam's* differ little from their final form. Thoreau later added the second paragraph of chapter 1 (although parts of this were in his February 1850 lecture), the paragraph on Greenland (60–61), two historical footnotes (15, 38), and a half dozen minor pieces of a sentence or two. These additions supplement rather than alter what is already in the chapters. Fields published two more chapters in the *Atlantic Monthly* for 1864, omitting (perhaps out of concern for the genteel sensibilities of the *Atlantic's* readers) only the passage from chapter 5 on breakfast foods that sustained "detriment from the old man's shots" (99). The complete book was also published in 1864.

Cape Cod thus dates substantially from 1849–52, with some additions from 1855. As with *A Week* and *Walden*, a considerable interval passed between the initial stimulus for the book and final publication of the whole, but Thoreau does not seem to have revised *Cape Cod* as often or as extensively as the two other works. He drafted it in the interstice after the C stage of *Walden* and expanded it when his more serious efforts were going into the D stage of his newly reconceived project. Instead of being a repudiation of *Walden*, then, most of the book was written before or concurrently with the crucial changes that turned *Walden* into a masterpiece. Although it shares many of *Walden's* themes, it does not treat them in the same way or in as much depth.

Among those themes are the related concerns about nature and perception. Those critics are surely correct who point out Thoreau's differing thematic emphases in the two books. Nature in *Cape Cod* is not the living, organic, divine force—potentially close to man—that it is in *Walden*. Rather, *Cape Cod* portrays a nature split into contradictory facets and mostly alienated from man. A basic duality emerges. On one hand, nature manifests itself from the start, as the notice informs Thoreau, in "Death!" (5). The ocean is a place of "butchery" (125) and its "fatal gripe is sure to come at last" (155); Cape Cod consists mainly of "exceedingly barren and desolate country" (25); and the shore, where ocean and Cape meet, is "a vast *morgue*" (186). On the other hand, nature also means life. The Cape contains fertile tracts (e.g., 37–38, 165) and the sea, with "its inexhaustible fertility" (120), is "the principal seat of life . . . the origin of all things" (127). Thus, the waves that wash ashore bodies from the wrecked *St. John* also bear seaweed, "valuable manure" for the Cape's farmers (8). At times Thoreau seems quite neoclassical in his sense of decorum violated: "What right has the sea to bear in its bosom such tender things as sea-jellies and mosses, when it has such a boisterous shore, that the stoutest fabrics are wrecked against it?" (70).

If the two faces of nature exist in uneasy, paradoxical tension, so also do Thoreau's attitudes toward nature's relations to man. He speaks of the treasures and gifts cast up for wreckers by the sea (115, 117), and maintains that "in the production of the necessaries of life Nature is ready enough to assist man" (219). But more often and more insistently he denies any relation between man and nature. Although Thoreau might sympathize with the "winds and waves" (11), nature does not respond in kind: the sea and its dead "necessarily left me out, with my snivelling sympathies" (108). To emphasize his theme of precarious human existence in alien nature, he frames the book with references to man-made iron structures that are "egg-shells" to the ocean (9, 263). The sea, he says, "appeared to have no relation to the friendly land" (123); "there is naked Nature—inhumanly sincere, wasting no thought on man" (187). The lack of relation between man and nature rules out a sense of correspondence. Although Thoreau occasionally uses natural facts as emblems and metaphors (e.g., weeds as "fabulous thoughts" [70], "the ocean of eternity" [p. 106]), he does not suggest that natural facts necessarily symbolize metaphysical realities or that facts will flower into truths.

Our sense of nature is, of course, always a function of perception. Where in *Walden* Thoreau perceives nature romantically, that is, through the unifying and vivifying power of imagination, in *Cape Cod* his perception is different. He approaches an Emersonian conception of the relation of dreams to reality when he claims, "The heroes and discoverers have found true more than was previously believed, only when they were expecting and dreaming of something more than their contemporaries dreamed of, or even themselves discovered, that is, when they were in a frame of mind fitted to behold the truth" (121). But in *Cape Cod* the term *imagination* refers to loose, aesthetic appreciation ("nor is the imagination contented with [Long Island's] southern aspect" [270]) or to false, misleading perception: "It was difficult," he claims, "for us landsmen to look out over the ocean without imagining land in the horizon" (65); the Wellfleet oysterman tells him that the ill effect of a clam "was all imagination" (94); and countries across the ocean "loomed to our imaginations by a common mirage" (178).

In *A Week* and *Walden*, mythologizing elevates and transforms—makes significant—the quotidian world. In *Cape Cod*, however, myth is not a vehicle for truth or a record of imaginative perception. Thoreau often alludes to classical and Judeo-Christian tales (e.g., Achilles [45], Neptune and Proteus [68], Scylla and Charybdis [163], Noah [189]), but the references are primarily decorative. Fables, instead of providing access to higher truths, are equated with lies, deceptions, "or a fish story" (68). He accuses the first New Englanders of "fabling" (236). Thoreau's allusions to myth and fable do not lead, as they do in *A Week* and *Walden*, to a sustained effort at his own mythologizing. Although he suggests the possibility of new American myths when he speaks of Cape Codders whose exploits "would cast the Argonautic expedition into the shade" (140–41) and when he mentions a semimythical "Mr. Bell (?)" whose wrecked ark planted America with seeds (167), he carries neither possibility beyond a paragraph. He says of the "voracious beach" that "the ancients would have represented it as a sea-monster with open jaws" (163), but the reference only emphasizes the absence of serious mythology in this modern book.

This absence is not owing to a lack of potential materials. If in *A Week* and *Walden* Thoreau could mythologize Concord farmers and local historical figures, he could have done the same with the early explorers and later inhabitants of *Cape Cod*. But Thoreau admires Champlain, one of the highest representatives of human culture in the book, because of his skill and adventuresomeness as a geographical explorer, not as an inward or spiritual quester. The stoic "wreckers" whom Thoreau also celebrates are heroic not because they have transfigured their lives imaginatively but because they simply survive (for a while) in a dangerous, desolate environment. The closest Thoreau comes to a significant mythical figure is the Wellfleet oysterman. The old man "was a sober Silenus, and we were the boys Chromis and Mnasilus, who listened to his story" (91). He dates back from the heroic age of American history, giving eyewitness accounts of General Washington (92). But the oysterman never approaches the spiritual status of the Tyne fisherman in *A Week*, "full of incommunicable thoughts . . . almost grown to be the sun's familiar" (*W* 24), or of Alex Therein in *Walden*. He is humble, entertaining, wise—an admirable figure, but not a hero. *Cape Cod* thus seems closer to Champlain's *Voyages* than to the "fabulous" histories of New England or even to Thoreau's other travels; in Champlain "we have a minute and faithful account, giving facts and dates . . . with scarcely one fable or traveler's story" (237).

As it was in "An Excursion to Canada," perception is important in *Cape Cod*. Thoreau frames the book with references to viewing the ocean (3, 269), and related references to looking, seeing, and observing dot each chapter. Also like "An Excursion to Canada," *Cape Cod* focuses often on blocked or distorted perception. The book is also framed by mention of "wide-open and staring eyes, yet lustreless, deadlights" (7) and the corresponding figure of the cook who "suggested how little some who voyaged round the world could manage to see" (263–64). Thoreau finds humor in the theme of misperception, as when he mistakes scarecrows for men (38) and vice versa (91), and when he and his companion anxiously try to see which dishes are contaminated by the Wellfleet oysterman's tobacco juice (99). But blocked or mistaken perception has its tragic side: in another pair of framing passages, waves prevent rescuers from seeing people on the *St. John* (10) and mist from the storm that wrecked the *St. John* causes the loss of a schooner (259).

Misperception occurs in connection with both realms of the book, nature and human culture. References to mirages abound; "to an inlander," Thoreau insists, "the Cape landscape is a constant mirage" (41).[5] Distortion also characterizes the records left by early representatives of human culture on the Cape. Thoreau

[5] See also 57, 63, 68, 107, 134, 172, 173, 175, 178, 190–93, 198, 200–201, et passim. As we have shown in ch. 7, misperception is a motif in "Excursion to Canada"; it will also appear as a theme in the late *Maine Woods* essays, which we treat in ch. 11.

often satirizes the Pilgrims whose "greenness . . . caused them to see green" (255).

To reduce the constant danger of mistaken perception, Thoreau proposes not romantic intuition into unified truth but an empirical determination of man's limits and the world's complexity. (If anything, Thoreau offers an ironic parody of the Transcendental moment of insight. He builds up the episode of the humane house [74–78] with references to "looking inward," "vision," "insight," "divine faculty," and Milton's "holy Light," only to turn the humane house anticlimactically into a symbol of "the wreck of all cosmological beauty" and of "inhumane humanity.") Instead of presenting moments of intuitive insight, Thoreau offers various perspectives on the ocean (i.e., nature) to capture as much as possible of its reality, "continually varying and shifting" like its colors (119). His central chapter emphasizes the difficulty of determining truth in a world of mirages and distorted visions (107). Yet Thoreau continues to strive for accurate, balanced perceptions, for a realistic sense of the sea's multiplicity: "this same placid ocean, as civil now as a city's harbor, a place for ships and commerce, will ere long be lashed into sudden fury, and all its caves and cliffs will resound with tumult. . . . This gentle ocean will toss and tear the rag of a man's body like the father of mad bulls, and his relatives may be seen seeking the remnants for weeks along the strand" (125).

Thoreau's perspective in the book is essentially fatalistic: "If this was the law of Nature, why waste any time in awe or pity?" (11). Although this attitude strikes his companion as unfeeling (78), it seems best calculated for survival in a complex, dangerous world. Thoreau's book thus parallels Melville's ocean masterpiece. In *Moby-Dick*, Ishmael counsels wisdom through the figure of the Catskill eagle "that can alike dive down into the blackest gorges, and soar out of them again and become invisible in the sunny spaces" (ch. 96). In his central chapter Thoreau offers an analogue to Melville's eagle: the phalarope which, though small and fragile, "would alight on the turbulent surface where the breakers were five or six feet high, and float buoyantly there like a duck, cunningly taking to its wings and lifting itself a few feet through the air over the foaming crest of each breaker, but sometimes outriding safely a considerable billow which hid it some seconds, when its instincts told it that it would not break" (113). The little creature "sporting" with the ocean serves as an emblem of a fatalistic, pragmatic approach to life in which one perceives the various "waves" of life clearly and survives by balancing on them.[6]

The waves that the bird sports with and that Thoreau returns to throughout *Cape Cod* provide an image for the book's structure. The rhythm in the flow of the tides, in the height and troughs of the sea, and in the waves breaking on the shore manifests itself, too, in the Cape's alternating moods. To convey the multiplicity of nature and of the perspectives necessary to avoid both illusory optimism and despair, Thoreau alternates vignettes of transience and permanence, sterility and fertility, life and death. His first chapter sets the pattern. He juxtaposes corpses with fertilizing seaweed (8); he presents in succession fatalistic, aesthetic, and religious consolations (12–14); then he moves rapidly from mention of a calm summer day (14), to a capsized vessel, to perfect sea bathing (16), to a reminder of shipwreck (17), to a "perfect seashore," to alewives rotting in a shallow lake, to a final, double view of Pleasant Cove as a graveyard for "many a shipwrecked man" and as a beautiful lakelike shore (18). The "ripple" and "wave" that he proposes as a device for the Hog Islanders' shield (15) could represent the order of his own book.

There is little beside this rhythm of alternation to structure *Cape Cod*, and the book's looseness indicates another important way in which it differs from Thoreau's more fully romantic works. Although *A Week* and *Walden* also contain digressive travel writing, history, and analysis of man's relationship with nature, they are structured primarily as spiritual quests for rebirth, heaven, or ultimate reality. Some hints in *Cape Cod* suggest a similar direction. For example, Thoreau announces in the first sentence his wish to view "another world" (3) and he speaks of the *St. John*'s passengers destined for a spiritual port (13). He occasionally alludes to the metaphysical importance of what he

---

[6] Compare the later Emerson of "Experience": "We live amid surfaces, and the true art of life is to skate well on them" (*CW* 3:35).

encounters on the beach (e.g., wreckers looking for treasure [115], a bottle of ale [117], anchors and chains [162]). But these passages are not developed far. He creates opportunities for epiphanies, but does not take advantage of them. For instance, the pure, life-sustaining springs of *A Week* (W 193–94) are recalled by the "unfailing spring" in Hull—but, Thoreau reports, "I did not visit it" (16). In "The Highland Light" he talks of a miraculously prolonged sunrise, with its obvious parallels to the account of sunrise on Saddleback in *A Week* and to the dawn imagery that pervades *Walden*. But Thoreau merely dismisses this sunrise as an interesting curiosity to be explained scientifically and used for a paragraph of playful moralizing (173–74).

Instead of structuring *Cape Cod*, then, the passages of metaphysical exploration decorate it. They do not seem numerous or substantial enough to support Joel Porte's claim that "it was not a scientific but a poetic attitude and religious expectation that Thoreau brought to 'the shore of the resounding sea.'"[7] Rather, they provide the "reflections" that are juxtaposed to "observations" in the tradition of eighteenth-century travel writing.[8] *Cape Cod* is a travel work unfertilized by mixture with other genres. Thoreau engages in no romance quest for the spirit that manifests itself in nature. He explores Cape Cod and the ocean partly as a devotee of the eighteenth-century sublime and picturesque and partly as an objective, scientific observer. Compared with *Walden*, *Cape Cod* resembles "The Pond in Winter," with its maps and empirical data, rather than "Spring," where imagination transfigures nature and the whole world is reborn.

Thoreau's early effort at combining travel writing with quest romance had been less than a popular success. In October 1853, four years after its publication, Munroe returned 706 copies of *A Week* (from a printing of 1000). There was, however, a considerable popular demand for travel writing. Noting the proliferation of such books in 1854, a writer for the *North American Review* commented, "Travelers in every zone and on every soil,

[7] Porte, p. 202.

[8] Batten, *Pleasurable Instruction: Form and Convention in Eighteenth-Century Travel Literature*, p. 116.

in their competition for literary fame, are treading one another down into oblivion"[9] *Cape Cod* appears to be Thoreau's entry into that crowded trek.

At the start of the book Thoreau places it in the tradition of historical and geographical studies of the Cape: "I at once got out my book, the eighth volume of the Collections of the Massachusetts Historical Society, printed in 1802, which contains some short notices of the Cape towns, and began to read up to where I was, for in the cars I could not read as fast as I traveled" (20). His other major reference is the gazetteer (25), but he mentions many supplementary sources throughout the book.[10] "The old accounts are the richest in topography," he writes, "which was what we wanted most" (42). He gives a great deal of topography in his own account, updating the old works and providing information, too, about flora and fauna, about the features and history of the towns, and about the various modes of making a living on the Cape. In this way his book goes beyond other modern accounts which consist, he claims, "in a great measure, of quotations, acknowledged and unacknowledged, from the older ones, without any additional information of equal interest" (42).[11]

Beside providing current information, Thoreau generates "equal interest" by contrasting his observations with those of past writers. For example, he plays his own experience of barrenness on the Cape off of early accounts that claim miraculous fertility for the land. The recurrent testing of the old histories and topographies provides material for his major theme of misperception.

---

[9] Anonymous review of H. B. Stowe, *Sunny Memories of Foreign Lands, North American Review* 79 (1854):423.

[10] For extensive lists of Thoreau's reading, see Suzanne Marie Strivings, "Thoreau and His Sources: A Reading of *Cape Cod*," Ph.D. diss., Texas, 1974, and Suzanne S. Lewis, "Thoreau's Use of Sources in *Cape Cod*," in Joel Myerson, ed., *Studies in the American Renaissance, 1978* (Boston: Twayne, 1978), pp. 421–28.

[11] Thoreau here points to a tradition explored in Percy G. Adams, *Travelers and Travel Liars 1660–1800* (Berkeley: Univ. of California Press, 1962).

He keeps insisting that past accounts can tyrannize over and distort perception in the present and that to reduce error one must test all previous accounts against one's own experience. Thus, he quotes with approval Thomas Browne, who refutes the popular tradition "of the tenth wave being 'greater or more dangerous than any other'" (157). Implicit in this theme is a challenge to the readers, who should test Thoreau's account for themselves. Indeed, the book is written primarily for "New-Englanders who really wish to visit the seaside" (272). Thoreau offers specific directions for those who would find the Cape a convenient six-hour train ride from Boston (269). He writes for an audience interested in the well-crafted and informational walking tour rather than romantic quests or Transcendental philosophy.

Although the vogue of aesthetic travel—of visiting places in search of the picturesque and sublime—had reached its peak in Britain by the 1780s and 1790s, it continued to be popular in America well into the nineteenth century. *The Home Book of the Picturesque*, America's most famous guide to aesthetic travel, appeared in 1852, as Thoreau was working on *Cape Cod*. Thoreau places his book clearly in this popular tradition.

The Wellfleet oysterman tells Thoreau of "English passengers who roamed over his grounds, and who, he said, thought the prospect from the high hill by the shore, 'the most delightsome they had ever seen'" (93–94). Thoreau himself travels with an eye toward picturesque views. He quotes Gilpin on "the brilliant hues which are continually playing on the surface of a quiet ocean" (119) and finds especially picturesque the unpainted houses of the Cape (80), the windmills (34), and the saltworks (23, 195). The last two structures, as they lapse into decay, remind Thoreau of the transience that is part of the picturesque effect and is another important theme throughout *Cape Cod*.[12]

Thoreau finds on *Cape Cod* even more of the sublime than the picturesque. He quotes a guidebook on the prospect from the hill of Scargo: "The view has not much of the beautiful in it, but it communicates a strong emotion of the sublime"; to which he

[12] See Price, "The Picturesque Moment," pp. 259–92.

adds, "That is the kind of communication which we love to have made to us" (27). Dennis is "sublimely dreary" (27), and Rev. Mr. Trout displays "a sublime and impressive style of eloquence" (50). Of course the ocean is the main source of awe. In his 1837 college essay "Sublimity," Thoreau listed the "tumult of the troubled ocean" among the primary sublime objects in nature (*EEM* 94). He argued then that sublimity produces not fear of death but "an inherent respect, or reverence, which certain objects are fitted to demand"; this emotion is "often attended by a consciousness of our own littleness" (*EEM* 96). A similar psychology operates throughout *Cape Cod*, especially in the first chapter. Thoreau reacts to the shipwreck not with fear but with a sense of man's impotence before "the power of the waves" (9) and with an aesthetic appreciation of the scene: "I saw that the beauty of the shore itself was wrecked for many a lonely walker there, until he could perceive, at last, how its beauty was enhanced by wrecks like this, and it acquired thus a rarer and sublimer beauty still" (12). Here the traditional vocabulary is pressed into the service of poetic consolation in the face of disaster.

With aesthetic travel, Thoreau combines another conventional mode of travel writing, the scientific. He lists the plants (111, 167), clams (110), and birds (131–32) that he found; he whittles up "a fathom or two" of seaweed "that I might become more intimately acquainted with it" (68); and he measures the lighthouse and banks with some improvised instruments (150). Like the French explorers whom he takes as his models, Thoreau goes about the Cape "measuring and sounding" (234).

The conventional nature of the travel writing helps to account for the book's loose, fragmentary nature.[13] It has the structure

---

[13] In an interesting deconstructive reading of *Cape Cod*, Mitchell Robert Breitwieser suggests that the fragmentation of the book results from the fact that "Thoreau writes in an age of the wreck of the Book, when miscellanies are not gathered into a new and perfect artifact" ("Thoreau and the Wreck on Cape Cod," *Studies in Romanticism* 20 [1981]:14). The book, he claims, is an analogue of Cape Cod itself. This thesis is compelling and gains some support from Thoreau's expressive use of fragmentation in *A Week* (see ch. 6).

expected in most travel books: a listing of the sights encountered at selected spots on his walking tour from the mainland to Provincetown, with some digressions in time as historical associations send Thoreau back to earlier periods. As straightforward travel writing, *Cape Cod* is, like the travel portions of *A Week*, somewhat dated. In it Thoreau puts greater emphasis on places and things than on the traveler traveling. What sparse information the narrator gives about himself comes when the Wellfleet oysterman grills him. Thoreau engages in little of the poetic heightening that characterizes romantic travel writing. And, as we have seen, he does not experiment here with merging travel and other genres.

The surviving manuscripts of *Cape Cod* indicate no major thematic or structural shifts in Thoreau's conception of the book. The "Course of Lectures" (HM 13206) shows Thoreau interlining to flesh out paragraphs with additional information, to improve style, and to turn his text from lecture into essay (e.g., a preliminary version of what became the last paragraph in chapter 3: "There was no better way to make ~~you~~ ⟨the reader⟩ realize how wide that plain was, and how long it took to traverse it than by ~~reading~~ ⟨inserting⟩ these long extracts in the midst of our narrative" [leaf numbered 79]). The surviving sheets reveal no pattern of cutting passages in order to focus better on a theme, as do the drafts for "Ktaadn," where Thoreau removes material on civilization to emphasize wildness, or those for "An Excursion to Canada," where he cuts positive descriptions of the waterfalls to leave a stronger impression of his disappointment with them. Many sheets in his draft of *Cape Cod* are lined through to indicate use; these sheets contain material that was rewritten or compressed, not eliminated from the narrative. For example, Thoreau cut eight lines of the poem by Herman Doane quoted in chapter 3 (sheet numbered 51; presumably these lines are excluded because they "have deceased" [*CC* 44]) and he compressed many extracts from early accounts of Cape Cod (e.g., sheets numbered 351, 355, and 357 and four adjacent leaves— material that contributed to the historical survey in chapter 10; scattered among the quotations are Thoreau's own observations on the areas described). The conventional travel piece that he was writing lent itself to a variety of topics and to structural looseness; he apparently did not revise the manuscript extensively to limit his material or to achieve a tighter form.

Even as he was writing *Cape Cod*, Thoreau was putting greater effort into revising a more complex kind of travel work—a kind which, as William C. Spengemann defines it, "simultaneously enacts and records a series of imagined experiences. As these experiences unfold, they bring the work into being, convey their creator into new states of mind, and reveal the principles of their own creative movement." This "true romantic travel narrative," Spengemann argues, "has dispensed with physical travel."[14] *Walden*, that work, is Thoreau's report "from a distant land" (*Wa* 3), from a place "as far off as many a region viewed nightly by astronomers" (88). By comparison, *Cape Cod* is rather tame and old fashioned.

If *Cape Cod* is not fully romantic, it is not necessarily, as some critics have argued, anti- or post-romantic. Just as Thoreau recorded imaginative encounters with and transformations of nature after his alienating experience on Katahdin his reaction to the wreck of the *St. John* and to the ocean at *Cape Cod* was not his final or only attitude toward nature. He claims in *Walden*, "We can never have enough of Nature. We must be refreshed by the sight of inexhaustible vigor, vast and Titanic features [Katahdin], the sea-coast with its wrecks [Cape Cod], the wilderness with its living and its decaying trees, the thunder cloud, and the rain which lasts three weeks and produces freshets" (*Wa* 318). What were initially causes of questioning and alienation eventually become sources of refreshment.

Thoreau, then, was not repudiating *Walden* as he composed *Cape Cod*. Rather, he was presenting different perspectives on nature and writing with limited aims for a more specialized readership. He was addressing a middle-class audience within traveling distance of the Cape who were more interested in concrete details than in mythic, poetic transformation. Apparently he was successful. Emerson noted that at one of Thoreau's lectures on

[14]*The Adventurous Muse* (New Haven: Yale Univ. Press, 1977), pp. 66–67.

Cape Cod, "Concord people laughed till they cried, when it was read to them" (C 255). And in his survey of critical reactions, John C. Broderick describes *Cape Cod* as the "most sympathetically received" of Thoreau's posthumous books.[15]

The third trip in 1855 led only to extensive Journal passages. Another expedition in 1857, perhaps a last try to put spirit into the manuscript, also produced Journal materials but nothing that Thoreau appropriated for the book. The *Cape Cod* project lay dormant until it found its audience in the 1860s.

[15]"American Reviews of Thoreau's Posthumous Books, 1863- 1866: Checklist and Analysis," *University of Texas Studies in English* 34 (1955):30.

9

"Walking" and Thoreau's Romantic Development as Reflected in the Journals

IN "WALKING" the sense of unlimited, subjective geography returns, and stands in direct contrast to the very restrictive and literal terrain Thoreau had just worked on in *Cape Cod*. Thus, a walk to local fences moves, within a single sentence, to the "middle of the prairie," and finally to "the midst of paradise" where we see the Prince of Darkness as the surveyor (*Ex* 212; ¶ 15; *J* 2:94–5).[1] The essay shows, as *Cape Cod* does not, Thoreau's growing commitment to a romantic conception of imagination and to myth as imaginative expression.

Despite his gauntlet proclamation in the first paragraph, Thoreau celebrates in "Walking" not so much physically wild nature as a psychologically "wild" way of looking at the woods and fields near his Concord home. This essay, coming as it does before Thoreau's final effort to complete *Walden*, points to a kind of resolution in his views of nature. We have seen the terrifying burnt lands from Mount Katahdin and a difficult mixture of corpses and plenitude at *Cape Cod*. While these features are definitely part of nature seen in its totality, they do not make for pleasant excursions. They may force us outdoors, but they hardly invite us there. Furthermore, if our encounters with nature result from the kind of psychological and physical control that Thoreau clearly wishes for himself (and recommends for his readers),

---

[1] As we will see later, one element in Thoreau's world that seems to restrain his subjectivity is political fact, which he feels is "but a narrow field." When the lecture was being drafted, Thomas Simms was captured (or, more properly, kidnapped) in Boston. The account of that event, later part of "Slavery in Massachusetts," appears in the Journals next to "Walking" material.

then we are better off threading our way along the unlimited pathways within twenty miles from our home.

Nature here is the abandoned Marlborough Road, which leads out of town. The phenomena the saunterer encounters are, by *Walden's* standards, rather vaguely defined. While the central section of the essay celebrates a West that is wilder and quite distant from New England, its major features are subsumed in an artist's diorama of the Mississippi valley. The West is a "strange and whimsical" compass point (217; ¶ 22) that leads not to the open lands Thoreau had read and heard about. Instead it is an "interior and ideal world" (217; ¶ 21)—a psychological or imaginative construction. People who move west physically, even to Australia, are in effect moving culturally backward, toward the east, toward Europe, toward civilization. But Thoreau's movement west is psychological and mythical—he wishes to recreate the Greeks' image of Atlantis, or Columbus seeking a New World, or Linnaeus and other Europeans who used America as an emblem of the perfect garden. In a paragraph added after he delivered "Walking" as a lecture, Thoreau celebrates America as a place where we will be creatively imaginative, think etherially, and experience a more comprehensive understanding (222–23; ¶ 32).

When Thoreau's discussion returns to the wild (224; ¶ 37), it is a forest, meadow, and a cornfield—eventually, the "impervious and quaking swamps" (226–27; ¶ 43) that surround the village. The ideal location is a township with one "primitive forest" above it while a second such forest "rots below" (229; ¶ 45). Thoreau's locale is, throughout this essay, the town or village that he can walk away from when he wants. The intellectual content is "the uncivilized free and wild thinking in Hamlet and the Iliad, in all the scriptures and mythologies, not learned in the schools" (231; ¶ 50). In effect, the wild is captured in the literature of the ancients, not the moderns—it requires a poet capable of organic expression (whose words "expand like the buds at the approach of spring") and occult "sympathy with surrounding Nature" (232; ¶ 53). No literature except mythology comes close to expressing "this yearning for the Wild" (232–33; ¶ 54). American mythology, then, will tell the story of American liberty, some time in the future.

Thoreau continues in this essay to depict the wild as being just a bit outside town, but definitely under man's control. His example of appropriate music, for instance, is "a bugle in a summer night"—appropriate because the horn reminds him of "wild beasts in their native forests" (234; ¶ 57). Significantly, "it is so much of their wildness as I can understand." To illustrate free expression of animal instincts, he chooses cattle who escaped a farmyard (234; ¶ 58).

In short, his celebration of "this vast, savage, howling mother of ours, Nature" (237; ¶ 65) turns out to be an appreciation of the untilled portion of the acreage which man has settled, that portion being meadow and forest, but decidedly not steppe or jungle. The final November sunset in the essay lights the horizons and makes them liable to new discovery. It is valuable, as are the other scenes in this essay, for illuminating the uninhabited meadows, marshes, and forests near town. Elysium, the wild to which one walks from town, is a subjective construction.

It is clear that "Walking" should not be taken as one of Thoreau's late works, even though it was first published in 1862. Thoreau accumulated the central ideas of the essay gradually. He used his notes for two different lectures, one in the spring of 1851 and the second for the 1856–57 season. Although he revised the essay before sending it to the *Atlantic* (11 March 1862), he had essentially completed the work by early 1857. In all, roughly one quarter of the essay originated in passages from the Journals—some 18 percent from before April 1851 and the rest between May of that year and the next November. The first lecture was called "The Wild" when delivered in Concord and, according to Harding, "Walking" when given in Worcester. The lecture for 1856 was called "Walking," and Thoreau explained to his Worcester sponsor, H. G. O. Blake, that he had divided the topic into two parts so that the public would hear new material.[2] Both titles ("Walking" and "The Wild") are penciled in at the top

---

[2] Letter of 6 February 1857. One wonders whether Thoreau's public, however devoted, would have recalled what he said six years earlier. The letter includes the phrase "I am able to read what before I omitted." His letter mentions his having read part of the lecture "to a private audience," presumably more recently than six years ago (C 465).

of Houghton manuscript AM 278.5 [21,B], portions of a lecture draft which Howarth dates before 23 April 1851 (*LMHDT* 145). The titles could have been added after 1851.

The essay treats the two topics implied by the alternative titles, with the West as their rhetorical and thematic link. In the final version of "Walking" we can trace the themes by Thoreau's ex-plicit inclusion of the words *walk, wild,* and *west* (and their mor-phological variants). Thoreau's introduction to the 1851 lecture better prepares the reader for what is to follow than his introduc-tions to either the 1857 lecture (CPL) or the published essay. In the earlier draft Thoreau mentions all three of his major themes—walking, the West, and the wild:

> Wordsworth on a pedestrian tour through Scotland, was one evening, just as the sun was setting with un-usual splendor, greeted by a woman of the country with the words "What, you are stepping west-ward!" and he says that such was the originality of the salutation, combined with the associations of the hour & place— that "stepping west-ward seemed to be a kind of *heav-enly* destiny."
>
> The sentences from my journal which I am agoing to read this evening, for want of a better rallying cry, may accept these words "stepping westward."
>
> I feel that I owe my audience an apology for speaking to them tonight on any other subject than the Fugitive Slave Law, on which every man is bound to express ~~his opinion~~ a distinct opinion; ⟨but I trust that something which I shall say will concern you⟩—~~but I had prepared myself to~~ ⟨I wish to⟩ speak a word now for *Nature*—for absolute freedom & wildness, as contrasted with a free-dom and culture simply civil. (AM 278.5 [21, B])

In the published version the first paragraph is about "absolute freedom and wildness," while the second is about the "art of Walking." As shown in figure 3, the essay is framed by the dis-cussion of walking (205–19 and 241–48; ¶ 2–24 and ¶ 76–87).

Thoreau establishes his special etymology and meaning for the word *saunter* in the second paragraph and elegantly returns to it at the very end; he also uses it in the section on the "Society for the Diffusion of Useful Knowledge" (239; ¶ 71, part in *J* 2:150) to make a rather tenuous link.

The left column shows the presence of the key words "wild," "walking," and "west" in each paragraph of the essay. For example, the transition in paragraph 22, where all three words appear, shows up clearly. Paragraph numbers are at the far left; the vertical scale is proportional to paragraph length. The actual count of key words, including all morphological variants (*walk, walks, walking,* etc.) is in the first column. The middle columns give the major sources—Journals before the date of the lecture, the 1851 lecture manuscript, and later Journals. These contributions are proportional; for example, the first third of paragraph two is in the early Journals. Related to these data are the presence of the paragraphs in the lecture manuscripts held at Concord Free Public Library—versions dated by Howarth 1851, 1857, 1861, and a later transcription by Sophia Thoreau during her editing of the text for publication.

In the "Wild" section three subtopics predominate, as shown by the three columns of the figure. The most important is Thoreau's linking of literature and myth to the wild (231–34; ¶ 50–57). In this subsection he recapitulates themes from *A Week*, particularly from "Sunday" and "Friday." Again he equates scripture, mythology, and the best literature: all three are "natural" and the expression of "Genius . . . which makes the darkness visible, like the lightning's flash" (231; ¶ 50; cf. *W* 58–61, 362–66, 375–77). As he had also done in *A Week*, Thoreau finds British literature to be "tame and civilized" (231; ¶ 51; *W* 392–93), he insists on the superiority of Homer (232; ¶ 52; *W* 56–57, 368), and he associates both literature and myth with dreams (233; ¶ 56; *W* 61), and with music (234; ¶ 57; *W* 174–77). The terms of Thoreau's aesthetic have not changed much; he is still fighting the neoclassical battle of the ancients versus the moderns, but in a context of more romantic approaches to mythology. He remains at a transitional stage of his aesthetic development. This section of the essay has only one passage from the Journals as an anteced-

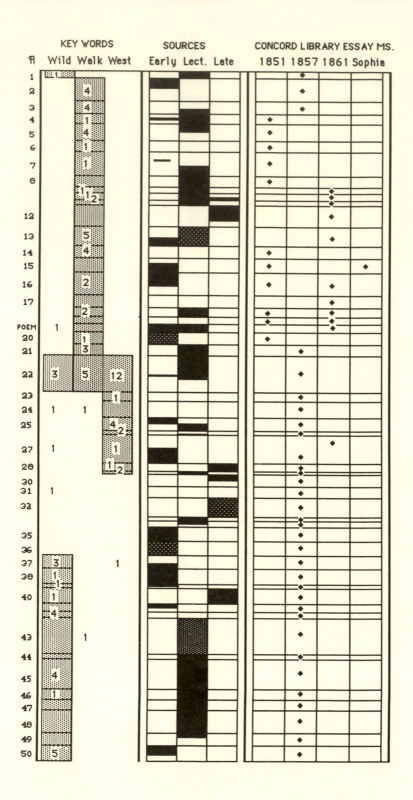

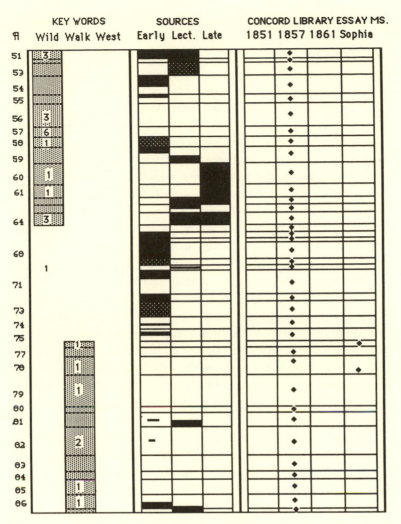

Figure 3: "Wild/Walking"

ent draft, and only paragraphs 51 through 53 appear in the 1851 lecture manuscript.

Mythology remains so important for Thoreau because it is not mere ornamentation (trivial, "civilized" excrescence); it is a source of truth: "The story of Romulus and Remus being suckled by a wolf is not a meaningless fable" (224; ¶ 37). Thoreau's attitude clearly grows out of the late eighteenth-and early nineteenth-century reevaluation of myth as being not just primitive religion superseded by Christianity but a legitimate and valuable part of Western culture and a link between that culture and the rest of humanity. Myth is primitive in the sense of its preceding civilized thought, but for Thoreau this precedence is positive. Myth expresses the "yearning for the Wild" that is one main focus of "Walking" (232; ¶ 54). By avoiding the distortions and compromises of civilization, myth puts us into contact with elemental, transcendent, unreflected truth. It gives unmediated "expression to Nature" (232; ¶ 53), which he has defined in the first sentence of the essay as "absolute freedom and wildness." Myth captures the "uncivilized free and wild thinking" (231; ¶ 50; J 2:97), the "pristine vigor" that is lost in artificial "culture" (232–33; ¶ 54). As in A Week, he discusses myth in terms of organic imagery and the psychology of the imagination. Mythology best expresses nature because it is "the crop which the Old World bore before its soil was exhausted, before the fancy and imagination were affected with blight" (232; ¶ 54). It appeals directly to the imagination, bypassing "common sense"; it ranks with "expressions of truth" that are "prophetic," as opposed to truths known from memory or directly from the senses ("sensible"). To support his point, he suggests, playfully, that modern science might ultimately confirm the "wild fancies" of the Hindu cosmological story (233–34; ¶ 56).

Thoreau returns in "Walking" to the mythos (or archetypal narrative derived from myth) that informs A Week. He advocates a romance quest for "the springs of life" (209; ¶ 10); the Journal source for this part comes from September 1851, after the lecture (J 2:472). He evokes the Holy Land or paradise that represents rebirth and "expanded consciousness, the sense of identity with God and nature which is the total human heritage."[3] Images of knights, crusades, and heroic adventures reappear (205, 206, 209, 224, 231), as they had throughout A Week, and Thoreau in both works draws on medieval fables of Robin Hood to illustrate wildness (207; ¶ 5; W 117, 170). But Robin Hood is not wild enough (231; ¶ 51; J 2:144, February 1851), and, furthermore, he is English, so Thoreau turns back to the more primitive and

[3]Frye, A Study of English Romanticism, p. 37. Frye considers this expanded consciousness "the most comprehensive and central of all Romantic themes."

fertile "Grecian mythology" (232; ¶ 54; *J* 2:145, February 1851). He identifies the goal of his quest with the search for Atlantis and the Hesperides (219; ¶ 25) and Elysium (247; ¶ 86; *J* 2:94). He also alludes to the rivers of the classic underworld, Lethe and the Styx (218; ¶ 23), and to Romulus and Remus (224; ¶ 37; *J* 2:151) and Cadmus (239; ¶ 70).

Because mythology and scripture are closely related for Thoreau, he alludes in "Walking" also to what he had characterized earlier as a "memorable addition to the old mythology, . . . the Christian fable" (*W* 66). He phrases his own call to redemption in terms borrowed from the gospels (206; ¶ 3; cf. Luke 14:26), and he characterizes his walking as a form of election (207; ¶ 5). He satirizes man's attempt to "improve" the land by picturing "some worldly miser" too greedy to notice that "heaven had taken place around him [suggesting that heaven is not a transcendent space but a psychological process that occurs in time], and he did not see the angels going to and fro, but was looking for an old posthole in the midst of paradise" while "the Prince of Darkness was his surveyor" (212; ¶ 15; *J* 2:94–5) Thoreau returns to the language of the Christian fable later when he takes exactly the opposite view about the value of cultivated land. From this different perspective, the American farmer not only wages his heroic battle with the land (230–31; ¶ 49), but "he *redeems* the meadow, and so makes himself stronger and in some respects more natural" than the Indian (230; ¶ 48). In the same vein Thoreau denounces remaining indoors "too late to redeem the day" as a "sin to be atoned for" (208; ¶ 7), and he sees emerging from the wild "the Reformer eating locusts and wild honey" (229; ¶ 45). Of course, Thoreau modifies Biblical myth to suit his own purposes. The "paradise" at the conclusion of "Walking" is not the orthodox heaven but a meadow on earth (247; ¶ 86; *J* 2:94), and one arrives at it not by faith or good works but by walking in an actual field (246; ¶ 85), by all that he has implied in the notion of "sauntering." The orthodox gospel of the New Testament gives way to "a newer testament,—the gospel according to this moment" (246; ¶ 83).

"Walking" ends with Thoreau sauntering in a suddenly illuminated place where "the air also was so warm and serene that nothing was wanting to make a paradise of that meadow" (247). He has discovered the heaven that throughout the essay has been the goal of his quest. Yet this is not the ultimate goal, a place to stop for good. Early in "Walking" he had poked fun at expeditions that "are but tours, and come round again at evening to the old hearth-side from which we set out. Half the walk is but retracing our steps" (206). At the end, although he has discovered "the boundary of Elysium," Thoreau himself is headed eastward and homeward, away from the western paradise: "the sun on our backs seemed like a gentle herdsman driving us home at evening" (247). Thus, as he does in *A Week* and *Walden*, Thoreau concludes "Walking" by looking beyond the boundary of the last page—by anticipating continued activity in the future: "So we saunter toward the Holy Land, till one day the sun shall shine more brightly than ever he has done, shall perchance shine into our minds and hearts, and light up our whole lives with a great awakening light, as warm and serene and golden as on a bankside in autumn" (247–48). And by switching to the first person plural, he involves us readers in the "walking" that may itself be heaven—a process rather than the more orthodox place.

The newer testament, the mythology that will replace the old fables and scriptures, will be American. Essential American nature, he claims, is better accounted for "in mythology than in any history of America" (214; ¶ 18; *J* 2:152). The American backwoodsman equals Adam in paradise (223; ¶ 33; *J* 2:152), and Native American myths of Dubuque and Wenona (*J* 2:146–7) figure in the panorama that indicates "*this was the heroic age itself*" (224; ¶ 36). Thus "the West is preparing to add its fables to those of the East" (233; ¶ 55; *J* 2:145), a theme that echoes from *A Week* (*W* 18, 54, 84, 102–3). He speaks of American liberty as being "to some extent a fiction of the present" (233). This fiction could be taken in the sense of hoax, when slavery and the other forms of servitude catalogued in the "Economy" chapter of *Walden* are considered,[4] but also "fiction" in the sense of an artis-

---

[4] One motif that runs through the essay is a series of related remarks on the discouraging political situation. Thoreau talks of "occasional and transient forays" into the state. Earlier he had seen politics as a "narrow

tic or imaginative design (from *fictus*: made, shaped). American freedom resembles the "beautiful idealisms of moral excellence" Shelley discusses in the preface to his own contribution to myth, *Prometheus Unbound*. When our liberty has become a "fiction of the past," Thoreau suggests, "the poets of the world will be inspired by American mythology" (233; ¶ 55)

A poet (maker) himself, Thoreau fashions his own myths. Just as he celebrated the godlike "respectable folks" at the "mythic center" of "Concord River" (*W* 7) and created imaginary guests to help him through the long *Walden* winter ("Former Inhabitants and Winter Visitors" (*Wa* 256–64), so too he calls up fabulous beings in both the "walking" and "wild" sections of the essay. Directly after commenting on American nature and its connection with mythology (214; ¶ 18), he turns to the Old Marlborough Road (214–16; ¶ 19; *J* 2:54–56), which is peopled by Martial Miles, Elijah Wood, and the "man of wild habits," Elisha Dugan. These men were actual Concordians, but Thoreau seems to have chosen them because their names suggest classical and biblical figures. They walk no ordinary road but a mythic or religious "living way" where life is "close to the bone." In the corresponding part of the "wild" (243–44; ¶ 79–80), Thoreau introduces the supernatural "shining family" that occupies Spaulding's Farm and embodies illumination, well-being, hilarity, serenity, naturalness, and music. These mythic figures appear "only after a long and serious effort to recollect my best thoughts," implying that they emerge from Thoreau's higher (i.e., mythmaking) consciousness. Thoreau canceled from an essay draft a paragraph which appeared shortly after the Spaulding's Farm passage and which also suggests mythmaking imagination: "It is not necessary for them to take the ether for exhilaration, who in their sane and waking hours are ever trans-

---

field" (213; ¶ 16) that a walk in the woods would help one forget. The "ancient and altogether admirable and shining family" at Spaulding's Farm "are of no politics" (243; ¶ 79). At the end, the life in the present that Thoreau celebrates will lead to a world without fugitive slave laws. As we will see, this world where politics can be ignored will be lost for Thoreau within less than two years, by the time he was able to complete *Walden*.

lated by a thought, nor for them to see with their hind heads, who sometimes see out of their fore-heads, nor for them to listen to the spiritual knockings, who attend to the intimations of reason and conscience" (CPL 92–93, which Howarth dates as composed in 1857 and revised in 1861–62 [*LMHDT* 150]; passage based on *J* 2:194).

This section of Thoreau's own mythmaking anticipates crucial additions to *Walden*, the next stage in the development of his attitude toward myth. In "Winter Visitors," for example, he tells of visits from the philosopher: "There we worked, revising mythology, rounding a fable here and there, and building castles in the air for which earth offered no worthy foundation. . . . Ah! such discourse we had, hermit and philosopher, and the old settler I have spoken of,—we three,—it expanded and racked my little house" (*Wa* 269–70; 14:22, E). Here, as in "Walking," Thoreau recapitulates the progress of myth in the eighteenth and nineteenth centuries and in his own career. He is first "revising" mythologies by adapting old myths, and also "seeing" myths "again" in new ways, and "rounding" fables, specifically about old people who lived in Concord, and thus perfecting previously existing myths. He ultimately moves on to "building castles in the air"—a metaphorical reference to creating new myths and to writing *Walden* itself. The philosopher here is both an idealized portrait of Alcott and another side of Thoreau. In coming together, the hermit and the philosopher prepare for the emergence of the poet at the spring climax of *Walden*. And the hermit and philosopher are joined in this work by the "old settler" who, Thoreau had previously hinted, is an avatar of God (*Wa* 137, 182). As he does in "Walking," Thoreau links myth with a perception of the divine. The passages on mythmaking originate in Journal entries mostly from February 1851, which suggests that Thoreau was thinking through the early draft of the essay during that winter.

After first delivering "The Wild" as a lecture in 1851, Thoreau provided a biographically and historically significant gloss that explains the experiences of the wild and West in explicitly romantic terms (222; ¶ 32; *J* 3:268, 2 February 1852): "If the moon looks larger here than in Europe . . . If the heavens of America appear infinitely higher, and the stars brighter, I trust that these facts are symbolical of the height to which the philosophy and poetry and religion of her inhabitants may one day soar. . . . I trust that we shall be more imaginative, that our thoughts will be clearer, fresher, and more ethereal." This passage, filled with moonlight and a sense of the imagination as the creative force behind symbols, all working with the poet to define America— this is the kernel of Thoreau's romanticism, which is part of the intellectual change that he underwent before and after he gave this lecture.

Conversion to Romanticism

Between the springs of 1851 and 1852, Thoreau's way of characterizing his own thoughts and his intellectual debts changed profoundly. He emerged from that year with a different vocabulary for describing his beliefs about nature and poetry. His attitudes changed toward Wordsworth and Coleridge, and even toward Emerson's writings. Finally, the process of identifying himself as an adherent of romantic or Transcendentalist philosophy seems to have led him to reassess his future quests and challenges. We have characterized the process as "conversion," but other metaphors such as crystallization, embrace, endorsement, or confirmation would do nearly as well.

Thoreau had certainly been exposed to the ideas of his Transcendentalist neighbors since he left Harvard. In the intellectual environment of Concord he picked up many of the prevailing attitudes. For example, throughout his adult life he advocated the subjective way of looking at and understanding nature, and disparaged the objectivity and rationality claimed by science. He consistently endorsed the individual's conscience and intuition as the only legitimate way to make ethical and political judgments.

In contrast, before 1851, when he described aesthetic experiences and the nature of poetry, he had tended to be conservative and to prefer classical works to those of his own century. His early writings both public and private show him retaining the older terminology and ideas about aesthetics that informed his college education. As "Walking" shows, his continued and close examination of myths led him eventually to a romantic view of mythology as a vehicle which mediates dynamically between the past and present and which points to a new role for the modern poet as a maker of myths, as a creative force in the world.

Between the two springs in question Thoreau settled on a single vocabulary to describe aesthetics, ethics, and epistemology—the vocabulary of Transcendentalism and romanticism. It was as if a conventional Christian, brought up in a Christian household and familiar with its doctrines and vocabulary, underwent the transforming experience of being "born again"—this time making the concerns and especially the language genuinely his own. During the year, he shows a mixture of enthusiasm about his discoveries and concern about his future. At the end of the process Thoreau could call himself a Transcendentalist and could chart the next step in his literary career, the completion of *Walden*.

We have based our argument chiefly on a reading of Thoreau's Journals, supplemented with evidence from works that were begun before the spring of 1852 and completed later on. The changes, especially in the Journals, involve different attitudes toward a few central ideas, such as imagination and sympathy, which Coleridge, Wordsworth, Emerson and their followers fostered and defined, or radically redefined from their neoclassical senses. The ideas, in their romantic sense, are virtually absent from Thoreau's Journals and manuscripts before the spring of 1851. Then passages start to appear in which he expresses a sense of discovery and enthusiasm, and a strong feeling that he is renewing his life, his intellectual growth, his relation to nature, and his career as a writer. That these thoughts occur when Thoreau was in his mid-thirties probably indicates the common psychological pattern today called the mid-life crisis.[5]

When Thoreau's published works are examined for these key words and poets' names, a significant pattern emerges. In *A Week on the Concord and Merrimack Rivers* and other writings

---

[5]For a detailed Eriksonian view of Thoreau's mid-life crisis, see Lebeaux, *Thoreau's Seasons.*

essentially drafted in the 1840s, the terms are used in their eighteenth-century sense. When we get to the final version of *Walden*, however, the vocabulary has distinctly shifted so that Thoreau's masterpiece is clearly a romantic book.

Thoreau returned from his two-year stay at Walden Pond with drafts of two books. *A Week* was circulating—it was ultimately turned down by four publishers—and parts of the *Walden* draft were used for lectures he gave first in Concord and eventually elsewhere in New England. During the following year, 1848, he worked heavily on *A Week*, expanding it by about a third, polishing and improving it until it was ready for another try. He spent some time in 1848 and 1849 adding a bit to the first draft of *Walden*. When *A Week* was published in May 1849, Thoreau announced the existence of his other book on a back page. He seems, however, to have abandoned *Walden* between late 1849 and the first months of 1852, or over two years. Then in 1852 he started again with the fourth (or D) stage, and during the next two years added substantially to the book, especially to the last nine chapters.[6]

Although Lawrence Buell argues that *A Week* is "Thoreau's most 'transcendental' work" and Charles R. Anderson calls it "a Transcendentalist book if ever there was one,"[7] we argued in chapter 3 that the language of Thoreau's first book is in important ways neoclassical. In form, it combines two eighteenth-century genres—Menippean satire and didactic travelogue. Like eighteenth-century works, it often separates observation and reflection, sketches generalized rather than particular natural scenes, and focuses very little on the traveler as a multidimensional individual whose traveling reveals and creates character.

In content, too, *A Week* remains rather "outdated." Throughout his scattered comments on poetry, Thoreau concentrates chiefly

[6] See ch. 10, below. Passages from *Walden* are cited by chapter, paragraph, and stage of the manuscript when the material was first introduced. The manuscript's history is documented in Clapper, "The Development of *Walden*: A Genetic Text."

[7] Buell, *Literary Transcendentalism*, p. 207, and Anderson, Introduction to the Limited Editions Club *Week* (1975).

on identifying Homer, Ossian, and Chaucer as original geniuses with a "yearning toward all wildness" (*W* 54). He continues to debate controversies (about the ancients and moderns and about natural and secondary genius) that dominated aesthetics from Addison to Johnson. Also, he uses important aesthetic terms in their neoclassical rather than romantic sense. For example, *imagination* in *A Week* refers to a mental power that combines past impressions with present experience; it is not a creative power operating "to idealize and to unify" (*Biographia Literaria*, ch. 13). Thus, Thoreau's view of the sunlit ocean of mist on Saddleback "required no aid from the imagination to render it impressive" (*W* 188). Imagination operates chiefly on neoclassically "sublime" scenes, and it implies false perception rather than romantic insight into essential truth (e.g., 192, 202). Thoreau's early aesthetic had often operated by juxtaposing ideas and images from diverse sources. As a result, *A Week* struck Lowell and other readers as fatally haphazard. Thoreau was working toward a unifying quest structure, but the number and variety of materials in his first book proved distracting to readers from the start. His later Coleridgean ideal of an organic unity leads to focusing such diversity better around a central image or metaphor. While the great romantic texts thrive on a multiplicity of materials, and foster a multiplicity of readings, they do so around a center that is at least physically well identified, even if its meanings are multiple and ambiguous. The obvious examples are Coleridge's albatross, Shelley's skylark, Melville's Moby-Dick, and, in our context, Walden Pond.

Thoreau's public lectures after release of *A Week* were the rather straightforward, factual account of his trip to Cape Cod, given during the 1849–50 lecture season, and "Walking," first in April 1851. "Walking" indicates that Thoreau was moving closer to full romanticism. This essay also deals with the place of mythology in the modern world, and with how myths are related to poetry. But the treatment uses romantic vocabulary only in the previously cited paragraph concerning moonlight, imagination, and "our inland seas" (*Ex* 222–23). This important section, with its clear romantic tone and terms, was not part of the lecture Thoreau gave in April 1851. Instead it was added to "Walking" from a Journal passage dated 2 February 1852 (*J* 3:268). That date occurs after his radical change, or conversion, to romanticism and Transcendentalism.

Thoreau announces the first step of his conversion in the Journal entry for 21 May 1851 (J 2:207) with a declaration of religious faith, discovered or confirmed quite recently: "Who shall say that there is no God, if there is a *just* man. It is only within a year that it has occurred to me that there is such a being actually existing on the globe." Thoreau seems quite sincere when expressing his faith in man and ultimately in God as something new. Transcendentalism is, among other things, a religious movement, and Thoreau's newfound faith is an important starting point toward his fully joining that movement. Within half a month he labels himself quite explicitly: "My practicalness [empiricism] is not to be trusted to the last. . . . I begin to be *transcendental* and show where my heart is" (J 2:228).[8] As far as we can tell, this is the first time he applies the label to himself unambiguously. The bulk of the entry for the day is a "credo" (both in form and content) that sets the Transcendental "instinct" against the bulwark of Rationalism, "common sense." The entry uses *transcendental* (with its variants) three times—for example, "with reference to the near past, we all occupy the region of common sense, but in the prospect of the future we are, by instinct, *transcendentalists*." It is unlikely that a person who had long and confidently held such beliefs about epistemology and its relation between the individual and his world would rehearse them in his private writings. We conclude that they were newly formulated and that Thoreau was trying them out.

The next stage is at once remarkable and straightforward. In the summer of 1851 Thoreau began to reread Wordsworth.[9] In July he wrote out a prose paraphrase that combines "Tintern Ab-

---

[8] Italics are added in all citations unless otherwise noted.

[9] Fergenson, "Was Thoreau Re-reading Wordsworth in 1851?," pp. 20–23. Fergenson suggests that the rereading might have been prompted by recent publication of *The Prelude* and that "perhaps also Thoreau turned again to the older poet to find what he remembered from his previous reading of Wordsworth, the expression of that longing for an earlier rapport with nature that was becoming poignantly pertinent to his own life" (23).

bey" and the "Immortality Ode," quoting from the latter so that his source is unmistakable. The passage is important because it demonstrates Thoreau's approval, in contrast to his condescending phrase from *A Week*, about "a simple pathos and feminine gentleness, which Wordsworth only occasionally approaches" (*W* 373, based on *PJ* 1:356–7). Probably more significant, Thoreau construes Wordsworth's texts with himself as the central character—it is *his* youth that was lost (*J* 2:306–07). A month later, Thoreau uses lines from "My Heart Leaps Up," the epigraph for the ode, in another striking passage filled with the enthusiasm of a person whose beliefs had recently changed: "I, whose life was but yesterday so desultory and shallow, suddenly recover my spirits, my spirituality, through my hearing. . . . Ah, I would walk, I would sit and sleep, with natural piety!" (*J* 2:390–393).

Thoreau's reactions to Emerson, the chief American spokesman for the romantics, also changed significantly during this period. While critics for nearly one hundred and fifty years have labeled Thoreau a disciple or pale imitator, Thoreau did not fully learn his Emerson lessons before 1851. In December of that year he says he opened "one of Emerson's books, which it happens that I rarely look at" (*J* 3:134), a statement the available evidence says we should take literally. Thoreau infrequently quotes from or alludes to Emerson's works in his earlier Journal or public writings, but in 1851 he seems to have turned intellectually toward his neighbor (ironically just as their friendship was cooling [*DHT* 298–302]). For example the entry for 25 December 1851 (*J* 3:154–56), is a prose paraphrase of "The Snow-Storm." More important for our purpose, the paraphrase is followed by a rehearsal of distinctions between the imagination and understanding:

> I witness a beauty in the form or coloring of the clouds
> which addresses itself to my *imagination*, for which
> you account scientifically to my understanding, but do
> not so account to my imagination. It is what it suggests
> and is the symbol of that I care for, and if, by any trick
> of science, you rob it of its symbolicalness, you do me
> no service and explain nothing. . . . If there is not some-
> thing mystical in your explanation, something unex-

plainable to the understanding, some elements of mystery, it is quite insufficient. If there is nothing in it which speaks to my *imagination*, what boots it?

Praise of the imagination had begun rather modestly, in July 1851: "Our feet must be *imaginative*, must know the earth in *imagination* only, as well as our heads" (J 2:300). During the next month the reliance of poetry on that faculty is rather well established by a contrast between the "man of intellect only, the prosaic man" and the poet: "What a faculty must that be which can paint the most barren landscape and humblest life in glorious colors! It is pure and invigorated senses reacting on a sound and strong *imagination*" (J 2:413). Thoreau asserts the hierarchy of intellectual powers: "We all have our states of fullness and of emptiness, but we overflow at different points. One overflows through sensual outlets, another through his heart, another through his head, and another perchance only through the higher part of his head, or his poetic faculty" (J 2:472). Earlier he talked of his "genius," which "makes distinctions which my understanding cannot, and which my senses do not report" (J 2:337; "genius" here is not the special trait of versifiers, but a universal potential of all persons).

In December a circling hawk becomes a "symbol of the thoughts. . . . But the majesty is in the *imagination* of the beholder." This personal imagination, roughly the equivalent of Emerson's "idealism," gives meaning, especially symbolic meaning, to nature. The bird's flight is described at length, then summarized as "the poetry of motion." The Journal passage concludes with a clear designation of its sources and psychological implications: "Flights of *imagination*, Coleridgean thoughts. So a man is said to soar in his thought, ever to fresh woods and pastures new. Rises as in thought" (J 3:143–44).

Concurrently with adopting Coleridge's definition of imagination Thoreau began to use *sympathy* quite frequently to describe an occult relation between nature and man.[10] Earlier, in *A Week*,

[10] See Roy Male, "Sympathy: A Key Word in American Romanticism," *ESQ* 35 (1964):19–23. Male argues that American romantics expanded the term *sympathy*, derived from late eighteenth-century rationalist eth-

the poem "Lately, alas, I knew a gentle boy" (*W* 260–61) employed the term to express close friendship, a nearly mystical bond between people. Elsewhere in his first book, Thoreau used the word in its ethical sense, especially for the essay on friendship. One exception may be the claim that "we could even *sympathize* with [the Merrimack River's] bouyant tide" (*W* 110). The first draft of *Walden* also employs various senses of the word, including the occult. "Sounds," chapter 5, includes the most important discussion of this term, since it links "the indescribable innocence and beneficence of Nature" to the "sympathy" which "sun and wind and rain . . . summer and winter" have with man (*Wa* 138; 5:17, A). More playful is Thoreau's "*sympathy* with the fluttering alder and poplar leaves" (*Wa* 129; 5:1, D), or the claim that "every little pine needle expanded and swelled with sympathy and befriended me" (*Wa* 132; 5:4, A).[11]

In the Journals, Thoreau treats the topic with occasional seriousness during the year we are examining. In July 1851, for example, he writes, "It is a test question affecting the youth of a person,—Have you knowledge of the morning? Do you *sympathize* with that season of nature? Are you abroad early, brushing the dews aside?" (*J* 2:315). Later: "The wind has fairly blown me outdoors; the elements were so lively and active, and I so *sympathized* with them, that I could not sit while the wind went by" (*J* 2:338). These sentiments continue in the long Journal entry which ends with a Wordsworthian comment that poetry "puts an interval between the impression and the expression,—waits till the seed germinates naturally" (*J* 2:341). At the start of the next year, the theme of sympathy seems to be treated quite seriously in a sermonlike passage on the text "obey the spur of the moment": "Let us preserve religiously, secure, protect the coincidence of our life with the life of nature. Else what are heat and cold, day and night, sun, moon, and stars to us? Was it not from *sympathy* with the present life of nature that we were born at this epoch rather than at another?" (*J* 3:231–32).

---

ics, to describe a mystical relation between one's emotions and natural events.

[11] See Donald Ross, Jr., "Composition as a Stylistic Feature," *Style* 4 (1970):1–10, for a discussion of this chapter of *Walden*.

The imagination not only links one sympathetically to nature but also leads to a vigorous faith in the vibrancy of the working mind. Thoreau during the period under focus often expresses a Faustian drive: "We forget to strive and aspire, to do better ever than is expected of us. I cannot stay to be congratulated. I would leave the world behind me" (J 3:187). In March, after reading "Purchas's Pilgrim's" he says, "I am conscious of having, in my sleep, *transcended* the limits of the individual. . . . As if in sleep our individual fell into the infinite mind" (J 3:354). This passage suggests an intriguing parallel to Coleridge's "Kubla Khan" headnote, but Thoreau gives no other hint about a possible link.

The Faustian quest was, more often than not, an internal, psychological challenge rather than an external, social one. So it is not surprising that Thoreau says, in July, soon after his conversion begins, "Let me forever go in search of myself; never for a moment think that I have found myself; be as a stranger to myself, never a familiar, seeking acquaintance still." His "aspiration" will be "the fountain of youth." This rejuvenation is especially significant since the passage is one of few in the Journals where Thoreau mentions his age, and middle-aged indeed he is: "Here I am thirty-four years old, and yet my life is almost wholly unexpanded. How much is in the germ!" His restlessness, finally, is important for anticipating the "different drummer" paragraph in *Walden*: "Let a man step to the music which he hears, however measured. . . . I will not be shipwrecked on a vain reality" (J 2:314–317; the passage was used in *Walden*, 326, 18:10, F). This spirit of eager enthusiasm carries through to the time when Thoreau started to work on *Walden* (his "melody," presumably) once more: "My life partakes of infinity. . . . I go forth to make new demands on life. I wish to begin this summer well; to do something in it worthy of it and of me; to *transcend* my daily routine and that of my townsmen. . . . May I dare as I have never done. . . . May my melody not be wanting this season!" (J 3:350–51).

The immediate result of Thoreau's changed way of thinking and talking about the key ideas of romanticism was a searching reassessment of his personal goals. In January 1852 he questioned both why he went to the woods and why he came back (J 3:214–6). Throughout the following spring, doubt and confidence were mixed. Doubts take the form of the lost youth motif familiar to Wordsworth's readers: "Perhaps we grow older and older till we no longer *sympathize* with the revolution of the seasons, and our winters never break up" (J 3:363);[12] "Once I was part and parcel of Nature; now I am observant of her" (J 3:378). The new faith that began this year returns with a stark realization: "For the first time I perceive this spring that the year is a circle. I see distinctly the spring arc thus far. It is drawn with a firm line. Every incident is a parable of the Great Teacher" (J 3:438).

His ability to write, specifically to start work on *Walden* again, went through a similar process of doubt followed by resolution and industriousness. In September 1851 he said, "I feel uncommonly prepared for *some* literary work, but I can select no work" (J 2:467; Thoreau's italics). After overcoming some of his personal doubts, he picked up *Walden* and moved it nearer to completion by April, when "Alcott wished me to name my book *Sylvania!*" (J 3:418). He began a quest for new ideas and even new facts: "How sweet is the perception of a new natural fact! suggesting what worlds remain to be unveiled. . . . I think that no man ever takes an original [*sic*; makes an original observation?], or detects a principle, without experiencing an inexpressible, as quite infinite and sane, pleasure, which advertises him of the dignity of that truth he has perceived" (J 3:441–2).

The resolution of the crisis in Thoreau's mental history, to use John Stuart Mill's phrase from an analogous context, was a comprehensive enthusiasm and hope. For a while, at least through the completion of *Walden* in 1854, Thoreau was able to channel this energy toward reconceiving his masterpiece.

---

[12]Compare the statement from 11 April 1852 (J 3:400), "If I am too cold for human friendship, I trust I shall not soon be too cold for natural influences. It appears to be a law that you cannot have a deep *sympathy* with both man and nature. Those qualities which bring you near to the one estrange you from the other."

10

The Endings of *Walden*

WE WISH TO speak a word for the second half of *Walden*, for its place in the evolution and structure of Thoreau's masterpiece. There are enough champions of the first half. Students in American literature survey courses read the opening three chapters in anthologies and see Thoreau as a social critic with a program for spiritual reform based on retirement from the town to live in the woods—an accurate view as far as it goes, but incomplete because it does not account for chapters 4 through 18. Academic critics get farther into the book. Matthiessen, Lane, and many others have noted the seasonal progression and other circle images throughout *Walden*.[1] Their insights help us appreciate the temporal structure, but they do not account in detail for other, more subtle developments in the physical and spiritual plot— why Thoreau remains at the pond for the time he does, and then why he leaves. Charles R. Anderson increases our sense of *Walden's* structure by detailing the importance of "The Ponds" (ch. 9). Anderson perceptively characterizes this chapter as a central focus, because it expresses Thoreau's mystical union with Walden Pond. Anderson also points to a "central triad of chapters" ("Baker Farm" [ch. 10], "Higher Laws" [ch. 11], and "Brute Neighbors" [ch. 12]) concerned with Thoreau's "attempted ascent to purity and perfection."[2] After his discussion of the middle of the book, though, Anderson's account becomes sketchy. He mentions that in the second half Thoreau reenters the world as a "poet seeking metaphors in the world's body,"[3] but his analysis

---

[1] See, for example, F. O. Matthiessen, *American Renaissance* (New York: Oxford Univ. Press, 1941), pp. 66–75; Lauriat Lane, Jr., "On the Organic Structure of *Walden*," *College English* 21 (1960):189–202; John C. Broderick, "Imagery in *Walden*," *University of Texas Studies in English* 33 (1954):80–89.

[2] Anderson, *Magic Circle of Walden*, p. 158.

[3] Ibid., p. 181.

of the last seven chapters is not nearly as thorough or insightful as his account of the first half.

A comprehensive account emerges from analyzing how the work developed—how Thoreau gradually focused on nineteenth-century, romantic ideas about the imagination and organicism. We then see that the first half of the book shows the imagination functioning, first to provide new moral and psychological perspectives on the material world. Once the mind perceives that world imaginatively, it is ready to approach directly the divine and transcendental essence of nature. The second part of the book then traces themes that can be glossed by the subtitle of Wordsworth's *Prelude*, the "growth of a poet's mind."[4] In the chapters after "Higher Laws" Thoreau defines his social vocation as that of the poet and myth-maker, and he eventually recognizes that the basic poetic metaphor for all natural phenomena is organicism.

In the light of these romantic themes, a view of *Walden*'s various and overlying structures emerges. The standard view, that the book is an account of seasonal changes from summer through spring, remains. But the book also employs linear structures to develop its themes. The first climax follows the progress from the false economics of Concord to the higher laws, and it celebrates the powers of imagination. After a relapse into spiritual anesthesia caused by winter, a second climax occurs when Thoreau, now a poet, recognizes the importance of organicism. An account of later stages of *Walden* shows how these structures developed and adds to previous critical readings of the book (see fig. 2, p. 58).

From the C stage of late 1849 until early 1851, a period of over two years, little seems to have happened to *Walden*. Thoreau spoke about Cape Cod in several towns during the 1849–50 and 1850–51 seasons, and he gave lectures, probably from "Economy," in Medford for the first time. In spring 1851 he presented in Concord and Worcester the lecture version of materials that now appear in "Walking" (*CL* 82). He took his second trip to Cape

---

[4] Perry Miller, "Thoreau in the Context of International Romanticism," *New England Quarterly* 34 (1961):157.

Cod (June 1850) and one to Canada (September 1850). Perhaps he decided that his efforts were most appreciated when he talked about his travels, and perhaps poor sales of *A Week* discouraged him from trying to publish *Walden*.[5] He did indicate in his Journal, however, a readiness for some major work: "I feel ripe for something, yet do nothing, can't discover what that thing is. I feel fertile merely. It is seedtime with me. I have lain fallow long enough" (*J* 2:101); "I feel myself uncommonly prepared for some literary work, but I can select no work. I am prepared not so much for contemplation, as for forceful expression. I am braced both physically and intellectually" (*J* 2:467–68). Sharon Cameron argues that at this time the Journal was not merely a sourcebook providing material for his public work but a "competitive, central task."[6]

During 1852 Thoreau was actively trying in his Journal to work out the full significance of his Walden experience. He was uncertain and troubled by what had happened. On 22 January 1852 he questioned his reasons for leaving, thereby anticipating the reader's natural inquiry: why leave the place where you have found authentic life outside of society? His uncertainty in the Journal is almost shocking:

> But why I changed? why I left the woods? I do not
> think that I can tell. I have often wished myself back. I
> do not know any better how I ever came to go there.
> Perhaps it is none of my business, even if it is yours.
> Perhaps I wanted a change. There was a little stagna-
> tion, it may be. . . . Perhaps if I lived there much longer,
> I might live there forever. One would think twice before

[5] He could have tried to publish the lecture text that had served him a dozen occasions, that is, to use "Economy" as a separate piece. "Reading" (ch. 3), the least changed part of *Walden* over the years, could also have become a separate magazine article even though it seems not to have been used as a lecture. On a practical level, the manuscript in early 1852 may have been too short to offer as a book (at 45% of its final length, or about 150 pages).

[6] *Writing Nature: Henry Thoreau's Journal* (New York: Oxford Univ. Press, 1985), pp. 159–60.

he accepted heaven on such terms. . . . I must say that
I do not know what made me leave the Pond. I left it as
unaccountably as I went to it. To speak sincerely, I went
there because I had got ready to go; I left it for the
same reason. (*J* 3:214–16)

On 18 April 1852 he recorded in his Journal a surprising discovery, and one important to the evolution of *Walden*: "For the
first time I perceive this spring that the year is a circle" (*J* 3:438).
The naturalist Thoreau knew, and had shown from the A stage,
that the seasons form a circle. Presumably he discovered for the
first time in 1852 the psychological and mythical importance of
spring for himself and his book; he had just begun to "count
one," and he had started to become "as wise as the day [he] was
born" (98, 2:23; A). Immediately after the Journal paragraph on
the discovery of the circular year, Thoreau poses a crucial question: "Why should just these sights and sounds accompany our
life? Why should I hear the chattering of blackbirds, why smell
the skunk each year? I would fain explore the mysterious relation between myself and these things. I would at least know
what these things unavoidably are, make a chart of our life,
know how its shores trend, what butterflies reappear and when,
know why just this circle of creatures completes the world. Can
I not by expectations affect the revolutions of nature, make a day
to bring forth something new?" (*J* 3:438). This is the crucial romantic question, posed also by Emerson in *Nature*,[7] that motivates the second half of *Walden*.

[7] Thoreau's question about how objects make a world and his hope for
a single phenomenon that illuminates all nature may be a response to
challenges first articulated in Emerson's *Nature*. In an atmosphere of
"solitude" both from society and from books, "the stars awaken a certain
reverence, . . . all natural objects make a kindred impression, when the
mind is open to their influence. . . . Nature never became a toy to a wise
spirit." This view illustrates the "poetical sense," and by it "we mean the
integrity of impression made by manifold natural objects" (*CW* 1:9). Just
a page earlier Emerson had claimed that "all science has one aim,
namely, to find a theory of nature. . . . Whenever a true theory appears,
it will be its own evidence. Its test is, that it will explain all phenomena"

Figure 4: Percentage of pages with drafts in the Journals

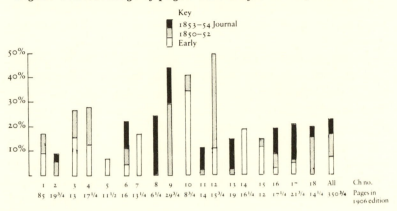

Prompted by his rethinking of the Walden experience, Thoreau returned to the manuscript in the first months of 1852, at the D stage, which has the largest ratio of new material to transcribed pieces. (With "Economy" removed, it is nearly three to one.) The Journal materials for this period (1850–52) provided substantial additions to the text, as figure 2 indicates.

Thoreau was not merely revising but was extending his book in important ways. For the first time he added significantly to what became the second half of the published *Walden*. He contributed important material to what we see as the first climax (the central triad of chs. 9 to 11, "The Ponds," "Baker Farm," and "Higher Laws"), to the turning point ("Brute Neighbors" ch. 12),

---

(8). In a fascinating reaction to these attitudes which he and Thoreau shared, Emerson commented in his eulogy on Thoreau (1862) that "the tendency to magnify the moment, to read all the laws of Nature in the one object or combination under your eye, is of course comic to those who do not share the philosopher's perception of identity" (*CE* 10:479). Their common attitude does not necessarily mean that Thoreau slavishly imitated Emerson. For one thing, Thoreau did not share Emerson's usual answer to this excellent question—namely, that the continued existence of a person's character will integrate and stabilize the sequence of perceptions. The question is raised by two independent thinkers who articulated an important problem with Romantic doctrine.

to the second climax ("Spring" ch. 17), and to the "Conclusion." Thus, with this stage, the basic shape began to come into focus; Thoreau demonstrated a growing sense of where his book was headed.

He had decided to go beyond the idea of the Walden experi- ence as a social protest, and beyond the manuscript's main rhe- torical function as an answer to local critics and doubters. As Anderson has shown, he wanted to give ordinary citizens of places like Concord a description of his mystical experiences, or the days of Transcendence, which personally justified his exper- iment.[8] The difficulty of his task is illustrated by what can be reconstructed about the composition of "The Ponds," the central mystical chapter. Only one tenth of the pages had been written in A, and none of that was copied into B or C. The next elements are Journal materials written between 1850 and 1852, which are drafts of over eight pages in the chapter. Especially instructive is the complex textual history of the fifth paragraph, where Tho- reau's effort to catch the colors of the water and the weather in- volves at least thirteen different Journal passages.[9] The D stage added one quarter to the final chapter (7½ pages) and E added the largest part (9 pages, or 30%).

Among the important specific passages that Thoreau added to "The Ponds" at the D stage are references linking the pond to the divine. Especially crucial is the poem in which Thoreau an- nounces, "I cannot come nearer to God and Heaven/Than I live to Walden even" (193, 9:25, D). The geographical center of the book was no longer the playfully described beanfield; it was the crystal-clear eye called "God's Drop" (194, 9:26, D), where Tho- reau reaches the height of moral purity. He added to the denun-

[8] Anderson, *Magic Circle of Walden*, chs. 3 and 5.

[9] From 24 January 1852 to 3 January 3 1853. We have compiled a list of all the Journal sources flagged in the footnotes to Torrey and Allen's edition; to these we have added items from a list compiled by J. Lyndon Shanley (personal communication) and our own suggestions and an- notations. All the information is in computer-retrievable form, and can be sent to interested scholars upon request; it comprises over 500 items and is 12 pages long. Write to Donald Ross, Jr., Dept. of English, Univ. of Minnesota, Lind Hall, 207 Church St. S.E., Minneapolis, MN 55455.

ciation of sensuality at the heart of "Higher Laws" and suggested a descent from the lofty, timeless realm of the central triad with the earthy parable of John Farmer, who must "let his mind descend into his body and redeem it" (222; 11:15, D).

In the E stage of *Walden*, between late 1852 and mid–1853, Thoreau again added significantly to "Higher Laws" and the crucial chapter that follows it.[10] He now begins "Higher Laws" by overtly pointing to the duality that pervades the chapter: "I found in myself, and still find, an instinct toward a higher, or, as it is named, spiritual life, as do most men, and another toward a primitive rank and savage one, and I reverence them both" (210; 11:1, E, F). Although this duality derives from traditional Christianity, it also comments on the realities of myth (e.g., the great

---

[10]The data from 9:5 suggest that Thoreau may have switched from D to E on 1 September 1853—Journal passages from this date appear in both D and E. The earliest Journal passage in E is dated 28 June 28 1852, but Thoreau could have gone back for this sometime in late 1852 or 1853.

Section of 9:5	*J* Source	*J* Date	Version
f	III, 223	24 Jan 52	D
d	III, 478	28 April 52	D
g	IV, 160	28 June 52	E (earliest in E)
d	IV, 321	27 Aug 52	D
b	IV, 322	27 Aug 52	D
d	IV, 337	1 Sept 52	interlined in D (latest in D)
a	IV, 341	1 Sept 52	E
e	IV, 387	13 Oct 52	E
e	IV, 401	26 Oct 52	E
e	IV, 407	2 Nov 52	E
e	IV, 408	2 Nov 52	E
c	IV, 447	3 Jan 53	interlined in E

Of two sentences in 9:16 that clearly parallel *J* 5:251 (14 June 1853), the longer was interlined in E and the other, though it appears in D, sounds like a cliché that probably ran through Thoreau's mind often when he thought about Walden ("The water laves the shore as it did a thousand years ago"). Perhaps the 1853 Journal entry is not the original source.

chain of being) and science. With this central passage, Thoreau anticipates the hope, which he added to the "Conclusion," that the new man will get "new, universal, and more liberal laws . . . and he will live with the license of a higher order of beings" (323; 18:5, E).

In "Higher Laws," Thoreau describes the ascetic regimen used to satisfy the spirit, along with the dichotomy between body and that spirit, and he insistently delegates the "imagination" as the arbiter of purity. In one of five examples he claims that the way of life he led, although not perfect, "went far enough to please my imagination. I believe that every man who has ever been earnest to preserve his *higher or poetic faculties* in the best condition has been particularly inclined to abstain from animal food, and from much food of any kind" (214–15; 11:5, E).

At this crucial stage, Thoreau incorporated the question about order and meaning in the world. It is part of "Brute Neighbors" (ch. 12), another turning point in the book. The movement begins with the dialogue, also added in E, between the Hermit and Poet, figures who represent two sides of Thoreau. This debate turns on the question, "Shall I go to heaven or a-fishing?" (224; 12:5, not in MS), one version of the Transcendental problem of vocation. Thoreau wonders whether he should remain a hermit at Walden Pond, the lofty and pure heaven he has discovered, or become a poet, a social being committed to life in this world, engaged in what from the perspective of "Higher Laws" appeared a lower occupation.

The dialogue has implications for the structure of *Walden*. When Thoreau debates whether he "should soon bring this meditation to an end" (224; 12:5, not in MS), the question applies to his book. If he is to remain a hermit at the mystical level of the central chapters, there is no reason to continue it, to go beyond "Higher Laws." But he chooses, of course, to go a-fishing—to descend once again and assume the mantle of poet. As a result, he is confronted with two further problems. The first is the question that he had debated in his Journal, which now appears in the E stage of *Walden* as, "Why do precisely these objects which we behold make a world?" (225; 12:8, E). That is, he sets out on a quest for unity or system in the world, to discover cosmos in the chaos of perceptions.

The other problem also grows out of his descent from the timeless realm of "Higher Laws" into the temporal world. With his commitment to earth, he is subject once more to time, change, seasonal and psychological phases. Thus, after the long summer of the first half of *Walden*, winter comes on and Thoreau feels life shrinking, withdrawing inward.

Through the rest of the book Thoreau explores these related problems of discovering a principle of unity in the world and of surviving the winter. He does so in his role as poet, as new materials in the E stage of the manuscript show. Immediately after he poses the crucial question about unity in the world, he adds, "I suspect that Pilpay & Co. have put animals to their best use, for they are all beasts of burden, in a sense, made to carry some portion of our thoughts" (225; 12:8, E). That is, his approach to the world and the life in it is poetic; his exploration of nature is the poet's search for enlightening metaphors. Thus, among the additions to E is the episode of the loon chase. Not only is the loon one piece of the chaos that Thoreau works to fit together into a cosmos, but the seriocomic chase also becomes a metaphor for Thoreau's quest to "drive life into a corner" (91; 2:17, A). Neither life nor the loon is easily cornered.

Thoreau also added to E such exercises in poetic thought as his accounts of former inhabitants. As a poet, he survives during the winter by his imagination. "There we worked," he says of himself and a philosophical visitor, "revising mythology, rounding a fable here and there, and building castles in the air" (269–70; 14:22, E).

Thematically, then, the E stage appears to be the most important for the whole rhythm and rhetoric of *Walden*. Other clues as well point to structural consolidation. The E stage constitutes the largest addition of material after A, and it is the first stage to have chapter divisions. It contains the largest number of first and last paragraphs for chapters (see table 2). By the end of 1852 Thoreau had plotted the overall movement of his book, and could thus focus on transitions among its parts.

Based on evidence from the Journals and Thoreau's previous habits, we guess that Thoreau took a vacation from work on the E stage in September when he went to Maine (13 to 28 Sept.). It seems unlikely that he would have taken much of the manu-

Table 2:   Chapter Openings and Closings

Chapter	First Manuscript Appearance	
	First Paragraph	Last Paragraph
1	C	A
2	D	A
3	A	none
4	A	A
5	A	A
6	A	E
7	A	A
8	A	C
9	A,E*	D
10	E	none
11	E	D
12	E	E
13	E	E
14	F	E
15	F	A
16	F	A
17	F	A
18	F	F

* The first sentence of 9:1 is in A.

script on the busy trip he later described in "Chesuncook." A month later the unsold copies of *A Week* were returned; perhaps the failure of his first book now helped inspire his final polishing of the second.

The F stage of the manuscript, as figure 2 reveals, helped fill out the last chapters of *Walden* and continued in the direction set by the previous stage. Thoreau added sections to "House-Warming" (ch. 13) to emphasize the restriction and diminishment associated with winter: "I withdrew yet farther into my shell, and endeavored to keep a bright fire both within my house and within my breast" (249; 13:12, E); "My dwelling was small, and I could hardly entertain an echo in it" (242; 13:6, F, G). He concentrated further on the quest for unity in the world, and sharpened the focus of the crucial question he had added to E. In "The Pond in Winter" (ch. 16) he now wrote, "If we knew all the laws of Nature, we should need only one fact, or the description of one actual phenomenon, to infer all the particular results at that point" (290; 16:12, F). This passage continues with the hope that one absolute form will replace the "infinite number of profiles" we mistakenly think are the real world (290–91, F). And to "Spring" he added that one form and phenomenon—the melting bankside. He discovered in the thawing sand and clay a metaphor for all life organically springing from one source, the pattern fashioned by "the Artist who made the world and me" (306; 17:7, F). "Thus it seemed," he added at the climax of the second half of *Walden*, "that this one hillside illustrated the principle of all the operations of Nature" (308; 17:9, F). Thoreau's effort to describe this hill is another example of a passage with a complex history of trial drafts in the Journals. Some twenty-three passages show up for paragraphs 6 through 9, nearly all having been written during the winter and spring of 1851–52, the time of his profound doubts about the reasons for leaving the pond.

In this climactic section, Thoreau regains the power that he feared was lost on Katahdin—the power to animate nature imaginatively, to join the spiritual and physical, the wild and the good. The sands of the melting bank mix together and obey "half way the law of currents, and half way that of vegetation," albeit "*grotesque* vegetation," until "converted into *banks*" by the water (305; 17:6, F, G). Once Thoreau gets "nearer to the vitals of the globe," he finds "an anticipation of the vegetable leaf." It is "no wonder that the earth expresses itself outwardly in leaves, it so labors with the idea inwardly. The atoms have already learned this law, and are pregnant by it" (306; 17:7, F). The leaf-vein form is seen in human blood vessels, and also, fancifully, in the development of hands and fingers, so that Thoreau asks, "What is man but a mass of thawing clay?" (307; 17:8, F, G), an echo of the Biblical story of creation. The organic imagery brings us back to the set of microcosmic parallels: "The whole tree itself is but one leaf, and rivers are still vaster leaves whose pulp is intervening earth" (307; 17:7, F).

Besides this climactic section, Thoreau also introduced more material connected with his chosen vocation of poet. He included in "The Ponds" the paragraph that explores various myths about the creation of Walden (182–83; 9:12, F), and he insisted later in the text that "mythology precedes regular poetry" (308; 17:9, F). Through imagination Thoreau intuits correspondences between microcosm and macrocosm. For example, the pickerel, with their "quite dazzling and *transcendent* beauty" seem "the pearls, the animalized *nuclei* or crystals of the Walden water. They, of course, are Walden all over and all through; are themselves small Waldens in the animal kingdom" (284; 16:5, F). Later, "the very globe continually *transcends* and translates itself, and becomes winged in its orbit" (306–7; 17:7, F; the only instances of *transcend* in the book). He spoke of the winged cat as "the right kind . . . for me to keep, if I had kept any; for why should not a poet's cat be winged as well as his horse?" (233; 12:15, F). And he incorporated in the "Conclusion" his defense of multisignificance and obscurity in his poetic account of the quest at Walden (325; 18:6, F, on "the volatile truth of our words").

Also in the F stage Thoreau formulated the answer to the question about leaving the woods: "I left the woods for as good a reason as I went there. Perhaps it seemed to me that I had several more lives to live, and could not spare any more time for that one" (323; 18:4, F). One of those lives, he learned, was that as a poet. Having discovered the explanation, or at least the metaphor for unity in the world (through organicism), having brought cosmos out of empiricism's chaos, he pictured himself returning to the town as a social being with a message for his townsmen.[11] This broader gospel goes beyond the social criticism, and even beyond the religious and personal vision of chapters 9–11, and it explores the unity of the universe in romantic, philosophical terms.

[11] Another "life to live" was that of abolitionist lecturer. Soon after returning from the pond he delivered "Resistance to Civil Government," his attempt to address national issues of the 1848 election campaign. Within a month after publication of *Walden* he gave his second abolitionist speech, "Slavery in Massachusetts," whose topical content is much more insistent and local, and whose tone is combative and engagé.

The G stage of the manuscript did not change, but it did clarify the direction of *Walden*. For example, Thoreau states explicitly the lesson of the thawing bank and the answer to the question posed in "Brute Neighbors": "There is nothing inorganic" (308; 17:9, G). He added a triumphant announcement of rebirth: "Walden was dead and is alive again" (311; 17:14, G). And, in his role as poet, he vigorously defends the book's style of *"extra vagance"* (324; 18:6, G)

What inferences can we draw, then, from examining the evolution of the *Walden* manuscript? First, *Walden* changed radically over the seven years of its development. Only in the sense that the seasonal structure and the rhetoric of defending his experiment in subsistence farming (chapters 1–8) still remain in the final version can we agree with Professor Shanley that "the essential nature of *Walden* did not change from first to last" (S 6)[12] Thoreau added gradually to the project until the fifth (or E), stage when he established a clear sense of its overall movement. Second, attention to the evolution of the manuscript helps us appreciate the second half of *Walden*, especially. We see how the latter part of the book grew from an appendix of "Economy" into a quest for unity in the world—for one principle that would illustrate and make significant all of nature. With his discovery of the organic principle, Thoreau the persona of *Walden* could leave the pond and return to the human community with his life-reviving message, the complete *Walden*.

An Outline of the Complete *Walden*

Matthiessen and many other critics have commented on the seasonal structure of *Walden*, but attention should also be paid to how the themes create other rhetorical structures that accom-

---

[12] Incidently, we do not find that the eight-year history of *Walden*'s composition is extraordinary. Many of our academic colleagues have publishing careers that match Thoreau's quite well—two studies drafted about halfway through in a two-year spurt, then lectures and short articles coming forth while first one and then the second book are seen through to publication.

pany the seasons. In a way it is quite ordinary to have a "nature book" follow the annual cycle; Thoreau's special place as an American romantic and his Transcendentalist's concern with finding a vocation make *Walden* less predictable. The idea of multiple structures and multiple meanings is consonant with his position in the final chapter: "'They pretend,' as I hear, 'that the verses of Kabir have four different senses; illusion, spirit, intellect, and the exoteric doctrine of the Vedas;' but in this part of the world it is considered a ground for complaint if a man's writings admit of more than one interpretation" (325; 18:7, F).

A comprehensive reading of *Walden* depends on recognizing both themes and the main structural divisions. A successful interpretation should account for the book's complexities, for how the parts interact, and for all the chapters. An outline follows of how the book might be read in the light of our previous discussion.

Walden has two major climactic sequences, framed by an introduction and a conclusion. The general outline makes chapters 1 to 3 the introduction, in which Thoreau explains socioeconomic truths (ch. 1), expresses hope for a vision (ch. 2), and warns the reader about reading (ch. 3). Chapters 4 to 11 present the path to moral purification (ch. 4), which clears the way to the concrete (ch. 9) and abstract (ch. 11) versions of the vision. In the second major part, chapters 12 to 17 show Thoreau recommiting himself to earth and losing his visionary ecstasy during the winter (chs. 12–16). With the coming of spring and the realization of the universality of organicism, Thoreau is reborn to a new way of life within the community as a poet (ch. 17). The last chapter (ch. 18) affirms the validity of the experiment and justifies the rhetorical methods necessary to convey the messages.

The first two chapters present the negative and positive impetus for the rest of *Walden*. In "Economy" (ch. 1) Thoreau conducts a "busk," rhetorically burning all obstacles to his quest for a more authentic life. He starts with the "lives of quiet desperation" that the wise man will avoid. Thoreau details through the rest of the chapter the many ways in which his readers waste their lives by accumulating surpluses of food, shelter, clothing,

and fuel. In the midst of this stinging, straightforward social criticism, he tells of his own withdrawal from society for a less costly
life in nature—but he does not yet indicate precisely what it
means "to adventure on life now" (15; 1:20, A).

The last paragraph of "Where I Lived" (ch. 2) implicitly comments on the shallow life and society that concern "Economy"
("time is but the stream I go a-fishing in"). Here Thoreau wishes
for a vision of eternity (and hence God, who "culminates in the
present moment" [97; 2:21, A]), which he expresses through the
extended metaphor of the need to find a body of water which is
not shallow, so that one can "fish in the sky." This paragraph
comments further on the incompleteness of life so far: "I cannot
count one. I know not the first letter of the alphabet." It concludes with the idea that one seeks the soul by getting down into
the earth (using the head as an organ for burrowing) (98; 2:23,
A). We need to be alert for the development of the images in this
paragraph, especially for echoes of the term "a-fishing."

In "Where I Lived" he sets out on his quest for "a higher life
than we fell asleep from" (89; 2:14, F). One achieves such
higher realms by the imagination, "a repetition in the finite mind
of the eternal act of creation in the infinite I AM."[13] The individual's imagination (or, as we now call it, intuition) opens up the
path to the transcendental, higher world. It shows up occult (or
metaphoric) links between disparate parts of the world and ultimately shows that all such links are organic. Thoreau uses
"imagination" often in *Walden*, and nearly always with rather
precise philosophic definition. The connotations of the term
gradually unfold. The imagination can liberate (8; 1:8, B), as it
does in "Resistance to Civil Government"; it can also simplify
(47; 1:67, D). With it Thoreau buys and sells local farms (81–82;
2:1–2, D), and it keeps his house "auroral" all day (85; 2:8, F).
Speaking more theoretically, he says, "When one man has re-

---

[13] Samuel Taylor Coleridge, *Biographia Literaria*, ed. John Shaw-
cross, 2 vol. (Oxford: Clarendon Press, 1907), 1:202. Thoreau, especially after 1852, uses imagination to mean a creative power, involving
will and conscious artistry—Coleridge's "secondary" form—although
Thoreau is not consistent in his terminology.

duced a fact of the *imagination* to be a fact to his understanding,
I foresee that all men will at length establish their lives on that
basis [i.e., of true knowledge]" (11; 1:15, B). The imagination is
the vehicle for the psychologically real time and space mentioned before, as Thoreau insists in chapter 2:

> Both place and time were changed, and I dwelt nearer
> to those parts of the universe and to those eras in his-
> tory which had most attracted me. Where I lived was as
> far off as many a region viewed nightly by astronomers.
> We are wont to *imagine* rare and delectable places in
> some remote and more celestial corner of the system,
> behind the constellation of Cassiopeia's Chair, far from
> noise and disturbance. I discovered ["imagined" in the
> first version of *Walden*] that my house actually had its
> site in such a withdrawn, but forever new and unpro-
> faned, part of the universe. (87–88; 2:13, A)

Thoreau's imaginative approach to time and space here link *Walden* with his other long major works, all travel books. Although
physically still in his home town, Thoreau travels farther—spiritually and intellectually—on his Walden adventure than he did
in New Hampshire, Maine, Canada, or on Cape Cod. He returns
to the theme of imaginative travel in the "Conclusion" (ch. 18)
as part of his frame for the book.

"Reading" (ch. 3), the last part of the introductory section, is
out of the seasonal pattern and out of time. Its comments, osten-
sibly about other books, are actually about *Walden*. The chapter
is a warning: "we must laboriously seek the meaning of each
word and line, conjecturing a larger sense than common use
permits out of what wisdom and valor and generosity we
have. . . . Books must be read as deliberately [thus an echo of "I
went to the woods because I wished to live deliberately" (90;
2:16, A)] and reservedly as they were written" (100–101; 3:3, A).
These comments are especially significant when one remembers
just how deliberately and reservedly *Walden* was written. To take
Thoreau literally, we should devote roughly seven years to the
text, the period he spent drafting and revising it. Many readers

take even longer, extending their deliberate reading over a life-time. "It is not all books that are as dull as their readers," Thoreau insists, as if anticipating and answering future generations of sophomores for whom *Walden* is required reading. He also antic-ipates the effect his masterpiece has on some of those sopho-mores and others: "How many a man has dated a new era in his life from the reading of a book" (107; 3:11, A). His comments in "Reading" pick up the themes of novelty and revolution recur-rent throughout the book and point to its concluding image of the morning star.

The chapters from "Sounds" (ch. 4) to "The Village" (ch. 8) move Thoreau further away from the shallow life and society of "Economy," deeper into the redemptive world of nature, and closer to the "eternity" and divinity that Thoreau has hinted to be the goal of his quest at Walden. These chapters explore the authentic life that he has deliberately set out to live near the pond. They present various disciplines or religious "ways" (via, Tao) by which Thoreau rises to the first climax of the book in the central triad of chapters ("The Ponds," "Baker Farm," and "Higher Laws"). Because these chapters have received most of the critical attention devoted to *Walden* (Anderson's *Magic Circle* is especially helpful), we will review them here only briefly.

Critics have long noted that chapters 3 through 8 are paired. While "Reading" obviously concerns books and human civili-zation, "Sounds" addresses experience of nature that is un-mediated by human language—what is "published" but not "printed" (111; 4:1, A). In this chapter Thoreau explores a con-templative, meditative approach to life. Having established "a broad margin to [his] life" (an image that plays on the books dis-cussed in "Reading"), he listens carefully to the world around him and discovers that "I grew in those seasons like corn in the night" (111; 4:2, A, F). Thoreau's meditations are interrupted by the sounds of the railroad and his consequent satirical musings on modern technology, but the chapter ends with his extensive catalog of animal sounds that "express the meaning of Nature" (126; 4:20, D); his translations and interpretations of these voices reveal that he is becoming more naturalized himself.

"Solitude" (ch. 5) and "Visitors" (ch. 6) are obviously paired

chapters. In the former Thoreau explores further the rewards of
meditation undistracted by society. Through his solitary contemplations, he approaches new states of consciousness: "With
thinking we may be beside ourselves in a sane sense" (134; 5:11,
D). Going beyond the naturalization he recounted in the previous chapter, he now insists, "We are not wholly involved in Nature. I may be either the drift-wood in the stream, or Indra in the
sky looking down on it" (135; 5:11, D). The title of this chapter
ultimately proves ironic, for Thoreau is anything but solitary at
the pond. He enjoys there not only the "sweet and beneficent
society in nature" (132; 5:4, A) but also supernatural visitors
such as the "old settler" and "elderly dame" (137; 5:16, A), ava-
tars of God the Father and Mother Nature. In "Visitors" Thoreau
turns to human society. He offers a cross-section of character
types, concentrating most on the Canadian woodchopper. His realistic portraits here form a scale of human development by
which he can chart his own progress at the pond. Their lives and
thoughts become a measure of his attempts to establish the true
"necessaries" of life and to adventure on life now.

The next two chapters, "The Bean-Field" (ch. 7) and "The Village" (ch. 8), contrast specific locations and all that they come to
represent. The first begins with Thoreau's attention to literal
beans but soon moves to their symbolic implications. As he labors meditatively in his field, Thoreau achieves moments of transcendence: "It was no longer beans that I hoed, nor I that hoed
beans" (159; 7:6, A). He turns the discussion to planting not
beans "but such seeds . . . as sincerity, truth, simplicity, faith,
innocence, and the like" (164; 7:15, A). He also uses his farming
experience for a self-reflexive reference to the writing of *Walden*:
"Some must work in fields if only for the sake of tropes and
expression, to serve a parable-maker one day" (162; 7:11, A). As
we will see, "parable-maker" is the role that Thoreau assumes
especially in the second half of the book. In contrast to the field
where he explores deeper life, "The Village" features a return
briefly to the society from which he has escaped and offers another measure of his progress beyond the superficial lives of the
regimented, bored, gossipy villagers he observes. The crucial
part of this chapter concerns not the location indicated by its title

but the "valuable experience" of being lost in the woods: "Not till we are lost, in other words, not till we have lost the world, do we begin to find ourselves, and realize where we are and the infinite extent of our relations" (171; 8:2, F). Thoreau thus prepares for the next major section of *Walden*, the central triad of chapters that concerns those relations to the infinity or eternity that he has been seeking.

"The Ponds" (ch. 9) is the book's symbolic center. The chapter starts with an account of fishing, considered first in social terms. However, Thoreau senses the "vibration" caused by "dull uncertain blundering purpose" at the end of the line; then the fish is brought to the "upper air," and the line is cast "upward into the air," and suddenly Thoreau is fishing in the sky, just as he had hoped at the end of chapter 2: "Thus I caught two fishes as it were with one hook" (175; 9:4, A, E). Thoreau's closeness and sympathy with nature are on a path that leads to his mystical vision of transcendent reality at Walden. The pond, which takes on various meanings in the book, gradually evolves into a symbol of the ultimate reality, the limitless bounds of man's mind, and the potential of nature—all that we might, for convenience, call the "oversoul," although Thoreau does not use the term.[14] The depth of the Pond is needed to satisfy the imagination, so that "not an inch of it can be spared" (287; 16:6, E). In imagined fact, it "dives deeper and soars higher than Nature goes" (288; 16:7, D). Thoreau plays often with the notion of the area of Walden Pond having contact with Arabia, the Ganges, and the stars; Thoreau's space as well as his time is defined imaginatively or psychologically.

Anderson and Lane have shown the importance of "The Ponds" for the meaning and structure of the book. Without re-

---

[14] In its flexibility as a symbol, the pond thus differs from a Swedenborgian "correspondence." Emerson complains that Swedenborg "fastens each natural object to a theologic notion" when "in nature, each individual symbol plays innumerable parts" (*CE* 4:121). In "The Poet," Emerson insists, "Here is the difference betwixt the poet and the mystic, that the last nails a symbol to one sense, which was a true sense for a moment, but soon becomes old and false. For all symbols are fluxional" (*CW* 3:20).

hearsing all the strategies Thoreau uses to explain how central Walden is, we will note only a proliferation of words that suggest the divinity of the pond: "pure," "Sky water," "a perfect forest mirror" (188; 9:19, E), "transparent and seemingly bottomless" (189; 9:21, E). It is seen "lying between the earth and the heavens" (E). It is an eye "blue mixed with the yellow of the sand. Such is the color of its iris" (176; 9:5, D), and this quietly introduced image leads to the remarkable notion that "a lake is the landscape's most beautiful and expressive feature. It is earth's eye; looking into which the beholder measures the depth of his own nature" (186; 9:17, F).[15] While most of these rhetorical extravagances appear in chapter 9, hints do occur later in the book. In "Pond in Winter," for example, Walden, "Like the marmots in the surrounding hills . . . closes its eye-lids and becomes dormant for three months or more" (282; 16:2, G).

No clearer statements of the pond's divinity exist than the sentence, "A field of water betrays the spirit that is in the air" (188; 9:20, E), and the climactic poem, which must be taken literally: "I cannot come nearer to God and Heaven/Than I live to Walden even" (193; 9:25, D). One is reminded of the "deep springs" (181; 9:10, D, F) that are the source of the pond. We are invited to translate the descriptive terms into metaphors, and, in a complicated way, to understand that they are not only metaphors for Thoreau but also a direct and literal account of his mystical experiences.

"Baker Farm" (ch. 10) is a humorous interlude between two very serious chapters. Here Thoreau establishes again the divine nature of Concord's ponds with his opening references to temples, druids, worship, Valhalla, swamp gods, fruits "too fair for mortal taste," shrines, and pagodas (201–202; 10:1, E). Here, too, he playfully indicates his spiritual progress when he mentions the halo of light around his shadow, an indication of divine favor that causes him to "fancy myself one of the elect" (202;

---

[15]James McIntosh, *Thoreau as Romantic Naturalist*, pp. 284–85, suggests that these passages echo the "transparent eyeball" paragraph from Emerson's *Nature*. We believe it significant that they were not introduced into *Walden* until after 1852, rather than in the earlier drafts.

10:2, E). But he soon changes from the chosen of the gods to "a poor unarmed fisherman" whom the gods rout with lightning (203; 10:3, not in MS). His subsequent talk with John Field constitutes another blow to his pride and self-conception. This part of the chapter recapitulates the social doctrines of "Economy" and perhaps expresses Thoreau's fears for the success of his book. Although Field listens to Thoreau's message (thus representing us readers), he cannot successfuly apply that message to his own life; he remains mired in his old "boggy ways" (209; 10:9, not in MS). The encounter with Field momentarily causes Thoreau to doubt his own way of life, but he recovers under the inspiration of his "Good Genius," who urges him to "grow wild according to thy nature" (207; 10:6, A). This crisis at the center of *Walden* prepares for the later discussion of the problem of vocation.

The third chapter of the central triad, "Higher Laws" (ch. 11), is striking for the dearth of references to the seasons and the classical elements. It thus escapes to a great extent time and space. Thoreau begins with a goal of balancing the "wild" and the "good," (210; 11:1, E, F) body and soul, matter and spirit. As the chapter develops, however, he loses that balance in his quest for purity. He lapses into an extreme asceticism that leaves him disgusted by physicality—by "this slimy beastly life, eating and drinking," and this "animal in us, which awakens in proportion as our higher nature slumbers. It is reptile and sensual, and perhaps cannot be wholly expelled; like the worms which, even in life and health, occupy our bodies" (218; 11:9, E; 219; 11:11, E). He sets an impossibly high, austere ideal that he himself cannot attain—"My practice is 'nowhere,' my opinion is here" (217; 11:8, E). The denials of body, space, and time are clearly a possible stopping place in *Walden*, but they are not Thoreau's final position. Just as he came down off the mountains of *A Week* to pursue the "purely sensuous" life on earth, Thoreau descends from the lofty spiritual elevations of "Higher Laws" and recommits himself to the balance that he advocated at the start of the chapter. In the final paragraph, the flute and voice (representing Thoreau himself) inspire John Farmer "to let his mind *descend* into his body and *redeem* it" (222; 11:15, D, emphasis added).

The discussion of structural implications in the remaining chapters needs to be a bit more detailed, since they have been essentially ignored by other critics.

In "Brute Neighbors" (ch. 12) the dialogue between the Hermit and Poet, with its crucial question, "Shall I go to heaven or a-fishing?" (224; 12:5, not in MS), recommits Thoreau to earth and sets the tone for the rest of the book. The debate is between two strong urges within Thoreau. It significantly echoes the fishing image that we have been tracing, and it alludes to the New Testament metaphor of fishing as an analogy to the saving of souls. The "Hermit alone" confesses, "I was as near being resolved into the essence of things as ever I was in my life" (224; 12:5, not in MS)—an allusion to the rarified stopping place he considered in the previous chapter. But Thoreau rejects the assumption that fishing and heaven are incompatible. He distances himself from the governor and his council who "are too old and dignified to go a-fishing, so they know it no more forever. Yet even they expect to go to heaven at last" (213; 11:4, F). The Poet wins the debate, and the Hermit asks, "Shall we to the Concord?" (225; 12:7, E), a key question—the village on the river is the place where they will find an audience, a group of people who will perhaps listen to the message that Thoreau, the Hermit-Poet, delivers.

The question that immediately follows the dialogue is also important, since finding the answer motivates the chapters through "Spring": "Why do precisely these objects which we behold make a world?" (225; 12:8, E). In romantic terms or those of idealist philosophy, how do we integrate the series of individual perceptions that flood our senses? More broadly, how do we satisfy our desire to order the "manifold natural objects" (*Nature*, CW 1:9). The question is not immediately answered. Instead, "Brute Neighbors" returns to the witty tone of the start of the book. The "brutes" are mice, and ants, and loons, yet they are wise (the loons) or they fight to mock-heroic strains (the ants). This and the following chapter ("House Warming," ch. 13) feature a descent into time and particularity, and the open metaphors and mysticism no longer hold sway. Thoreau recounts gathering foods and fuel "before I finally went into winter quarters." The cold forces him to close off his house (which "never pleased my eye so much after it was plastered" [242; 13:6, F]) and to some degree his life; "my dwelling was small, and I could hardly entertain an echo in it" (242; 13:6, F). The winter seems to restrict the imaginative as well as the physical possibilities: "I withdrew yet farther into my shell, and endeavored to keep a bright fire both within my house and within my breast" (249; 13:12, E).

Despite the beauty and precision of the descriptions in "Brute Neighbors" and "House-Warming," in the full narrative of the book they do not satisfy Thoreau. Not until the end of "Former Inhabitants" (ch. 14) does the pall start to rise. That chapter, it will be recalled, is a series of cameo portraits of Thoreau's sometimes neighbors, but these ordinary people are subtly given classical roles—Brister Freeman becomes Scipio; Wyman the younger is read about in Scripture; the alleged veteran, Hugh Quoil, puts a fresh woodchuck pelt on his house, "a trophy of his last Waterloo" (262; 14:11, E, F). Mythmaking, we are told later, "precedes regular poetry" (308; 17:9, F). At the end of the chapter Thoreau wades gently so "the fishes of thought were not scared from the stream" (another echo of the end of chapter 2 [269; 14:22, F]): "There we worked, revising mythology, rounding a fable here and there, and building castles in the air for which earth offered no worthy foundation" (269–70; 14:22, E); "with such reminiscences I repeopled the woods and lulled myself asleep" (264; 14:15, A). Through imagination the poet can escape the winter world, which tends so much to be limited to the sensuous events recorded in "Winter Animals" (ch. 15). Here even Walden loses some of its stature. The ice on Thoreau's "great bed-fellow" sounds at night as if "troubled with flatulancy and bad dreams" (272; 15:3, A). Among his observations on animals, Thoreau notes that "usually the red squirrel (*Sciurus Hudsonius*) waked me in the dawn" (273; 15:5, A)—an indication, perhaps, of unwonted lethargy in this season of his life. He does not yet "anticipate . . . the sunrise and the dawn" (17; 1:25, A). Like the foxes, both Walden and Thoreau seem to be "awaiting . . . transformation" (273; 15:4, A).

"The Pond in Winter" (ch. 16) refreshes the validity of the book's central symbol. As he had "fathomed" Walden earlier (179;

9:8, A [interlined], D), now he does so again (287; 16:6, E). With
the harvesting of ice he can study the bottom (246; 13:11, F)
and he is "thankful that this pond was made deep and pure for a
symbol. While men believe in the infinite some ponds will be
thought to be bottomless" (287; 16:6, E). But in a way the ice
forms a barrier between Thoreau and the living waters of Walden. The many measurements that he plots on his map (286)
suggest a mechanical, scientific approach to nature in this period of reduced life. Perhaps most important, the question about
perceived objects is getting more refined as the answer gets near,
especially in the passage quoted above: "If we knew all the laws
of Nature, we should need only one fact, or the description of
one actual phenomenon, to infer all the particular results at that
point" (290; 16:12, F). The ice harvest brings Thoreau back to
another metaphor from earlier pages, that Walden has communion with all the world, and, by implication, that a natural law
working at Thoreau's cabin would be universal.

Our previous discussion of "Spring" (ch. 17), the book's second
climax, has already revealed the solution to the problem. The
"actual phenomenon" is the melting bankside, and the truth
from which all others can be inferred is that "there is nothing
inorganic." The organic metaphor, the analogue between the
growing plant and the universe, is the core of the changed worldview that inspired the romantic movement. By the middle of the
nineteenth century, the metaphor had proliferated so that it began to appear in many other areas of thought than cosmology.

Thoreau sees man's moral life as upward growth from solid
roots (15–16; 1:20, A); later, he speaks of "hacking at the
branches of evil" (75; 1:105, G). The "new generation of men"
will let the seeds of virtue come up (164; 7:15, A). Men with
these "seeds of a better life" (213; 11:4, F) can "grow wild according to [their] nature" (207; 10:6, A). In "Higher Laws" the
organic nature of ethical improvement is clear: "The generative
energy, which, when we are loose, dissipates and makes us
unclean, when we are continent invigorates and inspires us.
Chastity is the flowering of man; and what are called Genius,
Heroism, Holiness, and the like, are but various fruits which
succeed it. Man flows at once to God" (219–20; 11:11, D). The

poem on correspondence in "Spring" talks of "seeds of cognate heaven" (314; 17:18, D). The use of this metaphor is infectious. Architecture is only good if it "has gradually grown from within outward" (47; 1:67, D); the names of ponds should arise from the animals they foster (196; 9:29, not in MS); ideally the houses will grow around the writer (85; 2:9, F, 242; 13:7, E, F). The most important passage for Thoreau's development of the organic metaphor describes his finding, during the spring thaw, organic forms in animal, vegetable, and mineral phenomena. That nearly all enter *Walden* in the D stage or later emphasizes again Thoreau's explicit adoption of the language of romanticism.

Here, finally, is the "the creation of Cosmos out of Chaos and the realization of the Golden Age" (313; 17:18, D). This discovery applies beyond nature, since "what I have observed of the pond is no less true in ethics" (291; 16:13, E, F). And this truth will be our freedom; it will redeem us, especially since the discovery accompanies the return of spring: "in a pleasant spring morning all men's sins are forgiven. Such a day is a truce to vice. While such a sun holds out to burn, the vilest sinner may return [a couplet in hymn meter]" (314; 17:19, D). Eden is again possible: "Through our own recovered innocence we discern the innocence of our neighbors . . . the sun shines bright and warm this first spring morning, re-creating the world and you . . . feel the spring influence with the innocence of infancy" (314; 17:19, D; in the next paragraph he quotes Mencius on "germs of virtues"). This account of redemption is prefigured by a passage from "The Ponds": "Perhaps on that spring morning when Adam and Eve were driven out of Eden Walden Pond was already in existence, and even then breaking up in a gentle spring rain" (179; 9:8, A). Finally, in the next-to-last paragraph, the seasons are perceived, *not* as a cycle, but as a progression: "And so the seasons went rolling on into the summer, as one rambles into higher and higher grass" (319; 17:25, A).

The "Conclusion" (Ch. 18) starts with a tour de force of Thoreau's imaginative world traveling. This introduces an answer to a question about vocation that Thoreau does not explicitly pose: "I left the woods for as good a reason as I went there. Perhaps it seemed to me that I had several more lives to live, and could not spare any more time for that one" (323; 18:4, F). It should be clear that one of the several lives is that of the artist, the poet, the writer of *Walden*. The vignette of the Artist of Kouroo, an obvious "mythic center" in Strauch's sense, points to the realization of the artist's dream.[16] The artist transcends time by his "perfect work," and makes "a new system in making a staff" (326–27; 18:11, D, E, F). As we might expect, this apparently Oriental tale has no outside source; it is the final myth that Thoreau invents for *Walden*.

A striking motif in the last chapter is an apologia for the rhetorical extravagance, the wandering beyond reality, that has characterized the book. *Walden* has been built on "the volatile truth of our words," since, if one merely "translates" reality, only a "literal monument" remains. Thoreau fears that he did not "exaggerate enough," did not "speak extravagantly" enough to "lay the foundation." This follows the metaphorical warning that reminds us of the whole argument about architecture that began in "Economy": "If you have built castles in the air, your work need not be lost; that is where they should be. Now put the foundations under them" (324; 18:5, E, F).

The frequently mentioned cycle of the rise and fall of Walden leads ultimately to the analogy between nature and man at the end of the book: "The life in us is like the water in the river. It may rise this year higher than man has ever known it, and flood the parched uplands; even this may be the eventful year, which will drown out all our muskrats" (332–33; 18:18, F). Here Thoreau picks up the theme of evolution that recurs throughout *Walden*. Earlier he had recalled the "aboriginal hunters" (180; 9:9, D) and the other "nations" that lived near Walden Pond (179; 9:8, A) at the time of "the infancy of the human race" (28; 1:43, C). These people he calls the "first fishers" (211; 11:3, E), and, building a metaphor between biology and anthropology, "the embryo man" who passed through the hunter stage (213; 11:4, F). He places himself on the continuum of development when he claims that his beanfield was "the connecting link between wild

[16] Carl F. Strauch, *American Literary Masters*, 1:473–79.

and cultivated fields" (158; 7:4, A). At the other end of history Thoreau celebrates the railroad for its celestialized sounds and visual effects (116; 4:8, A, 118; 4:11, A), and he anticipates future "ornamented grounds of villas which will one day be built" near the pond (180; 9:9, not in MS). These bits of fanciful history are augmented by a frequent plea for a "new generation [i.e., birth] of men" (164; 7:15, A), the new man whose possibility dominates the first two chapters, who will be the one finally to "live" in the richness of his humanity.

And in the final paragraph of *Walden* Thoreau invites each reader to become that new man for whom "there is more day to dawn" (333; 10:19, F).

11

"Chesuncook" and "The Allegash and East Branch"

IN AN 18 August 1857 letter to H. G. O. Blake, Thoreau described his final trip to Maine—an account considerably more upbeat than the one in "The Allegash and East Branch"—and then he added, "It is a great satisfaction to find that your oldest convictions are permanent. With regard to essentials, I have never had occasion to change my mind" (C 491). The two last Maine narratives suggest, however, that in important ways Thoreau did change. Both essays contain brief passages that celebrate imaginative (subjective, unifying, creative) perception and occult sympathy with and the higher uses of nature, but these moments affect the excursions very little. They are dwarfed by the surrounding sections in which Thoreau's perception is overwhelmingly scientific (objective, analytical, detached). Thoreau does not symbolically transform his last Maine trips into spiritual quests as he had in *A Week*, or interior explorations such as that depicted in *Walden*. Instead, he abandons his role of poet and mythmaker to become the naturalist and anthropologist of his later years. Nostalgically, Thoreau turns to "the Indian" as a type of romantic hero—the ideal Indian remains close to nature and enjoys mysterious, intuitive perception—but in "Chesuncook" he runs up against actual Joe Aitteon, half-corrupted by civilization, and in "The Allegash" he emphasizes his own distance from Joe Polis. In both essays, too, Thoreau explores (as he had in "Ktaadn") the destruction of the wilderness, which he now links with the end of poetry and mythology. The clearing of the Maine woods parallels his own loss of imaginative power.

Chesuncook

Thoreau made his second extended trip to Maine between 13 and 27 September 1853, probably at the end of work on the E draft of *Walden*. Upon returning to Concord he wrote a long account of the trip in his Journal (vol. 16, Morgan Library, MA 1302:22). On 2 December of that year he sent to Francis H. Underwood, editor of a proposed antislavery magazine, "a complete article of fifty-seven pages," which Harding and Bode suggest was probably "Chesuncook" (C 308). If so, it must have been only one portion of the Journal narrative, which runs over 100 manuscript pages. Underwood's magazine never materialized, but Thoreau used his Maine story for lectures over the next three years: December 1853 at Concord, November 1854 at Philadelphia, and October 1856 at Perth Amboy.

In summer 1857 Thoreau took his last trip to Maine. That November, James Russell Lowell offered to print the account of it in the *Atlantic Monthly*, but Thoreau declined out of consideration for Joe Polis, "my Indian guide, whose words & deeds I report very faithfully,—and they are the most interesting part of the story."[1] Instead, Thoreau offered "an account of an excursion into the Maine woods in '53; the subjects of which are the Moose, the Pine Tree & the Indian" (C 504). Unlike Polis, Joe Aitteon (Thoreau's guide on the 1853 trip) could not read and thus was not likely to be embarrassed by the publicity. When Lowell accepted, Thoreau began to revise the hundred-page manuscript ("or a lecture & a half, as I measure" [C 504]). On 5 May 1858 he sent "some 80 pages of my Maine Story" and promised "50 pages more of it" (C 509); he sent the rest on 18 May (C 514).

When "Chesuncook" appeared in the June, July, and August issues of the *Atlantic*, it caused a considerable rift between Thoreau and Lowell. Thoreau was initially upset about not being sent proofsheets of the first installment, as he had requested. Then he was outraged when a sentence that he specifically demanded to be retained "was, in a very mean and cowardly manner, omitted. I hardly need to say [he wrote to Lowell] that this is a liberty which I will not permit to be taken with my MS. . . . I

[1] Howarth argues that Thoreau's delay in publishing "The Allegash" had more to do with his reluctance to put it before readers: "He was safer writing his Book [i.e., his Journal] than taking chances with an unseen public" (*Book of Concord*, pp. 147, 157).

could excuse a man who was afraid of an uplifted fist, but if one habitually manifests fear at the utterance of a sincere thought, I must think that his life is a kind of nightmare continued into broad daylight" (*C* 515–16).

The omission is from the physical, temporal, and thematic center of "Chesuncook": "It [the pine tree] is as immortal as I am, and perchance will go to as high a heaven, there to tower above me still" (*MW* 122). This climactic section (118–22), following the "murder" of the moose, is the most philosophical part of the essay. In it Thoreau laments his part in "the afternoon's tragedy," which, "as it affected the innocence, destroyed the pleasure of my adventure" (119). He calls for an alternative to the hunter's and forester's sordid exploitation of nature—an imaginative, sympathetic vision of plants and animals: "Strange that so few ever come to the woods to see how the pine lives and grows and spires, lifting its evergreen arms to the light—to see its perfect success, but most are content to behold it in the shape of many broad boards brought to market, and deem *that* its true success!" (121). Other romantic elements in this central passage, beside the insistence on true perception, include emphasis on "higher" uses and laws, on nature as animated presence, and on sympathy as a mode of knowledge and a way of attaining unity. Thoreau insists that the poet best understands the nature of the pines because he "loves them as his own shadow in the air, and lets them stand. . . . It is the living spirit of the tree, not its spirit of turpentine, with which I sympathize, and which heals my cuts" (122).[2]

Before this passage insisting on poetic insight, Thoreau emphasizes objective, scientific perception. He carefully describes the geography of the Maine woods and lists the plants and animals to be found there, often giving their Linnean names. Even his relationship with Joe Aitteon is scientific, an exercise in what we would today call anthropology: "We had employed the Indian mainly that I might have an opportunity to study his ways" (95). In the essay's philosophical center, Thoreau distinguishes be-

[2] A playful reference to "occult sympathy" with nature, discussed in ch. 9.

tween hunters and foresters on one hand and poets (in the broad sense of imaginative creators) on the other: "For one that comes with a pencil to sketch or sing, a thousand come with an axe or rifle" (120). Sherman Paul claims that "Chesuncook" explores "the conflict between the hunter and poet-naturalist." While his companion hunted, "Thoreau went naturalizing, enacting that love of nature which distinguished the poet from the hunter and the lumberman."[3] However, we see a difference between the poet and naturalist. Thoreau carefully distinguishes himself from the hunters and woodsmen, but does not thus automatically become a poet. "Though I had not come a-hunting, and felt some compunctions about accompanying the hunters," he says, "I wished to see a moose near at hand, and was not sorry to learn how the Indian managed to kill one" (99). He perceives the moose not through sympathy or imagination but by scientifically examining its corpse. He may not carry a gun or ax into the wilderness, but neither does he bring a sketch pad or flute. Instead, his instrument is the tape measure. When the moose is killed, Thoreau measures it with the canoe's painter and later fashions a "two-foot rule of a thin and narrow strip of black ash" (113). He travels not as a poet but as a naturalist, a distinction that he makes explicit in his Journal for 9 September 1858 (a month after "Chesuncook" had appeared in print): "How differently the poet and the naturalist look at objects!" (J 11:153).[4] Ironically, for all his "pains" to measure accurately ("I did not wish to be obliged to say merely that the moose was very large" [113]), Thoreau botches one measurement (114). The mistake, one among many recorded in "Chesuncook," is a recurrent theme.[5] Such er-

[3] *The Shores of America*, pp. 362–63. Howarth also talks of Thoreau's "poetic sensibility" and claims that "his own character in 'Chesuncook' is that of a complacent lyric poet" (*Book of Concord*, p. 156).

[4] As early as 1851 Thoreau anticipated losing his poetic perspective: "I fear that the character of my knowledge is from year to year becoming more distinct and scientific; that, in exchange for views as wide as heaven's cope, I am being narrowed down to the field of the microscope. I see details, not wholes nor the shadow of the whole" (J 2:406).

[5] Examples of misperception appear on pp. 85, 86, 89, 94, 96, 99–100, 103, 114, 117, 118, 119, 123, and 153. As in "Excursion to Canada,"

rors suggest the limits of ordinary perception and contrast implicitly with the imaginative, intuitive grasp of truth celebrated at the journey's center.

After the section on poetic, sympathetic knowledge, we might expect a significant change in Thoreau's approach to nature—perhaps a substitution of poetry and mythology for measurement. Instead, even while denouncing the "coarse and imperfect use Indians and hunters make of nature," he examines "the botanical specimens which I had collected that afternoon" (120). Through the rest of the trip he goes on measuring ("my new black-ash rule was in constant use" [127]) and seizing opportunities "to botanize" (131). Biological, geographical, and anthropological data continue to dominate. The philosophical center, then, remains isolated; it does not affect the rest of the essay beyond stressing the disproportion of scientific to Transcendental material. Thoreau seems to value imaginative, sympathetic perception but to find it in 1858 beyond his own powers; he sees it as an ideal he can no longer attain.

If his own perception is scientific and therefore limited, perhaps the Indian's is closer to his earlier ideal. Thoreau explicitly contrasts himself with Joe Aitteon: "He had noticed that I was curious about distances, and had several maps. He, and Indians generally, with whom I have talked, are not able to describe dimensions or distances in our measures with any accuracy" (131). By this observation Thoreau does not necessarily disparage Indians, since their perceptions are often superior to the whites'. At Mount Kineo, for example, an unnamed Indian's "sharp eyes . . . detected a canoe with his boy in it far away under the mountain, though no one else could see it" (92), and Aitteon catches with his own "sharp eyes" a duck that Thoreau and his companion missed (98). But Aitteon is not an ideal, archetypal Indian; he has been corrupted by contact with the white civilization. He would fare better in a barn than the woods (85) because he can no longer live off the land (107), an indication of

---

Thoreau concentrates here on blocked or distorted perception without showing much faith in the power of the imagination to remedy what the senses confound.

his distance from nature. Thoreau is surprised to hear him "swear once mildly" (95; the Journal identifies the offending phrase as "Damn it" [MLJ 22:82]) and sing white songs (107); he is disappointed when the Indian cannot tell him about the construction of a canoe (107). Aitteon's perceptions, too, are not always those of the ideal Indian celebrated in *A Week*: he loses track of the wounded moose (113), misjudges the weight of a moosehide (116), and, in a humorous sequence, mistakes a hedgehog first for a bear and then for a beaver (117).

Thus, "Chesuncook" lacks a fully romantic hero (neither Thoreau nor Aitteon qualifies) and features only briefly and in a limited way the attitudes that characterize *Walden*. If the trip itself and the first draft date from 1853—the middle of Thoreau's most creative period and the time of his crucial revisions of *Walden*—why does "Chesuncook" not resemble his masterpiece more closely?

Perhaps the answer lies in the history of its composition and in Thoreau's choice of genre. Charles Norton Coe argues that Wordsworth required time for imagination to transform his own travels and readings in travel literature into the romantic experience of his poems.[6] In the same way, *Walden* developed slowly and changed significantly, as we have seen, through its seven drafts; only years after his experience at the Pond did Thoreau discover or create its full meaning. Bare facts flowered into imaginative truths during a long period of textual growth and reconception. Although five years separated Thoreau's second long Maine excursion from his published account of it, "Chesuncook" underwent relatively little revising (in the sense either of Thoreau's physically changing the text or returning to his experiences with new insights). The Journal account of 1853 is substantially the same as the *Atlantic Monthly* version of 1858.[7] Indeed, Torrey and Allen justify omitting this Maine narrative

---

[6] *Wordsworth and the Literature of Travel* (New York: Bookman Associates, 1953), ch. 1.

[7] And the posthumous 1864 version differs little from the *Atlantic Monthly* articles. In his Editorial Appendix, Moldenhauer lists only nine substantive changes, the most important of which involved restoring the passage Lowell had censored (*MW* 362).

from their 1906 edition of the Journal because "the story is told elsewhere, virtually in the language of the Journal" (J 5:424, 456). When he returned to his early draft in 1858, he added nothing equivalent to the late material that transformed the final versions of *A Week* and *Walden*.

Thoreau revised his earlier narrative for serial publication chiefly by omitting some materials, rearranging others, and supplementing his Journal account. He omitted information that had little to do with his major themes in "Chesuncook"—for example, single paragraphs on a conversation with General Capen (MLJ 22:75–76) and on a man recently lost in the area (MLJ 22:144)—and material from his visit to Orono after the crucial events in the woods—for example, five pages summarizing what old John Pennyweight taught him about building canoes (MLJ 22:151–55). He also dropped some of his naturalist's notes (e.g., MLJ 22:140–43), perhaps because they retarded the narrative. The paragraph on what Thoreau calls the "myrtle" bird (MLJ 22:141) survived until Thoreau canceled it in the manuscript that went to the printer in 1858—probably, Moldenhauer suggests, because Thoreau had only just discovered that the bird was actually a white-throated sparrow (*MW* 438–39).

Thoreau rearranged other materials because they went best together (thus, he joined scattered translations of Indian place-names [MLJ 22:136–38 and 148 to *MW* 140–42]) or because he wished to emphasize important points: he moved toward the center of his narrative early references to the "spiring" of trees (MLJ 22:85–86 to *MW* 109) and to living life "as tenderly & daintily as one would pluck a flower" (MLJ 22:79 to *MW* 120).

Thoreau revised "Chesuncook" most significantly by expanding the narrative that appears in the Journal. Some of these additions improved the structure, giving greater clarity and coherence. In the Journal, for example, Thoreau mentions a guidepost between Abbot and Monson "surmounted by a pair of large moose horns with a great many prongs" (MLJ 22:71). When revising the passage, Thoreau pointed it toward the climax of the story: "They are sometimes used for ornamental hat trees, together with deers' horns, in front entries; but, after the experience *which I shall relate*, I trust that I shall have a better excuse for killing a moose, than that I may hang my hat on his horns" (88, emphasis added). Also, Thoreau clarified his relationship with Joe Aitteon by expressing his intention to study the Indian's ways (95).

Thoreau added to the Journal account most of the humorous parts of the essay: the paragraph on "the days that tried dogs' noses" (127) and the puns involving General Atlas (86), Amphitrite (90), moose hides (116), and John Pennyweight (149). These were probably early additions, designed to entertain his lecture audiences. If his Philadelphia experience (21 November 1854) was representative, the bits of humor were not enough. W. H. Furness reported to Emerson that the lecture failed before an unreceptive audience (*DHT* 342). Thoreau spoke again the next month ("Life without Principle," delivered in Providence on 6 December), again unsuccessfully. He wrote in his Journal, "After lecturing twice this winter I feel that I am in danger of cheapening myself by trying to become a successful lecturer, i.e., to interest my audiences. I am disappointed to find that most that I am and value myself for is lost, or worse than lost on my audience. I fail to get even the attention of the mass. I should suit them better if I suited myself less" (*J* 7:79). We see here again the pressures of genre and audience on Thoreau. Lecture audiences and editors of magazines wanted conventional travel pieces, filled with adventures and exotic places and people. During the late 1840s and early 1850s, Thoreau was more interested in experimenting with and combining genres—turning travel into spiritual adventure and using objective observations as springboards for romantic philosophy. The fate of *A Week*, the slow start of *Walden's* sales, and the poor reception of some lectures may have discouraged him from further experimentation.[8]

The most important additions to the Journal account of "Chesuncook" concern the relation between nature and civilization. They show Thoreau moving away from the extreme celebration

---

[8] Seven hundred and six copies of *A Week* (from an edition of 1,000) were returned on 28 October 1853, a month after Thoreau got back from Chesuncook and during the time he was writing the Journal account of the trip.

of the wild he expressed in "Walking" and *Walden*. Although the evidence is sketchy, we suspect that the materials leaning toward a milder pastoralism and civilization were added when Thoreau revised the essay for serial publication in 1858—after his romanticism had begun to cool. The printer's copy for the last part of the essay (including the coda and section on Smith's clearing) is missing. However, the coda contains two Journal entries, both from 1858 (*J* 10:234, 286), which may suggest a late date for its composition.

To be sure, Thoreau did not eliminate his insistence on preserving the wilderness, a crucial theme in his essay from the start. He clearly revised to make the theme more prominent. He expanded the philosophical center of the essay to protest the exploitation of pines as well as moose. Although his attitude was implicit in the Journal account, with its many references to lumbermen and to "Veazies Mills where are 16 sets of saws &c &c" (*MLJ* 22:155), he revised the manuscript to make explicit his dissatisfaction with the "war against the pines" (*MW* 128). Also, he added as a frame to "Chesuncook" important references that merge the themes of perception and wilderness, both related to the theme of poetry. Starting his journey, he thinks he sees off Nahant "those features which the discoverers saw, apparently unchanged" (84). But on his return he admits that he first misperceived the peninsula; he saw it "but indistinctly in the twilight, when I steamed by it, and thought that it was unchanged since the discovery" (153). Consulting earlier accounts, he realizes that it has been stripped of its groves—"Now it is difficult to make a tree grow there" (154). Nahant inspires his terrifying vision of a barren America:

> a bald, staring town-house, or meeting-house, and a
> bare liberty-pole, as leafless as it is fruitless, for all I can
> see. We shall be obliged to import the timber for the
> last, hereafter, or splice such sticks as we have;—and
> our ideas of liberty are equally mean with these. The
> very willow-rows lopped every three years for fuel or
> powder,—and every sizable pine and oak, or other forest tree, cut down within the memory of man! . . . We

shall be reduced to gnaw the very crust of the earth for
nutriment. . . . At this rate, we shall all be obliged to let
our beards grow at least, if only to hide the nakedness
of the land and make a sylvan appearance. (154)

But Thoreau also added some sections that contrast with the
pro-wild position of his earlier works. In the 1853 Journal he described the "dreamy state" that he fell into after the "murder" of
the moose:

⟨most the time⟩
I seemed all the while to be floating through ornamental
⟨d⟩
grounds—for I associate the [fir] tops with such scenes—
⟨some⟩   ⟨beneath⟩
very high up [broadway] & bel through & between these
⟨between⟩
pyramidal tops I thought I saw an [endless] succession of
⟨cornices⟩   colu   ⟨verandas—& churches—⟩
ˌfacades & cornices—ˌporticoes & columns—ˌI did not
merely fancy this—but in my drowsy state in the moonlight—
such was the illusion—I fairly lost myself several times—
(MLJ 22:110)[9]

To this passage Thoreau later added, "still dreaming of that architecture and the nobility that dwelt behind and might issue
from it" (118). The new phrase makes the illusion unambiguously positive and tends to reduce the sordidness of the moose
killing. Although he is upset by the brutal slaughter and waste
that precede settlements, Thoreau comforts himself by flashing
forward hopefully in time, anticipating the "nobility" that might
eventually emerge from the coming of civilization. He echoes
here the hopes of Tocqueville: "Thoughts of the savage, natural
grandeur that is going to come to an end become mingled with
splendid anticipations of the triumphant march of civilization."[10]

[9]This vision is an illusion, not a poetic, imaginative transfiguration;
thus, the passage picks up the recurrent theme of misperception.

[10]Alexis de Tocqueville, *Journey to America* (Garden City, N.Y.:
Doubleday Anchor, 1971), p. 399.

Perhaps Maine in the future will not be a treeless wasteland but
a city of magnificent architecture.

A similar optimism pervades Thoreau's revisions of the section
devoted to Ansel Smith's clearing. Thoreau expanded this part
considerably, from seven handwritten pages in the Journal (MLJ
22:117–23) to seven pages of print (*MW* 123–30). Once again,
he reveals some ambivalence about the intrusion of civilization
into the wilderness. "I almost doubted," he writes, "if the lake
would be then the self-same lake,—preserve its form and identity, when the shores should be cleared and settled" (130). But,
although Smith's operation is part of the "war against the pines"
(128), Thoreau finds much to admire in it, especially the rough
pioneer architecture of the buildings. He added after the Journal
account almost all of the mythological references that appear in
"Chesuncook." In connection with Smith and his operations,
Thoreau refers to the Argo, Pandean pipes, forest gods (124),
Orpheus (125), Vulcan, Olympus (126), Hercules, and Apollo
and the flocks of Admetus (129).[11] These allusions elevate Smith
to near-mythical status, as do the references to American heroes
and places such as Ethan Allen, Ticonderoga, and Crown Point
(130).

Indeed, with the added material, this passage might be considered as an alternative center of the essay. If the moosehunting
occurs at the physical midpoint of "Chesuncook" and the temporal center of the excursion (fifth day of ten), the Smith passage
appears at the northernmost reach of the trip and shares an
equal claim to be the temporal center (the sixth day). The tension between these two possible centers illustrates the ambivalent structure of this essay in which Thoreau regrets what
hunters and foresters do to the wilderness, yet admires individual intruders and finds potential value in the civilization that
they herald.

Thoreau's pro-civilization stance, strongest in the sections

---

[11]The last reference occurs in a passage about versifiers going a-
hunting; here Thoreau appears to contradict his position at the center
(118–22) about the incompatibility of poetry and hunting—unless, of
course, he is being ironic.

added after the Journal account, is especially clear in the coda to "Chesuncook." Here, after warning against the possible wasteland that Maine might become, he comments: "Nevertheless, it was a relief to get back to our smooth, but still varied landscape. . . . The partially cultivated country it is which chiefly has inspired, and will continue to inspire, the strain of poets, such as compose the mass of any literature. . . . The poet's, commonly, is not a logger's path, but a woodman's. The logger and pioneer have preceded him, like John the Baptist; eaten the wild honey, it may be, but the locusts also; banished decaying wood and the spongy mosses which feed on it, and built hearths and humanized Nature for him" (155–56).[12] This conclusion marks a considerable distance from Thoreau's scorn for "civilized" pastoral poetry in *A Week* (56, 366–67) and especially in "Walking," his apologia "for absolute freedom and wildness" (*Ex* 205). "Give me a wildness whose glance no civilization can endure," Thoreau demanded in that earlier essay (225), which he delivered as "The Wild" in the spring of 1851. As in *A Week*, he there criticized "essentially tame and civilized literature" and claimed that "in literature it is only the wild that attracts us" (*Ex* 231).

Thoreau does insist at the end of "Chesuncook" that the wilderness is necessary "for a resource and a background, the raw material of all our civilization" (155), and is especially important to the poet who "must, from time to time, travel the logger's path and the Indian's trail, to drink at some new and more bracing fountain of the Muses, far in the recesses of the wilderness" (156). But by 1858 Thoreau's earlier radicalism has muted considerably. He prescribes for the poet in an essay that reveals himself to be essentially a naturalist. His call for the creation of "national preserves" (156) is rightly recognized as an early manifestation of environmentalism, but it also suggests Thoreau's distance from his earlier stance. In "Walking," for example, physical place was not necessarily important because "wildness" was essentially an individual, imagined, and portable state: "The

---

[12] The banishing of decayed wood is especially important, since a "decayed stump" provides Thoreau with his one mystical episode in "The Allegash" (179–82).

most alive is the wildest" (*Ex* 226). Thus, "the West" in that earlier piece is not California, where the literal-minded had gone gold-grubbing, but a psychological state and a return to one's senses (*Ex* 246). Thoreau's call in "Chesuncook" for national action is a subtle political plea that takes him further from the earlier hopes of both himself and Emerson that self-reform would produce all the needed changes for a better world.

The Allegash and East Branch

Thoreau took his final trip to Maine between 20 July and 8 August 1857, four years after the Chesuncook excursion. As we have seen, however, the basic work on the third *Maine Woods* essay was contemporary with, and may even have preceded, his finishing the draft of "Chesuncook." On 1 January 1858 he reported to George Thatcher, his companion of 1853, "I have written out a long account of my last Maine journey—part of which I shall read to our Lyceum—but I do not know how soon I shall print it" (*C* 502). He delivered the promised lecture on 25 February 1858, but delayed publishing "The Allegash" because of the previously mentioned concern for Joe Polis. In late winter and spring 1858 he completed "Chesuncook" for the *Atlantic* and later indicated in a letter to G. W. Curtis his intention to publish "another and a larger slice" of his Maine adventures (*C* 519).

As with "Chesuncook," Thoreau did not revise "The Allegash" as radically as he had *A Week* or *Walden*. The final version is close enough to the Journal account (volumes 23 and 24, Morgan Library MA 1302: 29 and 30) that Torrey and Allen again omitted a transcript since it seemed to them merely to repeat what was available in volume 3 of the 1906 *Writings*, *The Maine Woods*. A closer comparison does reveal several changes of varying degrees of importance. Thoreau omitted some passages that could retard the flow of the narrative and would probably have lost his readers' interest (e.g., naturalist's notes [MLJ 29:211–13, 327–29; 30:4–5] and further instructions on making canoes [MLJ 29:252–53]). Other Journal materials are more interesting, such as the sketches of Maine residents and of a Revolutionary War soldier (MLJ 29:292–94), but Thoreau dropped them apparently to avoid distracting from his portrait of Polis. He omitted, too, a passage reminiscent of the epistemological and aesthetic theorizing in his earlier works, a paragraph that argues that "the most valuable communications—or news consists of hints & suggestions" that reveal "an almost wholly new world" (MLJ 29: 309).

Revising his narrative, Thoreau also expanded the original Journal. Most of the added materials concern Joe Polis, who clearly becomes the main focus of attention. Thus, in the process of revision Thoreau seems to have discovered that "the Indian" was his true subject.

Thoreau, as we have noted, was working on another revision of "The Allegash" and the other Maine essays close to his death. Howarth insists that "he had never written a proper conclusion to the narrative; it simply ended with his last glimpse of Joe Polis. He told Channing on April 23 [1862] that the paper was 'in a knot I cannot untie.'"[13] The lack of a coda for "The Allegash," in contrast to the other two parts, suggests to Robert Sattlemeyer, also, that the work should be considered unfinished, but Joseph Moldenhauer argues that "when Thoreau died he left something very much like a finished (though not a fair) copy of the last essay."[14]

In a letter to Blake shortly after his return from the Allegash, Thoreau gave an upbeat, positive account of the trip:

> I have made a short excursion into the new world
> which the Indian dwells in, or is. He begins where we
> leave off. It is worth the while to detect new faculties in
> man,—he is so much the more divine; and anything
> that fairly excites our admiration expands us. The In-
> dian, who can find his way so wonderfully in the
> woods, possesses so much intelligence which the white
> man does not,—and it increases my own capacity, as
> well as faith, to observe it. I rejoice to find that intelli-

[13] Howarth, *Book of Concord*, p. 218.

[14] Sattelmeyer, "Away from Concord: The Travel Writings of Henry Thoreau"; Moldenhauer, *MW* 364.

gence flows in other channels than I knew. It redeems
for me portions of what seemed brutish before. (C 491)

Absent from the letter but clear in "The Allegash" is a strong
pessimistic undercurrent that points to the changes in Thoreau's
view of the world in the late 1850s. "The Allegash" takes up
again the important topics of epistemology, myth, and the relation of civilization to the wilderness, but the treatment here
shows Thoreau moving in new directions.

If Thoreau dropped from the Allegash Journal one entry that
approaches his old sense of perceiving best through indirection
and suggestion (which allow full play of the imagination), he
retained an important section that seems quite romantic—that
on phosphorescent wood (179–82). Up to this point, Thoreau,
as he did in "Chesuncook," took every opportunity "to botanize."
He provides even more geographical information and lists of
plants and animals than he had in the previous essay. Once again
his instrument is the tape measure rather than the flute or
sketch book. But in discovering phosphorescent wood he "let science slide, and rejoiced in that light as if it had been a fellow-
creature" (181). He reacts to the light not as a biologist but as a
poet and mythmaker; he gives it metaphorical and religious significance and responds to it sympathetically. After quoting
Wordsworth's "'a *pagan* suckled in a creed'" he provides a thoroughly Transcendental account of his enlightenment: "It suggested to me that there was something to be seen if one had eyes.
It made a believer of me more than before. I believed that the
woods were not tenantless, but choke-full of honest spirits as
good as myself any day,—not an empty chamber, in which chemistry was left to work alone, but an inhabited house,—and for a
few moments I enjoyed fellowship with them" (181).

This moment of sympathetic perception resembles the one at
the midpoint of "Chesuncook," but it occurs on the first night of
wilderness travel; it is far from the spatial or temporal center of
the essay. The discovery of phosphorescent wood may historically have occurred early in the trip, but in a more imaginative
work Thoreau would not have felt bound by the tryanny of fact.
In both *A Week* and *Walden* he rearranged chronology to fit his
rhetorical purposes. He even placed at the temporal center of *A*

Week ("Tuesday") an epiphanic moment (sunrise on Saddleback) that occurred five years after the excursion recounted in the book. "I have no respect for facts," he then claimed, "even except when I would use them, and for the most part I am independent of those which I hear, and can afford to be inaccurate, or, in other words, to substitute more present and pressing facts in their place" (*W* 363). Thoreau, then, could have made this episode more central physically and thematically to "The Allegash." By placing it so early in the essay, he de-emphasizes it. The mystic light gleams briefly; it does not illuminate the rest of the excursion. In this respect, too, the episode resembles the philosophical passage in "Chesuncook" (118–22). Both segments contrast conspicuously with the other materials in the essays. The moments of imaginative perception fade quickly without affecting subsequent events on the excursions. Thus, Thoreau ends his discussion of the symbolic light on a note of disappointment: "I kept those little chips and wet them again the next night, but they emitted no light" (182). He even rearranged the Journal materials to conclude thus rather than with the more positive ending in his original narrative: "It suggested to me how unexplored still are the realms of nature—that what we know & have seen is always an insignificant portion—We may any day take a walk as strange as Dante's imaginary one to L'Inferno or Paradiso" (MLJ 29:242–43; MS only).

Thoreau resumes his excursion, looking not with a new poetic perspective but scientifically, through "surveyor's eyes" (252). He does not even seem as troubled as he had been in "Chesuncook" by the change. When Polis kills a moose, Thoreau says nothing of higher, more imaginative uses of nature; he just measures the carcass (266). (During his final revisions of "The Allegash" [April-May 1862], Thoreau dropped from the manuscript what little protest he had ventured: "I had a short talk with him about killing moose for their hides in which he used the common white man's argument about the necessity of one supporting his family.")[15] When he uses the term *imagination* in "The Alle-

---

[15] Houghton AM 278.5 [17, A], page numbered 219. Subsequent references to Thoreau's last revisions of "The Allegash" are to this manuscript.

gash," it most often means not intuitive perception of essential truth but misperception or illusion. For example, infected by "the associations of the settlements," he cannot perceive the wilderness clearly: "The waterfalls which I heard were not without their dams and mills to my imagination,—and several times I found that I had been regarding the steady rushing sound of the wind from over the woods beyond the rivers as that of a train of cars,—the cars at Quebec. Our minds anywhere, when left to themselves, are always thus busily drawing conclusions from false premises" (203). Later in the narrative he comments, "Generally speaking, a howling wilderness does not howl: it is the imagination of the traveler that does the howling" (219).

The contrast is quite striking between the first essay in *The Maine Woods*, "Ktaadn," and these pieces. The manuscript of "Ktaadn" and even the final text were filled with Thoreau's doubts about his personal and social abilities even to survive in the face of titanic nature. In the later essays Thoreau comes through more like a Victorian gentleman moving toward a scientific and anthropological way of looking at Polis and the other Indians. His previous ease at introducing mythology (both classical and invented) as a way to explain or to forestall the press of nature is gone. The continued progress of civilization seems to take the mystery out of the world. Maine is a day's trip from Boston, and the traveler does not leave his guide or his traveling companions to challenge the heights. The most memorable travail of this journey is the Mud Pond carry.

In one instance, however, Thoreau once more links the imagination with mythmaking. In a particularly wild part of the area, he comments: "My imagination personified the slopes themselves, as if by their very length they would waylay you, and compel you to camp again on them before night. Some invisible glutton would seem to drop from the trees and gnaw at the heart of the solitary hunter who threaded those woods; and yet I was tempted to walk there" (184). The perception could be an illusion or it could be, with its personification (a start toward mythology), an expression of the kind of essential truth that imagination and myth provided in *A Week* or *Walden*. But myth in "The Allegash" is not very extensively or well developed. The essay contains but one allusion to classical myth—the wilderness "reminded me of Prometheus Bound" (235)—and Thoreau does not explore this reference as he had in "Ktaadn." Also different from "Ktaadn" is his presentation of Indian mythology. By the end of his first Maine excursion Thoreau took quite seriously what the Indians said about Mount Katahdin. Here, though, he mocks Polis's story of how a moose was metamorphosed into Mount Kineo. In dismissing the myth, Thoreau comments, "An Indian tells such a story as if he thought it deserved to have a good deal said about it, only he has not got it to say" (172). Such a passage, were it to have appeared in, say, the "Reading" chapter of *Walden*, could be interpreted as a call for the reader's own creativity.[16] Here it is part of the Indian's "deficiency," which he makes up for "by a drawling tone, long-windedness, and a dumb wonder which he hopes will be contagious" (172). If there is not much mythmaking in "The Allegash," there is little hope for any in the future: Thoreau complains of "the Anglo American" who "cannot read the poetry and mythology which retire as he advances. He ignorantly erases mythological tablets in order to print his handbills and town meeting warrants on them" (229).[17]

Ironically, while Polis is not a very good teller of myths, he does approach in "The Allegash" the status of a mythic hero. Thoreau imagines him going heroically through the woods and "contending day and night, night and day, with the shaggy demon Vegetation" (236). This part was added to the Journal draft, and Thoreau's other additions suggest that he revised the narrative mainly to focus on Polis, to give him a more prominent—indeed, leading—role in the story. The finished piece is a more thorough,

[16] See Thoreau's defense of the suggestiveness of myth and his concluding call for the reader's creativity in *A Week* (58–61, 392–93) and his insistence in *Walden* that "we must laboriously seek the meaning of each word and line, conjecturing a larger sense than common use permits out of what wisdom and valor and generosity we have" (100).

[17] In his late revisions Thoreau canceled two sentences that followed this passage: "This wilderness is a great mythic poem worth a thousand of Spenser's Faery Queens & Dante's Divine Comedies. Spenser and Dante translated only such sheets[?] of it as came round their grounds."

detailed study of "the Indian" than was the Journal account, and the revisions especially emphasize differences between Polis and the whites. For example, the Journal for 22 July concludes, "At 8 PM Polis arrived in the cars & I led the way—while he followed me ¾ of a mile to Thatcher's with the canoe on his head" (MLJ 29:219). In revising, Thoreau added, "I tried to enter into conversation with him, but as he was puffing under the weight of his canoe, not having the usual apparatus for carrying it, but, above all, [since he] was an Indian, I might as well have been thumping on the bottom of his birch the while. In answer to the various observations which I made by way of breaking the ice, he only grunted vaguely from beneath his canoe once or twice, so that I knew he was there" (159). He resumes the theme of the Indian's silences later, adding to the Journal account a paragraph on Polis's desire "to get along with the least possible communication and ado" (272).

Not all the material devoted to Polis either in the Journal or the later additions is positive or flattering. Polis is not the abstract, idealized Indian of the earlier works.[18] Thoreau is disappointed to find him a conventional Christian, a land speculator, occasionally moody, self-pitying in illness, and selfishly reluctant to help Thoreau search for his lost companion.

But Polis is the closest that Thoreau comes in the last Maine essays to the near-mythic hero he let himself play in his earlier works. Also, in his political involvement (293–94), Polis anticipates somewhat John Brown, Thoreau's last major hero. Unlike Joe Aitteon, the Indian half-corrupted by civilization, Joe Polis exemplifies "an Indian availing himself cunningly of the advantages of civilization, without losing any of his woodcraft" (201). Familiar with the "mystic lore of the wilderness" (230), he can travel through the woods surely (184–85, 235, 276) and live there self-sufficiently. Thoreau describes Polis's knowledge in terms that recall the romantic imagination. "The Indian," as Thoreau often calls Polis, making him a kind of representative man, possesses a mysterious, intuitive intelligence that differs from

[18] For an account of how Thoreau's attitudes toward Indians changed, see Sayre, *Thoreau and the American Indian.*

"the other sort of knowledge, all labelled and arranged."[19] It is spontaneous and independent (he "relies on himself at the moment," an echo of Emerson's "Self-Reliance"). It resembles animal instinct, perhaps "a sharpened and educated sense" (185), and, indeed, Polis at one point seems "suddenly to have quite forsaken humanity, and gone over to the musquash side" (207), an example of sympathetic identification with nature. Unlike Aitteon, Polis rarely misperceives. He may be wrong about a sign that Thoreau would marry (210), but most of the essay concentrates on his remarkable "sharp eyes" (276) and knowledge of the woods. Thoreau associates his own brief moment of imaginative perception with the Indians, who witness such "unimagined phenomena" as phosphorescent wood because "they are abroad at all hours and seasons in scenes so unfrequented by white men. Nature must have made a thousand revelations to them which are still secrets to us." Thoreau concludes from the episode, "I have much to learn of the Indian, nothing of the missionary" (181).

Thoreau's motive in "The Allegash" is to learn from Polis, with whom he makes a bargain at the start of the trip: "I told him that in this voyage I would tell him all I knew, and he should tell me all he knew, to which he readily agreed" (168). But although he does learn much from Polis and even briefly approaches the Indian's special way of perceiving, Thoreau emphasizes throughout the narrative his distance from the Indian. He even reveals that Polis violated their seriocomic bargain. Polis refuses to tell him how to make pitch from materials taken on the excursion ("there were some things which a man did not tell even his wife" [205]), and we are left wondering how much more the Indian would not, or could not, reveal. "The Allegash" thus contrasts with *A Week*, where Thoreau incorporated Indian qualities into

[19]Throughout the late revisions, Thoreau changed "Polis" to "the Indian" (e.g., Houghton AM 278.5 [17, A] pages numbered 215, 218, 221). In "Thoreau's Maine Woods Indians: More Representative Men" (*American Literature* 49 [1977]:366–84), Philip Gura explores Thoreau's search for universal genius in American Indians rather than the European models that Emerson chose for *Representative Men* (1850).

his own synthesizing role of the poet, and with *Walden*, where he portrayed himself as a successor to the Indian, planting where the Indian once planted and mediating between wild and civilized. "Great difference between me and white man" (185), Polis himself insists, and he reinforces the distinction by never saying "we" to whites (167). As we have seen, that distinction is mainly between white and Indian ways of viewing the wilderness.

Thoreau's scientific approach turns out not to be very practical in the woods, since he gets lost on a number of occasions when Polis does not guide him. Going around a fall after Grand Lake, for example, Thoreau keeps losing the shore because Polis "did not call often enough, forgetting that we were not Indians. He seemed to be very saving of his breath,—yet he would be surprised if we went by, or did not strike the right spot" (272). At the temporal center of the two-week trip (July 27), Thoreau presents another such episode. He narrates how, without Polis to guide them, he and his companion become lost on the carry from Umbazookskis Lake to Mud Pond. Confused by the numerous paths, they miss the right one and wander into "an arbor-vitae wilderness of the grimmest character" (213). The episode, which may be the thematic center as well, emphasizes the crucial distinction between the two races' perception of and relation to the wilderness. When Polis finds them, he is "greatly surprised that we should have taken what he called a 'tow' (i.e. tote or toting or supply) road, instead of a carry path,—that we had not followed his tracks,—said it was 'strange,' and evidently thought little of our woodcraft" (217). The whites continue on through a swamp where they expect to hear "the growl of a bear, the howl of a wolf, or the scream of a panther," but where actually "it is the imagination of the traveler that does the howling" (219).

As with "Chesuncook," there is another thematic center in this narrative—the account of the next day, 28 July, which marks the spatial extreme ("my furthest northern point" [235]), and entry to the Allegash River. It also coincides with the physical center of the essay (the middle pages). Earlier Thoreau spoke of the wilderness "invaded by the lumbering army" (210), a major theme, also, of the two other *Maine Woods* essays. Now, at the far reach of his journey, in a passage that he expanded considerably from the Journal (MLJ 29:286–87 to *MW* 228–30), he denounces the loggers as "vermin gnawing at the base of her [the wilderness's] noblest trees" (228) and he emphasizes especially the destruction caused by dams, which create around each lake a border of dead trees and so make the shores inaccessible.[20] He presents here a scene equivalent to the vision of barren America that closes "Chesuncook": "For half a dozen rods in width it was a perfect maze of submerged trees, all dead and bare and bleaching. . . . Imagine the wharves of the largest city in the world, decayed, and the earth and planking washed away, leaving the spiles standing in loose order . . . while there rises from the water's edge the densest and grimmest wilderness, ready to supply more material when the former fails, and you may get a faint idea of that coast" (238–39). The scene telescopes the rise and fall of civilization; in this wilderness being cleared to erect future cities, Thoreau already sees the cities of his illusion (118) in ruin. In the late Maine essays Thoreau uses trees, with Thomas Cole, to sketch his own "Course of Empire." The "endless succession of porticoes and columns" that he hallucinated on the Chesuncook trip (118) gives way to the "bare liberty-pole" (154) of the near future and finally to the total wreck that he presents at the center of "The Allegash."

Anticipating the destruction of the physical wilderness and ultimately of civilization, Thoreau takes a little comfort by pointing to an internal, metaphorical wilderness within men: "some are nearer the frontiers on feather-beds in the towns than others on fir-twigs in the backwoods" (200). More often and emphatically, he laments the passing of the actual Maine woods and associates

[20] The passage was even longer before Thoreau canceled in his last revisions a page-long satire on cutting trees for oxen to stand on the stumps. He may have thought that references to California redwoods were out of place in *The Maine Woods*, or, more likely, he might have felt that the humorous, satirical treatment clashed with the dominant tone of this section. Channing reports that Thoreau "showed an anxiety to correct" his last pieces by removing the humor "that formerly had luxuriated amid the serious pages" (*Thoreau: The Poet-Naturalist*, p. 232).

with it the end of imaginative perception—the disappearance of poetry and mythology. As in "Chesuncook," this prophecy is expressed in a work that conspicuously lacks the poetry and mythology that characterized his earlier works. Despite his insistence to Blake that he had not changed, then, both the late Maine essays reveal a nostalgia for an earlier period when imagination transfigured the world and when he could look forward to the junction of heaven and earth rather than to a barren wasteland.

12

"Resistance to Civil Government" and the Reform Essays of 1854–1860

IN JOURNAL sheets that survive from fragmentary volume "I" (*PJ* 2:381–85), there appears a remarkable conflux of passages all tied together that later became part of *A Week*, *Walden*, and "Ktaadn." These pages presage the unfolding of Thoreau's major early works and remind us of the directions they would take— the narrative of the Maine trip, the complex word fugue of *A Week*, and the personal memoir of the first version of *Walden*. At the end of the *Walden* struggle in 1854, we again can see a diversity of texts in the process of being written. "Chesuncook," the companion narrative to "Ktaadn," seems to have come easily together following Thoreau's 1853 trip, and was being used for lectures. The other two works, "Slavery in Massachusetts" and "Life without Principle," were organized and drafted almost concurrently. Five years later the arrest and execution of John Brown prompted Thoreau to write again about his relationship to the state. In this chapter we will examine these various reform papers in the light of Thoreau's developing political consciousness.

The Night in Jail (1846) and "Resistance to Civil Government" (1848)

Thoreau's earlier works had expressed his antislavery sentiments. *A Week* contains important passages that show his views about politics and slavery during the mid 1840s. In "Monday" he recounts his night at the Concord jail (July 1846) and explains the motive for his protest: he does not want to be "associated with Massachusetts, either in holding slaves or in conquering Mexico" (*W* 130–31). The same paragraph mocks the inability of institutions, including the state, to make much difference—a man may easily proclaim that his individual liberty is more significant than the "political commonweal," and his friends will tolerate that defiance, but the distant state will not. The discussion begins with Thoreau exposing the irrelevance and even nonexistence of the whole system: "To one who habitually endeavors to contemplate the true state of things, the political state can hardly be said to have any existence whatever" (*W* 129).

This charming indifference to the political world was expressed more extravagantly in "Resistance to Civil Government," where Thoreau could eliminate the state psychologically by taking his shoe to the cobbler, then picking huckleberries. In 1848 "the State was nowhere to be seen" (*RP* 84). "Resistance to Civil Government" is unusual from the perspective of our study in that it has virtually no manuscript history. None of the other major works and few of the short ones have evidenced so little their being in Thoreau's mind. We find no Journal passages that echo sentences or even phrases. While Thoreau does remark on his jailing in *A Week* (130) and *Walden* (171; 8:3, C), the phrasing and even many of the sentiments are quite different from those in "Resistance." There may have been a separate notebook (now lost) in which Thoreau drafted the text, and earlier versions could be among the missing parts of the gutted Journals from 1846–49. But if Thoreau worked extensively on the piece, only fragments of lecture and essay drafts have survived, making a genetic study of "Resistance" impossible.

"Resistance to Civil Government" was not, as is often implied, given in the heat of Thoreau's tax refusal. Thoreau was jailed in July 1846, but the lecture that concerns that night was not delivered until a year and a half later. At that time Thoreau was joining the lively debate about the 1848 election with a lecture (later printed as an essay)[1] concerning the issues that he wanted poli-

---

[1] In *Aesthetic Papers*, a potential sequel to the *Dial* that realized only one issue. The full title of the lecture (delivered in January and February 1848) was "The Rights and Duties of the Individual in Relation to Government"; in the book it was changed to "Resistance to Civil Government." Compare the language of the Declaration of Independence: "But when a long train of abuses and usurpations, pursuing invariably the

ticians to address—primarily the question of slavery as it affected the lands about to be acquired through the Mexican War.[2] Thoreau treats the current political situation with a series of overstatements about governments, nominating and voting, that express his despair about the failures of the system even to consider slavery. He must have hoped to appeal to Whigs, because Massachusetts under Webster's leadership had voted for Whigs or anti-Jacksonian candidates since Thoreau's college years, and because the Democrats both north and south had been committed to the expansion of slavery all along.[3]

Thoreau's rhetorical strategy in "Resistance to Civil Government" is to allude to this general political climate in the context of a narrative of his personal experience as a tax refuser. Thus, he implies that his essentially private act of getting arrested in the early months of the Mexican War was a symbol of his despair and a token of his long opposition to that war. In the lecture Thoreau connects taxes directly to the war and slavery, even though his refusal to pay the poll tax should be seen as a general reaction to government. He says, "I do not care to trace the course of my dollar, if I could, till it buys a man, or a musket to shoot one with,—the dollar is innocent,—but I am concerned to trace the effects of my allegiance" (84).

In assessing the political realities of Thoreau's speech, we find nothing to suggest that people were persuaded by it to stop paying taxes or to enter jail. Clearly the signing of a peace treaty one week after Thoreau first delivered his lecture made protesting the war moot, and the discovery of gold at Sutter's mill on 24 January made the spoils of the war even more attractive. The issues for abolitionists in 1848 proved to be too abstract and the relation between the Mexican War and slavery too poorly de-

---

same object, evinces a design to reduce [the governed] under absolute despotism, it is their right, it is their duty to throw off such government, and to provide new guards for their future security."

[2] See Donald Ross, Jr., "The Historical Context of 'Resistance to Civil Government,'" unpublished manuscript.

[3] Joel H. Silbey, *Congressional Voting Behavior, 1841–1852* (Pittsburgh: Univ. of Pittsburgh Press, 1967).

fined. Emerson's judgment in 1846 proved correct, "The United States will conquer Mexico, but it will be as the man swallows the arsenic, which brings him down in turn. Mexico will poison us" (*JMN* 9:430–31). Three years after "Resistance to Civil Government," the full impact of the Compromise of 1850 came home to Boston with the arrest of Thomas Simms, and serious law-breaking occurred with an attack on Federal marshalls.

Thoreau's rhetoric may have been doomed to fail. The narrow range of practical alternatives advocated during the 1840s and 1850s is striking. Thoreau rejects the nominating process and elections. He senses the possible value of flooding the prison system, but does not concern himself with promoting and organizing this "peaceable revolution" (76). With most other antislavery people, he seemed not only out of sympathy but out of touch with the parties and realistic politics. Abolitionists tended to argue along the lines of Thoreau's essay—individual moral purity was the precondition, and then, by some undefined path, a nation of purified individuals would make slavery and other social ills disappear. The demand for immediate abolition made moral sense, but it was not backed up with a serious discussion of how the economic loss to slaveholders or the economic disadvantage of the freed slaves would be resolved. Even more rarely mentioned was the fact of racial difference between slaves and their owners. Hawthorne, in the 1852 biography of Pierce, captures the sentiment nicely: "Providence," he hopes, will make slavery "vanish like a dream."[4] Morison and Commager single out Emerson for "the only constructive proposal" given at a New York Antislavery Society meeting (6 February 1855), which was, using the British Empire model, to compensate slave owners through the sale of federal and state lands and private donations. He even computed the cost, $200 million.[5] Even though the dollar amount was probably low (less than $100 a person), Morison and Commager note

---

[4] Nathaniel Hawthorne, "Life of Franklin Pierce" in *Complete Works of Nathaniel Hawthorne* (Boston: Riverside, 1888), 12:417.

[5] Samuel Eliot Morison and Henry Steel Commager, *The Growth of the American Republic* (New York: Oxford, 1962), 1:649.

how cheap any plan would have been compared to the $3 million a day the Civil War wound up costing by 1864.

Perhaps Thoreau and other reformers could not find alternatives because the parties' political positions at least through the Civil War were variants of the conservative, tory way of looking at the world. In John Stuart Mill's formulation of the difference between the Benthamite, liberal views and Coleridgean, conservative ones, America never saw a serious advocacy of the former. American leaders were apparently unable to think about institutional or collective solutions to problems, injustice, or national plans. To use the cliché, they did not see the ending of slavery as being "the greatest good for the greatest number." The Wilmot Proviso, the closest to an antislavery bill to get out of Congress, mutely accepted slavery where it already existed. Emerson, in "Politics" (composed 1837–40), dismisses the Whig position as "timid, and merely defensive of property. It vindicates no right, it aspires to no real good, it brands no crime, it proposes no generous policy; it does not build, nor write, nor cherish the arts, nor foster religion, nor establish schools, nor encourage science, nor emancipate the slave, nor befriend the poor, or the Indian, or the immigrant" (CW 3:123). This list anticipates the second paragraph of "Resistance to Civil Government": the state "does not keep the country free. It does not settle the West. It does not educate" (64). Thoreau's point is that only individuals do whatever good exists. Between laissez-faire on the right and individualism and intuitive morality on the left, the range was small, and it hardly gave Thoreau many choices to recommend.

At this stage of his career, however, Thoreau finds himself attending to politics only briefly. Although his lecture explores serious concerns about the election campaign of 1848 and its implications for slavery and for the lands about to be taken from Mexico, Thoreau finds it possible for the individual to transcend the state, or imagine it out of existence, or find more meaning and satisfaction in picking huckleberries than in paying taxes and voting. The topical dimension in "Resistance" points clearly to his later political works, where concern with and disgust for the state rather eclipsed his ability to ignore its actions. Eventually, the pressing problems of slavery and the failure of individual protest to effect change moved Thoreau toward more radical remedies and away from the celebration of divinity in man and nature that characterized his crucial years of spiritual renewal.

Reform Essays from 1854

Walden has rather few moments where Thoreau shows any concern about politics, and only a couple where the problem of slavery seems important. The major sustained comment comes early in "Economy" (7–8; 1:8, A, 1847) with the contrast between the "many keen and subtle masters" who enslave both north and south, including the individuals who enslave themselves by too much concern for their jobs. This rather frivolous linking (at least frivolous by abolitionist standards) culminates in the idea that "self-emancipation" can exist in the "West Indian provinces of the fancy and imagination," a gentle mockery in the first draft of abolitionist efforts and hopes. Thoreau refers twice in *Walden* to the underground railroad to Canada—once poetically to the "fugitive slave [who] keeps the polestar in his eye" (71; 1:99, A). The second time is more detailed, and clearly shows Thoreau's active commitment—in "Visitors" he alludes to his personal effort to assist one person through, a "runaway slave, among the rest, whom I helped to forward toward the northstar" (152; 6:16, D). This confession (as it was in 1852) of having violated federal law betokens Thoreau's change. Three anecdotes about former slaves initiate the mythologizing section of "Former Inhabitants" (257–58; 14:2–4, E). A late, significant addition to this minor theme of *Walden* is a biting attack at the end of "Economy" on the hateful hypocrisy of the "pious slavebreeder devoting the proceeds of every tenth slave to buy a Sunday's liberty for the rest." This reference is one of a series which shows us a world "hacking at the branches of evil" in contrast to what is needed: "striking at the root" (75; 1:105, G interlined; G itself has a phrase, later dropped, which mutes the criticism by bringing in British wage slavery).

Most of Thoreau's published writings after *Walden* were to a growing degree skewed by his concerns with the politics, first, of the Fugitive Slave Act, then of its enforcement in Massachusetts, and, finally of the nation's movement toward war.[6] (Recall that we are talking about periods between wars, from Mexico to Kansas, 1848–54, and from Kansas to Fort Sumter, 1854–60). The major intellectual and emotional development we see in Thoreau's public writings from 1854 onward is a slipping away from the world of redemptive nature into the world of revenge and violence proclaimed in the John Brown lectures. His private Journals are for the most part immune from politics on one hand and from extended celebration of nature's spiritual lessons on the other.[7]

Thoreau's interest in politics after he finished *Walden* is spotty (to say the least, and to accept his word for it). On 18 February 1854, he notes: "I read some of the speeches in Congress about the Nebraska Bill,—a thing the like of which I have not done for a year. What trifling upon a serious subject! while honest men are sawing wood for them outside. Your Congress halls have an ale-house odor,—a place for stale jokes and vulgar wit. It compels me to think of my fellow-creatures as apes and baboons" (*J* 6:129). In August he wrote to H. G. O. Blake, "Methinks I have spent a rather unprofitable summer thus far. I have been too much with the world, as the poet might say. . . . I find it, as ever, very unprofitable to have much to do with men" (cf. the alternative lecture title for "Life without Principle," "What does it profit?") (*C* 330).

He spent several days during that "unprofitable summer" unburdening himself about the Burns affair in his Journal and then weaving those entries together with the earlier Simms material into the lecture and finally the essay "Slavery in Massachusetts." The work was put together from two places in the Journals. In 1851 Thomas Simms, an escaped person, was caught and dis-

---

[6] At the start of the Journal section on Simms, Thoreau says with heavy irony, "I do not believe that the North will soon come to blows with the South on this question. It would be too bright a page to be written in the history of the race at present" (*J* 2:174).

[7] For a more sanguine assessment of Thoreau's later Journals, see Howarth, *Book of Concord*, Cameron, *Writing Nature: Henry Thoreau's Journal*, and Richardson, *Henry Thoreau: A Life of the Mind*.

played on the steps of the Boston Court House; the event occurred near the time Thoreau first delivered "The Wild" lecture
(23 April), and, in a preface to that, he apologizes for not talking
about the Fugitive Slave Law (Houghton AM 278.5 [21, B]). He
expressed a detailed but private reaction in the Journal (2:173–
85). During the middle of 1854, when *Walden* was in final production stages,[8] another fugitive, Anthony Burns, was captured
in Boston and Thoreau again wrote extensively in the Journal
(6:313–70). This time he went to the public immediately, with a
speech at a large rally in Framingham (July 4), and went a step
further by sending the speech to the *Liberator* where it appeared
in much its present form on 21 July 1854.

"Slavery in Massachusetts," when viewed from the history of
its composition, consists of a general introduction, half of which
is in the 1854 Journal, a section of retrospect on Simms (paragraphs 12–30), and a final section on Burns. Most of the second
half of the speech is represented by Journal passages written in
May and June. Unlike "Walking," even though this essay was
composed directly from passages written three years apart, it
does not have any obvious seams. Thoreau successfully merged
the Simms and Burns episodes so that only a specialist (or one
who knows the Journal sources) would be able to tell which was
being discussed. This blending is so smooth partly because the
Journals from both periods share a common political theory and
a satirical tone about the government of Massachusetts.

Thoreau's strategy here is to use the ironic parallel of the two
events to point up the unpleasant continuity of Massachusetts
state governments in their upholding of the Fugitive Slave Act.
His attacks are, from a twentieth-century perspective, quite topical, since he devotes much attention to the failures of individual
governors and state officials to rise above their official statures.
The outrage here, though, is vicious and ad hominem. A purist,
who would like to have seen Thoreau continue with the high
idealism of "Resistance to Civil Government," could only be dis-

---

[8] The last Journal passage to go into *Walden* was from February 1854
(*Wa* 253, 13:18; *J* 6:102–3). The first proofs arrived on 28 March (*J*
6:176), and the book was published on 9 August (*J* 6:429).

appointed. Thoreau does not in these later writings suggest that elusive doctrines such as the "majority" of one should prevail, or recommend that all just people commit themselves to prison. Instead, he uses the sarcastic rhetoric of abolitionist infighting. It is thus unlikely that his essay would have stood out on the *Liberator*'s pages—it fits in nicely with the tone which Garrison had developed over the years.

From the perspective of Thoreau's intellectual change, the ending deserves special comment. The key paragraphs start with the vision of Massachusetts as a Miltonic region "morally covered with volcanic scoriae and cinders," which makes him feel he lives *"wholly within* hell" (*RP* 106, ¶ 46, *J* 6:355–6). The fugitives' captures make him feel a "sense of having suffered a vast and indefinite loss. . . . what I had lost was a country" (the last clause is not in the Journal). This sense of total despair with the political process sounds completely sincere. It invites us to take quite seriously the implied hope of "Resistance to Civil Government" that something might be done to affect the nominating and election process at the national level. Now, in 1854, in the midst of the controversy about the Nebraska Act and the Kansas civil war, Thoreau can see hope of influence neither along party lines nor within the generally "liberal" government of Massachusetts.

He alludes directly to his postponed errand from 1846: the State "has not only interrupted me in my passage through Court street on errands of trade, but it has interrupted me and every man on his onward and upward path" (107, ¶ 47). After the direct expression of his grief, Thoreau presents an extended image of the lovely water lily in the swamp. The flower itself had appeared several times over the years in his Journal, always with a view of its striking pure whiteness.[9] In the passage Thoreau used directly for "Slavery in Massachusetts" (*J* 6:352–3) the lily's purity of fragrance and color remains prominent. But, we have been warned, "when we are not serene, we go not to [the lakes]" (108, ¶ 49). The lily may be still lovely, but its swamp setting is

[9]Journal passages with lillies: 2:331; 4:147–49, 162, 167–69, 172, 205, 216–17; 5:283; 6:434, 469, and 470.

a place of "slime and muck," and we find that "the foul slime stands for the sloth and vice of man, the decay of humanity; the fragrant flower that springs from it, for the purity and courage which are immortal" (108–9, ¶ 50). Thoreau is unable to focus long on a natural setting and he certainly gives nothing parallel to the psychological escape from jail in "Resistance to Civil Government." Here the state is everywhere—he cannot take his thoughts from it.

The same problem of politics hindering authentic life concerns "Life without Principle," which was written at the same time as "Slavery in Massachusetts" and was composed in much the same way—Thoreau went back to his Journals from the early 1850s, drafted other sections during early 1854, and completed the essay in the weeks before he delivered it. It is tempting to see "Life without Principle" as a survey of theoretical notions that are applied in "Slavery in Massachusetts." The former essay, however, has few direct references to the political scene. It qualifies as a "reform paper," presumably, because of Thoreau's explicit comments about slavery and greed and his implicit assumption that reform of the individual will ultimately affect social change. The piece was first given as a lecture in New Bedford on 26 December 1854 under the title "Getting a Living" (CL 84).[10] The sources for about two-thirds of the essay can be found in the Journal from as early as May 1850, but mostly between November 1850 and July 1852 (during the hiatus between *Walden* C and D). Journal sources seem to end in June 1854, or exactly the time of "Slavery in Massachusetts."[11] We assume that Thoreau spent the summer and fall of 1854 putting the lecture together for the 1854–55 winter "season." For once Thoreau judged his audience well; the material was successful enough for him to use at least six times in various cities on the east coast (even in Perth Amboy).

[10]Glick calls this his first "Life without Principle" lecture, but Harding's item for 20–21 November in Philadelphia looks like a possible earlier candidate.

[11]The only Journal sources for "Life without Principle" after J 6:335–6 were the account of Australian gold explorations in J 7:491–501 for October 1855, and a passing echo from 16 November 1858 (J 11:325).

"Life without Principle" is important as an indication of Thoreau's philosophy at the time he completed *Walden*, but it is not so well organized as its contemporary works. It does not seem to have major divisions in content—some paragraphs yoke together Journal passages from two to three years apart, and it is difficult to extract a coherent outline. One might think of it as a statement on the Transcendental problem of "vocation," but even then the bits of the discussion are scattered. Thoreau seems to have assembled the ideas for it without much concern for overall structure. Perhaps the original occasions for the notes, the various times he lectured on these topics, evoked a fragmented, modular approach. His listeners could respond to "Life without Principle" as a series of effective aphorisms and not be bothered by a lack of tight coherence in the whole work.

The essay is a sermon, purely secular, on how the natural state of man is corrupted by society (*RP* 163). The Gold Rush and the visit of Kossuth are dramatic events which highlight the problem, while reading newspapers or getting mail are daily substitutes for self-awareness and self-knowledge (169–70).[12] The figure who must deal with such a world is occasionally a poet, prophet, or philosopher—Thoreau gathered remarks from several Journal entries on the difficulty of a poet's earning a living (see *J* 2:472, 164; 5:19; and *RP* 156, 160–61, ¶ 4, 12–13 and 15, respectively, for examples). The ending especially brings us back to the political intrusions into Thoreau's (or the poet's) life. He expresses his abolitionist views (174–75; ¶ 40–43) in straightforward terms. In the final paragraph (178, ¶ 47), he insists that

---

[12] Thoreau to Parker Pillsbury, 10 April 1861: "That [i.e., ignoring Fort Sumter and Lincoln] is just the most fatal and indeed the only fatal, weapon you can direct against evil, ever. . . . I do not so much regret the present condition of things in this country (provided I regret it at all) as I do that I ever heard of it. . . . Blessed were the days before you read a president's message. . . . Blessed are they who never read a newspaper, for they shall see Nature, and through her, God" (*C* 611).
The early Journal drafts which went into this essay are mostly about the triviality of newspapers and books (1850-January 1852). Passages from June-July 1852 and from March-August 1853 are on the idea of a vocation, especially on the poet's needing pay. There is a hiatus in relevant Journal passages from July 1852 to March 1853.

"politics and the daily routine" should really be performed "unconsciously," as if they were bodily functions. The paragraph, in part from *J* 3:103, continues to call politics the "gizzard of society." Then Thoreau paraphrases Wordsworth's Immortality "Ode": "our life is not altogether a forgetting, but also, alas! to a great extent, a remembering of that which we should never have been conscious of" (179). In an essay nearly void of any reference to nature, the words of romantic poetry explain the need to suffer the world viscerally, not the chance to explore it with poetic imagination. The events entailed in a president's message or the newspapers produce the same effects as poor digestion: they seem to take over even the "ever glorious morning" (179). That remark resonates quite profoundly, and quite ironically, with the ending of *Walden*: "Only that day dawns to which we are awake. There is more day to dawn. The sun is but a morning star" (333, 18:19, F).

The problem at this stage is the failure of Thoreau's elaborate set of psychological defenses against the state and its immoralities. The defenses were mostly personal; he used his creative imagination to get himself away from the jail cell or the Mexican war, but he also tried to provide a line of protection for his fellows through the resilience of nature. Now both imagination and nature appear unable to transform society or free Thoreau from it. In the reform essays of 1854 we find the liberal program of "Resistance to Civil Government" in apparent shambles. The earlier essay took a strong position against war and soldiers, against political parties and the institution of voting, and against the extension of slavery and expansion of the U.S. territory. Even though that essay began with an apparently absolute stand of the anarchist, it is clear by the end that Thoreau wished rather to have government (at all levels) limited to those institutions which he approves (roads, yes; established churches, no). In "Slavery in Massachusetts," five years later, we find only the opposition to slavery at the level of an absolute principle. Pacifism is not an issue, nor is expansion, and Thoreau does allow that the voting majority might be a better vehicle than other elements of the government: "I would much rather trust to the sentiment of the people. In their vote, you would get something of some value, at least, however small" (97, ¶ 20; *J* 2:177). The narrowing of Thoreau's political morality to the single issue of slavery continues in the John Brown essays, where we see even more of a reversal of the 1848 liberal program.

In both "Slavery in Massachusetts" and "Life without Principle" Thoreau is explicit and self-conscious about his rhetoric. He insists that these are genuine and personal statements, that the issues of finding a living or halting slavery are important to the speaker-writer. Others of Thoreau's works take similar trouble to argue for a less literal rhetorical stance—*Walden*, with its famous passage about retaining the "I, or first person," establishes the context for an extended poet's autobiography, along the same rhetorical line Wordsworth staked out in *The Prelude*. "Walking," in its first paragraph also argues for its "extreme" claims.

No matter how well the speaking voice has been established in the two later essays, it is clear that Thoreau does not define his expository pathway in narrative terms. Like "Walking" and "Resistance to Civil Government," these essays are episodic and static. There is no quest, no spiritual or emotional progress toward a vision. The discussions in this chapter do not diminish the values of these essays, but they do point out a fact of their composition—namely that, especially for "Life without Principle," the pieces that came from the Journals do not need to "fit" into a sequence of moral or poetic advance. They can remain fixed. They can depend upon the kind of hard-working sentences (and paragraphs) that Thoreau admired—he wrote of Carlyle's work, "It resounds with emphatic, natural, lively, stirring tones, muttering, rattling, exploding, like shells and shot, and with like execution" (*EEM* 226).

In these 1854 essays, Thoreau still casts himself as hero, as he did in *Walden*. The speaker-writer remains the protagonist of his own works—the man who takes risks by speaking his own person in the face of social opposition. But these writings do not approach the level of *Walden*. "Slavery in Massachusetts" takes political but not aesthetic risks; it is written in conventional, utilitarian prose that does not tap the readers' own creativity. "Life without Principle" lacks a mythos that might have fused and elevated its central concerns, which are closer to those of *Walden*.

John Brown Essays (1859–60)

In John Brown, Thoreau finally created a mythic hero who could crystalize his concern about the collapse of his nation. Thoreau's vision of John Brown· represents almost classic mythmaking. Brown was a person, a historical reality—he had been to Concord and met Thoreau and some of his friends. Over the years Brown had been in the public eye, backing up abolitionist rhetoric with various acts of daring or bravado. The facts about Brown, however, from the atrocities to his moral courage, are not relevant to the mythic Brown that Thoreau created in his lectures and essays.[13] To invent his mythic John Brown, Thoreau started with the figure of the captured revolutionary that the abolitionist press presented. The mythic transformation first involved a fanciful biographical sketch that is subtly laced with allusions to Christ and Cromwell. These preliminaries are followed by a more systematic link between Brown and Christ until Thoreau can end the first essay with quotations from Brown offered as if they were the new gospel.

In his early writing Thoreau rarely focuses much on characters other than himself. Examples from his later years include Governor Loring, the villain from "Slavery in Massachusetts," and Joe Polis, from "The Allegash and East Branch." Loring is ultimately but a functionary of the political system who could not rise to the obvious evils around him. Joe Polis, owing to his ethnic differences from the whites, is at times shown to have an extraordinary understanding of nature, but his status as a potential mythic figure is undercut by his occasional technical blunders and civilized traits. Brown remains the only person to match Thoreau himself. Thoreau's narrating persona has been the dominating figure of the earlier books and essays. Those works portray two different sides of Thoreau: the humble quester whose charge to himself was to "simplify, simplify," and the bold saun-

[13] For an account of Thoreau's knowledge about the real Brown, see Michael Meyer, "Thoreau's Rescue of John Brown from History," in *Studies in the American Renaissance, 1980*, ed. Joel Myerson (Boston: Twayne, 1980), pp. 301–16.

terer with acute insight into the workings of the natural world. His Journals from 1855 on reveal a narrowing of the gap, as the modesty of the observations takes over the bulk of most entries, and inferences become more scientific, less subjective and daring, and infrequently metaphysical or Transcendental.

In the three John Brown essays, even the narrating self diminishes. Thoreau does not present the events as a personal witness (as he had in "Slavery in Massachusetts"). Instead, he tries to project the collective views of Concord and he evokes general memories of Brown's visit in 1857. Thoreau also narrows the politics of 1859; he does not deal with issues of race or economics, and he barely deals with the notion of "section" (North versus South) that was to precipitate the war.

The John Brown offered parallels in many ways the narrator of "Resistance to Civil Government." For both, opposition comes from newspaper editors, political parties and conventions, and hypocritical church leaders. Thoreau's night in jail becomes a symbolic protest, and, as we have seen, the time of the lecture and essay displaces the event from its meaning. Brown, even at the time of the "Plea," is clearly in serious trouble, and his commitment to the causes he represented more than verbal.

Thoreau directs "A Plea for Captain John Brown" rhetorically toward redressing the inadequacies of newspaper accounts, which, he says, systematically excluded Brown's words and thus the valid and true positions Brown espoused. Having set that challenge, he fittingly closes the speech with several quotations from Brown. The motif of a debate with the papers continues throughout the piece—only a dozen or so paragraphs present more general or abstract discussions of the ethics of antislavery.

The first section (paragraphs 1 to 17) provides a revisionist biography of Brown, which brings him through an early pacifist stage to the point where he decided he had to fight in order to make headway against slavery. This account rehearses Thoreau's own radicalization, even though he never says so explicitly. [14]

[14] Thoreau may have tried (unconsciously or not) to project his own image onto Brown. He cites Brown's work as a surveyor and presents him as a New Englander with Spartan habits (*RP* 112, 115–16). Other

Brown in these paragraphs emerges as the heir first of the American political tradition of Concord Bridge and Bunker Hill (*RP* 113; ¶ 6), but even further back, of Cromwell and the Puritans. In all this is an echo of the perennial fosterer of freedom, the sort of abstract personage found in Hawthorne's story from the 1840s, "The Gray Champion": "He died lately in the time of Cromwell, but he reappeared here" (113; ¶ 8).

The biographical prologue ends with a brief transition as Thoreau promises to deal with Brown's "last act," ambiguously his arrest or his death. Here begins Thoreau's direct rebuttal of the current newspaper stories, which he quotes and alludes to quite often. They err first in questioning the wisdom of Brown's tactics, as if that were the issue, rather than the moral position which Brown advocated. The newspapers outrage Thoreau most often with the charge that Brown is insane—he refers to it about half a dozen times and then turns it *ad papyrum* into a questioning of the sanity of the papers themselves or the society they represent.

The first part of the rebuttal (¶ 18–27) includes a three-paragraph commentary on the role of churches (¶ 24–26), and the first explicit association of Brown with Christ: "A church that can never have done with excommunicating Christ while it exists!" (120; ¶ 25). The next section of the newspaper material explicitly condemns them for not quoting Brown directly, a failure likened to a publisher who would "reject the manuscript of the New Testament" (122; ¶ 28). Most of the paragraphs are rather straightforward editorial street fighting. In only a couple of places does Thoreau rise above his tactics. He wishes to escape "at a distance in history or space" from the "crowded society" of the American world. Under Brown's influence, we live, says Thoreau, in "a city of magnificent distances" (121; ¶ 27). Another sustained metaphor sees the whole country as a "slave-

---

phrases emphasize the parallel: "He had his eyes about him, and made many original observations" (112), he was "deliberate and practical" (112–13), "a transcendentalist above all, a man of ideas and principles" who kept "a reserve of force and meaning" rhetorically (115), and he maintained his "obedience to an infinitely higher command" (119).

ship . . . crowded with its dying victims" (124; ¶ 34).

This assault ends with a reminder, both personal and to the lecture's audience, that Thoreau had been treating Brown as if he were physically dead (125; ¶ 38), a clear sign that the point of this speech was to turn Brown into a martyr, not just to defend his record before a public court. The insanity charge soon echoes again, but this time the parallels between Brown and Christ are more insistent. Brown has his "twelve disciples" (126; ¶ 41); his prosecutors with their "temples" are likened to "Pilate, and Gessler, and the Inquisition" (126; ¶ 42). Insanity is not a serious charge; it is "a mere trope" (126; ¶ 41). In the midst of the general failure to quote Brown, the *New York Herald* blundered by quoting Brown verbatim, thus making those words immortal. Governor Wise, of Virginia, is finally cited as the authority on Brown's ultimate sanity. By widening his focus beyond the newspapers and churches to include the government, Thoreau also politicizes his association of Brown with Christ—"A government that pretends to be Christian and crucifies a million Christs every day!" (129–30; ¶ 51). The states, including Massachusetts, commit a collective sin, and the only remedy is the "Vigilant Committee" and its Underground Railroad which has "tunnelled under the whole breadth of the land." (131; ¶ 54).

The final parts of the speech justify violence as the way to clear the temple (133; ¶ 58) and to "create a revival" and bring the "best news" (134–5; ¶ 61). Brown's death, compared again with "Christ crucified" (136; ¶ 66, and 137; ¶ 68), leads to Thoreau's "fear" that Brown might be delivered. The gesture is one of apotheosis. One writer sees him "'as a supernatural being,'" and Thoreau concurs: "He shows himself superior to nature. He has a spark of divinity in him" (135; ¶ 62); "He is not Old Brown any longer; he is an Angel of Light" (137, ¶ 68). After the passages quoted from Brown, called now a "testament" (138; ¶ 74), Thoreau offers a final version of how the future will treat the hero. The painter, poet, and historian will present Brown and place his image in American iconography next to "the Landing of the Pilgrims and the Declaration of Independence" (138; ¶ 77). This patriotic diorama will clearly give us not the historical Brown but a mythic and symbolic figure. In this speech, Thoreau takes a rather routine attack on slanted journalism and elevates his discussion to the level of what he perceives to be Brown's moral superiority. His vehicle is a formal mythologizing of the controversial figure into a fully dressed American hero.

Between Brown's arrest on 18 October and the first delivery of the "Plea" on the thirtieth, in three relatively long passages Thoreau drafted nearly all of the lecture in his Journal, interspersed with brief, typical accounts of his afternoon walks. The Journal draft of the "Plea" reveals much about Thoreau's writing. We have tried to show the complexity of the process by charting the Journal source (by page) for each of the seventy-seven paragraphs of the speech. Remarkably, most of the paragraphs have several sources, and many of the Journal paragraphs were broken up to contribute to several parts of the speech. Thus, for example, the first relevant section of the Journal contributed to paragraphs 49, 20, 52, 28, 57, and 49. The first paragraph is made up of a new sentence, one from 22 October, redrafted later (J 12:424 and 433), and the final two sentences from 21 October (414)(see fig. 5).

In his Journal, Thoreau initially reacts to Brown's arrest by characterizing it as an instance of tyranny like that conducted by France and Austria. He then records a brief conversation with the postmaster, and takes down notes from the newspapers. Thoreau quotes his townspeople as questioning Brown's sanity, a theme, as we noticed, which appears often in the Journal and in the final speech. Like other Journal passages devoted to a major topic, the entry includes aphorisms ("A government that pretends to be Christian and crucifies a million Christs every day!") which Thoreau integrated into his longer paragraphs, although their balanced phrasing would have stood out when the speech was delivered. This particular phrase introduces Thoreau's linking of Brown and Christ, and, in effect nearly all of the explicit references to Christ appear during the first day's entries. After a few more quotations from newspapers, some without context, the day's contributions end with what sounds like the start of a companion essay to "Resistance to Civil Government": "The only government that I recognize is that power that established justice in the land, never that which establishes injustice" (J 12:409).

After a day's pause, "Oct. 20 P.M.—To Ripple Lake," Thoreau resumes work on his topic again. Now, it seems very much more like an impassioned speech, with paragraphs that begin with exclamations and direct questions and even commands ("Read his admirable answers . . ."). These passages liberally use first person (singular and plural) and second person pronouns as Thoreau warms rhetorically to the prospect of a lecture hall address. The quotations and paragraphs are mostly short, and it is hard to see a clear theme emerge in this second set of materials. It does contain the series of quotations from Brown that conclude the speech.

Entries under the date of 22 October comprise the bulk of the draft, and, since the next dated entry is 28 October, were likely written over several evenings. Thoreau says in the essay, "I put a piece of paper and a pencil under my pillow, and when I could not sleep, I wrote in the dark" (RP 118). The paragraphs now tend to be complete (as determined by what happened to them in the speech), or to conclude speech paragraphs which were started on earlier days. These Journal paragraphs are longer than before, and material from newspapers enters as key words or phrases rather than bald quotations. Figure 5 shows that the biography of John Brown (paragraphs 1–17) emerged chiefly from this set of drafts, a good sign that the general form of the speech was crystalizing.

In the days before the lecture on Sunday, 30 October, Thoreau clearly had to rework these paragraphs and fragments into the reading draft, which was also the printer's copy. Glick reports that the speech was written on sixty sheets, thirteen of which are preserved. There is evidence, based on two of the sheets, that at least part of the text was revised, although there might have been an interim draft.[15] Given the very short notice, Thoreau probably resequenced the material from memory, unless he copied the Journal draft and then used "scissors and paste" to assemble the materials. In this essay, at least, we clearly see Thoreau, under a deadline, drafting a rather long essay by a collage or mosaic technique until he determined its final structure.

[15] Glick's General Introduction, RP 230. See also 341 for the Textual Introduction.

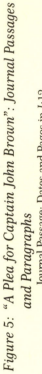

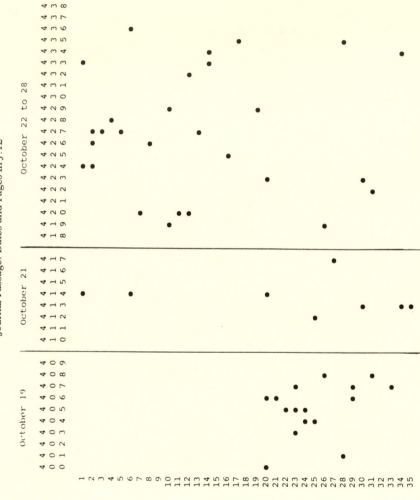

Figure 5: "A Plea for Captain John Brown": Journal Passages and Paragraphs

Journal Passage: Dates and Pages in J:12

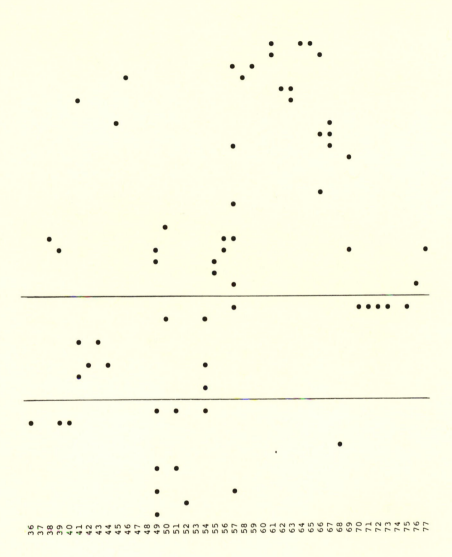

Understandably, most material not in the Journal is transitional—the first sentences of paragraphs 1, 2, 14, etc., the final sentences of paragraphs 3, 7, 10, etc., the one-sentence transition between the biography and the attack on newspapers (¶ 18).

"The Martyrdom of John Brown," the middle piece of the series, is a minor effort. It consists of a brief introduction followed by Ralegh's "The Soul's Errand" and a passage which Thoreau translated from Tacitus. Roughly half of the introduction appears in *J* 12:445–6. Apparently Thoreau felt he had to be ready on short notice to participate in a memorial service after Brown's hanging. The Journal passage says, "Almost any noble verse may be read either as his elegy or eulogy or be made the text of an oration on him." On 30 November he lists the committee nominated to toll the parish bell and conduct the service. By that occasion, Thoreau's political condemnation, that "no church *which is wedded to the state*" can provide a service appropriate to a martyr, had been muted by dropping the emphasized words (139).

"The Last Days of John Brown" offers another chance to explore Thoreau's composing process in detail. The "Plea" lecture was given three times, on 30 October and 1 and 3 November. The Journal entries from 28 October and 12 November are not political; a few of them even include brief field notes left over from the week of 21–28 October, when the lecture was being written. As mentioned, the entry for 15 November includes material for the eulogy—the likelihood of Brown's execution had politicized Thoreau again. Entries for 15 and 18 November have passages that later appeared in "Last Days."

Thoreau worked seriously on "Last Days" from 5 December through the ninth, that is, the days after the hanging. In effect all but one brief paragraph from the essay and a few lines here or there were not present in the Journal. Alternatively, Thoreau wrote just a few paragraphs about Brown that he decided not to use in the essay. The Journal paragraphs were kept essentially intact—verb tenses were regularized to the past, and adverbs were added to smooth some transitions or heighten some of the descriptions. The interesting feature is the degree to which the composing sequence did not resemble the final sequence:

Date:	15 Nov	17 Nov	18 Nov	5 Dec
Para:	13,2	3	14	1,20,7,21,23,8
J 12:	445	447	448	13:6–7

Date:	6 [–7?] Dec	8 Dec
Para:	22,16,17,18,4,8,9,16,21,5,6,8	10,11,cf.19
J 13:	10–14	14–15

Date:	9 Dec
Para:	12
J 13:	18–19

Relatively sustained, long Journal entries for 5 and 6 December reveal Thoreau's original intentions. The former emphasizes the mystical or religious "translation" of John Brown's spirit. In the face of his enemies (mostly preachers), the theatrical hangings have insured his immortality. As a result, the North became "all Transcendental" and able to understand "eternal justice and glory." The longer passage, dated 6 December, presents a different theme—that Brown's own words are his best praise. Thoreau had argued in the "Plea" that Brown's messages from jail constituted a sacred text and he ended that speech with a series of quotations. Now, Thoreau insists, Brown's additional letters in the six weeks of his captivity show a remarkable "variety of themes"; his words regarding "the education of his daughters . . . deserve to be framed and hung over every mantelpiece in the land." Brown's thoughts, when quoted at memorial services (such as, presumably, the one Thoreau and Emerson sponsored), will change the views of doubters and convert even the preachers.

This Journal draft is an effort at hagiography, clearly presenting Brown as a saintly person whose words are inspired. The resulting essay seems to be about Brown's place in (secular) history.[16] The paragraph about the memorial service (145–46, ¶ 5)

[16] For a contrasting view, see Abraham Lincoln, Address at Cooper Institute, 27 February 1860: "John Brown's effort was peculiar. It was not a slave insurrection. It was an attempt by white men to get up a

states the general case, while the bulk of the essay traces the various institutions that Brown's example of nobility and heroism have affected: preachers and churches, the Massachusetts legislature, the Church of England, and literary "gentlemen, editors, and critics." Thoreau probably changed the essay's structure because he was writing for the public, perhaps even for a national audience. The themes that dominated the Journal draft provide the conclusion (151–53, ¶ 20–23): Brown's enemies blundered by failing to suppress his words; his victory was of "pure spirit." Only the last two paragraphs discuss Brown as a saint or as Christ, his body "cut down from the gallows-tree," but the religious tone is muted. The final message is patriotic and political: "He works in public, and in the clearest light that shines on this land" (153, ¶ 23; not in *J* 13:7).[17]

The brief history of these essays reveals Thoreau working as an anti-slavery journalist, writing competently for a particular occasion. They also show him in the heat of a genuinely emotional response—his anger and his call for revenge contrast with the philosophical and distanced posture that appears in his other writings. While political events cut sharply into the Journals on three major ocasions, most of Thoreau's private writings from 1854 on concern the facts of the natural world. He observes that world and catalogs it impersonally and without as much obvious passion. The history of his works after 1854 demonstrate, too, that Thoreau moved away from using himself as his central figure. We have seen that, in the "Allegash" essay (*The Maine*

---

revolt among slaves, in which the slaves refused to participate. In fact, it was so absurd that the slaves, with all their ignorance, saw plainly enough it could not succeed. That affair, in its philosophy, corresponds with the many attempts, related in history, at the assassination of kings and emperors. An enthusiast broods over the oppression of a people till he fancies himself commissioned by Heaven to liberate them" (*The Collected Works of Abraham Lincoln*, ed. Roy P. Basler et al. [New Brunswick, N.J.: Rutgers Univ. Press, 1953], 3:54). Thoreau addresses the slave insurrection issue, with apparent approval, in "Last Days" (149).

[17]See *J* 14:291–92 for an account of a conversation Thoreau had, defending Brown against Walcott's and Staples's charge that he did wrong by dying. Thoreau again likened Brown's death to the Crucifixion.

Woods, drafted 1857), he went to some trouble to keep our focus on Polis as a hero of nearly primitive and nearly mythic proportions. In the John Brown speeches from 1859, Thoreau set Brown up on a pedestal as a mythic figure of national stature. And in the late natural history essays, nature herself becomes the "hero" and Thoreau the observer and chronicler.

13

Coda: The Late
Natural History Essays

ON THE BACKS of handbills announcing a memorial service for
Brown, Thoreau polished Journal entries about wild fruits.[1]
These notes are part of related major projects during his last
years—an undertaking the Brown writings only temporarily interrupted. Thoreau was apparently planning large-scale works
on "The Fall of the Leaf," "Wild Fruits," and "The Dispersion of
Seeds." He was abstracting materials for these projects from the
"Kalendar" that he had been gathering in his Journal for years (J
12:389). The root idea goes back to the time of crucial revisions
to the *Walden* manuscript: "Why should just these sights and
sounds accompany our life? Why should I hear the chattering
of blackbirds, why smell the skunk each year? I would fain explore the mysterious relation between myself and these things. I
would at least know what these things unavoidably are, make a
chart of our life, know how its shores trend, that butterflies reappear and when, know just why this circle of creatures completes
the world. Can I not by expectation affect the revolutions of nature, make a day to bring forth something new?" (J 3:438). As
we have seen, Thoreau worked parts of this entry into "Brute
Neighbors," where the passage helps motivate the quest in the
second half of *Walden* and leads ultimately to the climactic discovery of organicism, the principle that unites and animates all.
In his last works Thoreau continues to explore organicism and
its significance for man's life.

But for various reasons Thoreau was unable to finish his late
work on natural history. From the larger projects, he managed to
produce only four lectures, three of which he readied for publication shortly before his death. We will glance at these pieces

[1] Howarth, *Book of Concord*, p. 181.

only briefly because they have been handled well by James McIntosh, William Howarth, Robert Sattelmeyer, and John Hildebilde,[2] and because, despite recent claims for them, we do not consider them major works. They are wise, charming, informative, well crafted examples of familiar essays and scientific studies leavened with poetic and humanistic perspectives, but they do not go much beyond *Walden*. They remain fragments of what might possibly have become works even greater than *Walden*, had Thoreau been able to complete them.

As early as 1853 Thoreau considered making a book that consisted entirely of brilliantly colored leaf shapes—"a book which should be a memorial of October, be entitled October Hues or Autumnal Tints" (*J* 5:516; revised slightly for inclusion in "Autumnal Tints," [*Ex* 251]). Not until 1858 did he get around to writing a lecture on the topic, which he delivered several times in 1859 and 1860 (*CL* 86–87). Apparently "Autumnal Tints" was successful enough for Thoreau to begin expanding it into a larger work, "The Fall of the Leaf," but he did not get far into this project (few of the notes for it remain). In 1862 he returned to "Autumnal Tints," revising his lecture draft (now part of his notes for the larger project) into an essay for the *Atlantic*. He added no new Journal material at this stage; the latest entry in it dates from 21 November 1858. The essay consists of reworked Journal passages mostly from 1857–58, with about one-quarter representing materials from prior Journals.

In this pleasant, witty, colorful essay, Thoreau returns to some of the themes and feelings from *Walden*. He concentrates primarily on organicism, perception (especially aesthetic perception), and correspondences between nature and the life of man. This is the most poetic of the late natural history essays. Here Thoreau approaches nearest his goal of synthesizing art and science. The piece is filled with Linnean classifications, technical

[2]McIntosh, *Thoreau as Romantic Naturalist*, Ch. 8; Howarth, *Book of Concord*, Ch. 8, 9; Introduction to Henry David Thoreau, *The Natural History Essays*, ed. Robert Sattelmeyer (Salt Lake City: Peregrine Smith, 1980), pp. vii–xxxviii; Hildebilde, *Thoreau: A Naturalist's Liberty*, Ch. 4.

vocabulary from physiology, and closely observed natural details; but it is concerned even more with beauty and with metaphorical uses of nature. It does differ significantly from Thoreau's earlier writings, however. As in the other late scientific essays, nature moves to the fore as the hero while Thoreau plays the skilled observer. The piece is not structured like the earlier excursions or romance quests, where dramatic interest derives from the quester-hero's struggles, intellectual adventures, and growth. Rather, Thoreau begins now to employ a calendar structure, arranging his sections chronologically.[3] Finally, although myth receives occasional mention (*Ex* 259, 266, 267), it does not play a large role in the structure or content of the essay.

As he worked on "The Fall of the Leaf" in 1859, Thoreau was also gathering notes on fruits, another part of his natural history project. The following January he extracted a lecture, "Wild Apples," which he delivered as his last before the Concord Lyceum (*CL* 87; revised slightly for publication in 1862). The piece uses Journal entries mainly from before 1854, which helps account for its nostalgic character. Thoreau here reworks materials from the *Walden* era. He uses this treatise on wild apples as the vehicle for thoughts about his favorite subjects from the early 1850s: wildness, heightened perception, sauntering, ripening, cultivation of the senses, aesthetic versus utilitarian uses of nature, and American history and destiny. This piece, unlike the other late nature essays, also seems nostalgic in its pervasive reliance on myth.[4] But if it picks up again the concerns and style of the earlier works, the piece differs from them in that Thoreau no longer plays the hero. Instead, the wild apple itself takes that role; Thoreau taps conventions of myth and romance to picture

[3] Howarth suggests that "Autumnal Tints" is also structured by an "evolutionary rationale"; "it moves from the simple, widely distributed grasses to more complex and localized trees of the deciduous forest" (*Book of Concord*, p. 170).

[4] For mythic readings of the essay, see Hildebilde, *Thoreau: A Naturalist's Liberty*, pp. 83–93, and Kevin P. Van Anglen, "A Paradise Regained: Thoreau's 'Wild Apples' and the Myth of the American Adam," *ESQ* 27 (1981):28–37.

the wild apple as a "prince in disguise" (*Ex* 307) who contends with demon cold, "wandering kine, and other adverse circumstances" in its quest for survival and propagation (306).

Later in 1860 Thoreau began compiling notes for a work "on the Dispersion of Seeds" (*C* 590). He extracted from this long project the lecture he gave in September before the Middlesex Agricultural Society, "The Succession of Forest Trees." Although he begins this address by identifying himself as "a transcendentalist," he quickly moves to his role as surveyor and naturalist addressing "a purely scientific subject" (*Ex* 185). "Succession" answers the question of why a pine wood appears when an oak wood is cut down, and vice versa. More generally, it concerns the themes—familiar from *Walden*—of organicism, generation, and nature's wonderful economy. Thoreau aims this basically scientific essay at laymen, leavening his facts with analogies, humor, and a concluding paean to the miraculousness of common seeds. Once again, he remains in the background as an observer while Nature takes over as heroine of the piece. She "can persuade us to do almost anything when she would compass her ends" (188); she provides men with a model for using pines to cultivate hardwoods (194); she shows how best to pack and plant seeds (197); and so on.

At the beginning of 1861 Thoreau extracted another lecture from his larger "Wild Fruits" project. He never completed or delivered "Huckleberries," although his drafts were ready for final revision.[5] More than the other late pieces, this lecture consists of naturalist notes and observations, although Thoreau does broaden his scope to include metaphorical explorations of anthropology, American history, and "berrying" as a special way of life. He ends the lecture by calling for public parks to save the wildness that he sees disappearing from an America obsessed with private property.

When he extracted "Huckleberries," Thoreau had not worked on the rest of "Wild Fruits" for close to a year, and the larger project remained unfinished. Conducting further research on

[5] The lecture has been edited and published by Leo Stoller (New York: NYPL, 1970).

seeds and trees in December 1860, Thoreau caught the cold that began his final series of illnesses. He worked on "The Dispersion of Seeds" at intervals throughout his last months, amassing a considerable number of notes toward it (the major portion of the manuscript, Berg 70B, contains over three hundred leaves), but this project, also, remained incomplete at his death in 1862.

Why did Thoreau not finish more of his late natural history work?

The easy answer is that he simply did not have the time. As Emerson claimed in his ambivalent eulogy for Thoreau, "The scale on which his studies proceeded was so large as to require longevity" (CE 10:484). If A Week did not reach its full shape and meaning until the third major draft and much revision over ten years, and if Walden did not finally coalesce until the seventh draft in nine years, it is not surprising that "The Fall of the Leaf," "Wild Fruits," and "The Dispersion of Seeds" were nowhere near completion in the five or so years that Thoreau worked intermittently on them. Not only were those years few, but they were full of distractions. We have seen how politics interrupted Thoreau's work during late 1859. He was also surveying frequently and working for the family's plumbago business. Finally, his illnesses halted his work completely during some weeks and reduced his efficiency during others. He just did not have time for the leisurely "re-vision" that produced his best writing.

Some other possibilities suggest themselves for Thoreau's failure to publish more of the late projects. After poor reception of his earlier work, he might well have felt discouraged from marching directly into print with more. As Howarth and Sharon Cameron argue, he turned increasingly to his Journal as an end in itself rather than as the workbook it was before—the source of materials to be mined for the ultimate goal of public lectures, essays, and books.[6] He seems to have been satisfied recording careful observations of nature in his Journal, without the need to justify them through inclusion in other works of art. By this time he had given up his early ambition to be a successful published

---

[6] Howarth, Book of Concord, and Cameron, Writing Nature: Henry Thoreau's Journal.

writer, and perhaps he was satisfied that *Walden* contained most of what he wanted to put before the public anyway.

Also, as he did try to work some of his observations into the late projects, he encountered trouble organizing them on a large scale. As we have shown, he was moving away from myth and excursion as structural principles, but he had not yet discovered an adequate substitute, an alternative way of organizing entries into complex, multisignificant texts. The calendar form fits the chronological nature of his observations, but it was fairly predictable and mechanical, and natural cycles were turning out to be less regular than he might have hoped.

Finally, we see a problem of inspiration, too, in the late materials. A current revisionist movement seeks to elevate the later works, to counter a view that Thoreau's writing declined toward the end. For example, John Hildebilde claims, "It is the sheer bulk of this material, and the meticulousness with which Thoreau compiled it—especially those tables and indexes that he culled from his journal—which make it hard to credit the idea that Thoreau's intellectual energies were somehow on the wane after *Walden*."[7] The late Journals do evidence abundant energy, but we cannot help noticing a difference in the kind of entries Thoreau was writing. Where the Journals of the early and mid 1850s combine facts and poetry in imaginative syntheses—the subjective transfiguring and making significant the objective— the later Journals record page after page of facts and observations with, by contrast, relatively little reflection. Thoreau may have been gathering materials for ultimate reworking, but he seems not yet to have found the inspiration and fresh perspectives that would transform those facts into art. These late entries resemble *Walden*'s "The Pond in Winter," with its map of scientific measurements, more than "Spring," where the natural observations inspire myth and poetry.

Thoreau's goal appears not to have changed from the early days. Just as he urged in "Natural History of Massachusetts," "Let us not underrate the value of a fact; it will one day flower in a truth" (*Ex* 130), and just as he wrote in 1853 at the height of

---

[7] Hildebilde, p. 69.

his conversion, "I pray for such inward experience as will make nature significant" (J 5:135), so he argues along similar lines in his late Journal: "A fact stated barely is dry. It must be the vehicle of some humanity in order to interest us. . . . It must be warm, moist, incarnated,—have been breathed on at last" (J 13:160). But the facts recorded in the late Journals are not yet warm, moist, incarnated. They remain mostly dry, bare statements that have yet to become vehicles of humanity. "With regard to such [natural] objects," Thoreau wrote, "I find that it is not they themselves (with which the men of science deal) that concern me; the point of interest is somewhere *between* me and them (i.e. the objects)" (J 10:165). That crucial, vivifying subjectivity is not nearly so evident in the later Journals as in the earlier.

Nina Baym has pointed to a paradox in the late Journals—that they "are at once more scientific in content and more opposed to science in comment." According to Baym, Thoreau's early hope that science and Transcendentalism would lead to the same truths faltered; he rejected science when he found that it pointed to "the irrelevance of man in the universe."[8] But Thoreau's views about science seem inconsistent and contradictory to the end. He does complain often about the dryness and deadliness of scientific perception, but he also argues that science aids subjective, aesthetic, poetic perception. For example, in the last year of his Journal he writes:

> How much of beauty—of color, as well as form—on
> which our eyes daily rest goes unperceived by us! No
> one but a botanist is likely to distinguish nicely the dif-
> ferent shades of green with which the open surface of
> the earth is clothed,—not even a landscape-painter if
> he does not know the species of sedges and grasses
> which paint it. With respect to the color of grass, most
> of those even who attend peculiarly to the aspects of
> Nature only observe that it is more or less dark or light,
> green or brown, or velvety, fresh or parched, etc. But if

[8]"Thoreau's View of Science," *Journal of the History of Ideas* 26 (1965):221, 234.

> you are studying grasses you look for another and dif-
> ferent beauty, and you find it, in the wonderful variety
> of color, etc., presented by the various species. (J 14:3)

Perhaps this mutual reinforcement of science and poetry did not occur often enough at the end for Thoreau to complete the last projects. He had earlier expressed his hopes for the Journal materials: "I trust there will appear in this Journal some flow, some gradual filling of the springs and raising of the streams, that the accumulating grists may be ground" (J 10:126). Perhaps that spring flood of inspiration that did facilitate the completion of *Walden* in the early 1850s simply did not come for the later works. The Journals remain "accumulating grists" that, for the reasons we have listed, Thoreau did not finally grind.

Again, this is not to argue that, under different circumstances, Thoreau could not have produced great works. We are looking at projects in an unfinished state; *Walden* at a similar stage, say the C or even D version, was nowhere near the complete masterpiece. But Thoreau did not complete these last projects, and the parts that he did manage to polish into essays do not suggest to us a major movement beyond his aesthetic and intellectual development in the mid–1850s.

The John Brown and late natural history essays serve to remind us of how important the paragraph is as the unit of composition in nearly all of Thoreau's works. His ability to move blocks of a draft around into a new sequence without apparent major disruptions is quite remarkable. In the broader view, writing lectures and essays by putting Journal passages together poses clear risks in terms of the ultimate coherence and flow of the final presentation. One might guess that the conditions of the mid-nineteenth-century lecture hall tended to mask the difficulties from the speaker.

Twice in his career, in *A Week* and *Walden*, Thoreau put those small pieces together into works that were both collections of individual insights and coherent, skillfully orchestrated large texts. A number of factors led to his sustained performance in these two books. First, Thoreau spent a great deal of time and effort on each. They evolved over a number of years and through the course of many drafts. As we have shown, tracing the evolution of these works furthers our understanding of them. We can see them take shape, change purpose, and gain meaning at each stage of their development. By returning again and again to events from his past for "re-vision," Thoreau was able both to discover and create what he ultimately had to say about them. We can see in the major works fine examples of what composition theory calls a "recursive" process—where editing, drafting, and revising are essentially simultaneous events, and where the writer explores what he wants to say by trying to say it.[9] It is important to notice that Thoreau had a wide range of composing practices, suited to the diversity of his writing occasions, and (perhaps) to the diversity of genres he used. It may not be accidental that the demands on the reader turn out to match quite closely the difficulty or ease of Thoreau's composing process. We may, in fact, read books "as deliberately and reservedly as they were written" in a *literal* sense. The multiple meanings and interpretations that readers have made in response to Thoreau's great works may actually have been caused, albeit somewhat inadvertently, by what Thoreau suffered in composing those works. In them he approaches closest to his own Artist of Kouroo, taking abundant time to select and polish his materials. He did not allow people or events to pressure him into publishing too soon.

Nor did he allow any other pressures—whether editors, genre, or popular market—to interfere with the books. While he felt constrained to meet public expectations of rather conventional travel writing in *The Maine Woods* and *Cape Cod*, he felt free in *A Week* and *Walden* to create new, experimental forms by combining and altering old genres, challenging his readers' expectations in order to channel them in new directions. He could balance the centrifugal and centripetal forces in his works—that is, he could use the form supplied by genre conventions and his underlying narratives to control and shape the individual in-

[9] J. Emig, "Writing as a Mode of Learning," *College Composition and Communication* 28 (1977):122–28.

sights (often from Journal passages having nothing to do with the vacation trip of 1839 or the Walden years) that threaten the overall coherence of his other writings. He achieves in these works both the disrupting, epiphanic moments that he values as the only genuine source of truth and a larger structure that binds these moments into coherent narratives that are more than the sums of their individual parts.

In *A Week* and *Walden*, Thoreau used myth most seriously and most extensively. We have seen how he recapitulated the progress of myth in the late eighteenth and early nineteenth centuries, employing it decoratively in his early essays and then taking it quite seriously in these two major works. Here Thoreau used myth both as a means of gaining and communicating special insights and as a way of providing structure. His extensive use of myth gives these works more unity and architectonic control than, for example, "Walking," a shorter yet less coherent work that touches several of the same themes. Thoreau is also most effective in these two works at creating his own myths and portraying himself as the central mythic hero.

In these two books, Thoreau most successfully tapped his readers' own resources. Unlike his apprentice pieces with their prefabricated morals or the John Brown essays with their clearly defined topical agenda, *A Week* and *Walden* are "scriptable"— that is, they are written to evoke a corresponding creativity on the part of their readers. In *A Week* Thoreau challenges us to take up the informing quest for ourselves; in *Walden* he insists that we discover our own pond, an alternative life that will let us see clearly what our routine life tends to hide. Thoreau is explicit in both works about what he expects from us. At the end of *A Week* he encourages us to write a sequel more valuable than the work he has just concluded, and the third chapter of *Walden* ("Reading") calls upon our own imagination and generosity in reading properly the book that is before us. Both works are rich and layered, complex and multisignificant. Each natural fact blossoms with a variety of significances. His symbols are not Swedenborgian correspondences but are fluxional, suggestive, designed to stimulate our imagination rather than convey a fixed or allegorical truth. In Richard Poirier's image, Thoreau has created "jungle gyms" on which his readers can play or perform.[10] Meaning emerges in *process* as the reader confronts Thoreau's texts imaginatively.

Finally, *A Week* and *Walden* came at the right time in Thoreau's personal development. He worked on them (especially on *Walden*) at a stage when his conversion to romanticism provided new energy for artistic creation. He was caught up in the excitement of acknowledging the spiritual, philosophical, and moral vision that he had sensed for years but was just in the process of making his own through the ability to name that vision and to recognize its components. The ideas now *felt* new to him. He even comprehended intellectually and emotionally the full impact of spring. The world was pervaded with wonder, novelty, and freshness that he was able to capture, finally, in parts of *A Week* and in most of *Walden*. He was not yet hampered by politics, since the state did not occupy much space in his personal landscape, and he could even make it disappear by walking away from it.

Romanticism provided an aesthetic that gave him a loose, flexible structure for long works (a mythic quest with the poet as hero) and justification for freely leaving and returning to that loose frame for those moments of insight that alone offered living, vibrant truth. As he puts it in "Life without Principle," "Knowledge does not come to us by details, but in flashes of light from heaven" (*RP* 173).

If Thoreau was most successful as he approached (*A Week*) and underwent (*Walden*) his conversion to romanticism, we do not mean to imply that these works are superior simply because they are in varying degrees romantic. They are superior to his other works, but for different and complex reasons. In his early pieces, for example, Thoreau does not yet have much of his own to say, nor does he know how to say it well. His travel pieces are not so rich and suggestive as *A Week* and *Walden* because Thoreau bows to the forces of audience and genre; he writes inter-

---

[10] See "The Performing Self" in *The Performing Self: Compositions and Decompositions in the Languages of Contemporary Life* (New York: Oxford Univ. Press, 1971), pp. 86–111.

esting but not unusual or very complex material because he employs the expected conventions. These works follow, or perhaps are tyrannized by, the sequence of events that the actual excursions included. While items were deleted to focus on a theme, they were rarely added. Also, he wrote these pieces without much revising, either in the mechanical sense of putting them through many drafts or in the creative sense of viewing again, with new eyes and insights, the significance of his travels. Although they were published years after the events they treat, these straight travel pieces did not benefit from Thoreau's attention during the intervening years.[11]

The political pieces are bristling propaganda, but, again, they result from little prolonged effort and they are limited in their aims and scope. "Resistance to Civil Government," of course, has stood out from the other essays because the issues of pacifism and of the individual's relation to the state rode out the Civil War and the Thirteenth Amendment. In both the travel and political works, our role as readers is restricted; we are not expected to join Thoreau on a creative journey that makes us cocreators of the works' meaning, nor does the journey extend beyond the last page.

Thoreau's writings after *Walden* reveal a sense of anticlimax, as if he had said much of what he wanted to in his greatest work. He felt discouraged, perhaps, by his failure to find or establish an audience for the kind of writing which most interested him and which suited his talents best. His later Journals reveal that scientific studies were replacing his mythic-poetic approach to the world around him. His later speeches betray a strong ambivalence about the lecture as a medium for sincere expression. The world had lost its freshness and glory, as Thoreau suggests by his recurrent references to Wordsworth's "Immortality Ode." He was rapidly becoming secularized, losing the artistic and spiritual en-

---

[11] These works reveal stasis both in their process of writing and as written products. Perhaps their static nature contributed to Thoreau's delay—up to his deathbed—in preparing them for book publication, even though Greeley and others showed over the years continued interest in publishing them.

ergy that characterized his best works. *Walden*, then, and to a lesser extent *A Week*, represent the pinnacle of Thoreau's writing career when all the many and complex forces that make for great writing came mysteriously together to create, if not eternal art like the Artist of Kouroo's stick, at least art as close to it as we can come.

Appendix: Chronologies of Thoreau's Works

The chronologies below trace the development of the works that are discussed in the body of this study. The dates and materials are drawn from the works listed in Abbreviations, supplemented by the following resources:

Walter Harding and Michael Meyer, *The New Thoreau Handbook* (New York: New York Univ. Press, 1980);

Hubert Hoeltje, "Thoreau as Lecturer," *New England Quarterly* 19 (1946):485–94;

William L. Howarth, *The Book of Concord: Thoreau's Life as a Writer* (New York: Viking Press, 1982);

Sherman Paul, *The Shores of America: Thoreau's Inward Exploration* (Urbana: Univ. of Illinois Press, 1958).

Additional sources of information for specific pieces are listed before the chronologies for those works.

The Development of *A Week*

[Additional sources: Linck C. Johnson, Historical Introduction, Princeton *Week*, and *Thoreau's Complex Weave: The Writing of A Week on the Concord and Merrimack Rivers, with the Text of the first draft* (Charlottesville: University Press of Virginia, 1986).]

31 August–13 September 1839
    The trip: Thoreau kept a brief log.
1840
    June: Copies notes on trip into Journal, adding description of equipment, preparation, departure, etc. (*PJ* 1:124–37 ff.), perhaps preparing for lecture or essay "Memoirs of a Tour—

a Chit-chat with Nature" (Huntington HM 945); also lists
topics for writings that were later included in *Week*.

1841

Transcribes gleanings from original Journal into MS Journal
II (Pierpont Morgan MA 1302:2).

Summer: draws up a new list of topics, headed by "Merrimack & Musketaquid" (Huntington HM 945).

1842

11 January: John dies.

Fall: drafts passages for projected essay or book about voyage; began to transcribe river entries from earlier Journal
into Long Book (Pierpont Morgan MA 1303); transcribes
(into Pierpont Morgan MA 608) entries on "Hindoo Scriptures" and "Books & Style."

1843

October: Drafts Agiocochook section (*PJ* 1:476).

1844

April: last issue of *Dial*, forcing Thoreau to seek other outlets.

Preparing to go to Walden: revises and copies relevant Journal entries into Long Book; drafts original passages of nar-
ration and description; incorporates Journal entries (1837–
44) not originally related to trip.

1845

25 March: lecture "Concord River."

Numbers Long Book entries according to designated chapters in *Week*.

July-Fall: completes first draft at *Walden*.

1846

Spring: expands first draft, using passages from Journal,
lectures and essays ("Sir Walter Raleigh," "The Service");
combines two "Thursday" chapters.

July: Emerson presses for publication, but Thoreau preparing further additions to Second Draft.

August: seven-page account of Agiocochook (Berg MS).

September: Katahdin trip.

Late Fall: Thoreau decides not to domesticate account of
Agiocochook; expands Saddleback episode.

1847

Working on drafts of both *Week* and *Walden*, using recent Journal passages on memory, history, fable, religion; probably inserted revised versions of "Dark Ages" and "Homer. Ossian. Chaucer." from *Dial*.

February: second draft has expanded to nearly twice first draft length.

March: Emerson offers *Week* to Duyckinck (of Wiley & Putnam); Thoreau drafts Hannah Dustan section, continues to revise throughout the spring.

May: sends MS to Duyckinck.

June: recalls MS for further revisions.

July: resubmits MS to Duyckinck.

August: Emerson offers *Week* to W. H. Furness; MS apparently has expanded from 70,000 to 90,000 words since March.

November: Thoreau records rejections by Wiley & Putnam, Munroe, Harpers, Crosby & Nichols.

1848

March: after eight-month interval, returns to *Week*, adding expanded "Friendship," corrected version of "Aulus Persius Flaccus," critique of Christianity and Bhagavad-Geeta, materials on Colonial history; excises incongruities and redundancies.

Late Summer: walking tour to New Hampshire provides new materials for *Week*.

Fall & Winter: drafts Journal entries on reformers, great men, the East, Greece & Rome.

1849

February: Ticknor agrees to publish *Week* at Thoreau's expense; Thoreau refuses, but accepts offer from Munroe to pay costs out of expected sales; may have been drafting or revising later portions of text even as earlier sections were being typeset (MS lost).

March: proof sheets arrive.

April: returns corrected proof sheets (1000 changes).

30 May: *Week* officially published.

1850s
>Continues to revise *Week*.

28 October 1853
>Munroe returns 706 unsold copies of *Week* from printing of 1000.

1855
>Thoreau tries to convince Ticknor & Fields to reissue *Week*.

1862
>Thoreau revises *Week* shortly before his death in May; Ticknor & Fields reissues *Week* (new title page on 1849 copies).

1868
>Ticknor & Fields issues "new and revised" edition of *Week* (400 changes in words, 1000 in punctuation: "Friendship" altered; fourth epigraph and critique of clergymen added).

The Development of *Walden*

[Additional sources: Walter Harding, *Walden and Civil Disobedience: The Variorum Editions* (New York: Washington Square Press, 1968); J. Lyndon Shanley, Historical Introduction to Princeton *Walden*; Phillip Van Doren Stern, *The Annotated Walden* (New York: Clarkson N. Potter, 1970).]

4 September 1841
>Possible original idea for the book in proposal for "a poem to be called 'Concord'" (*PJ* 1:330).

March 1845
>Began to work on the cabin in March; regular residency from July 4.

Before 13 March 1846 (?)—Lecture (?)
>"After I lectured here before ["Carlyle" on 4 February], this winter, I heard that some of my townsmen had expected of me some account of my life at the pond. This I will endeavor to give to-night" (*PJ* 2:142); implies that the first Walden lecture was given in 1846, not 1847.

Late 1846 to September 1847—Draft
>A version of *Walden*.

3 February 1847—Lecture (?)
    Thoreau may have delivered a Walden lecture, and it may
    have been in Concord (*CL* 80).
10 February 1847—Lecture, No. 1 from "Economy"
    "The History of Myself" at Concord Lyceum.
17 February 1847—Lecture, No. 2 from "Economy"
    At Concord Lyceum on "Same as last week" according to
    Lyceum records.
6 September 1847
    Left pond.
19 May 1848—Newspaper Extract
    Letter based on 1:98 published by Greeley in New York
    Tribune.
Mid 1848 to Late Summer 1849—Draft
    B and C versions of *Walden*: B is partly a fair copy of A with
    some additions; C involves some rewriting; revisions inter-
    lined in B suggest that Thoreau now viewed the manuscript
    as a book rather than a series of lectures.
22 November 1848—Lecture, No. 1 (?)
    "Student life in New England, its economy" at Salem Ly-
    ceum—portion of "Economy."
20 December 1848—Lecture No. 1 (?)
    "Student life" repeated at Gloucester.
3 January 1849—Lecture, No. 3
    "White Beans and Walden Pond" at Concord Lyceum—
    probably "Bean-Field."
8 February 1849
    Ticknor letter to Thoreau implies that a manuscript was
    completed.
28 February 1849—Lecture, No. 1 or No. 3 (?)
    "Life in the woods" at Salem—either "Economy" or "Where
    I lived"; see review quoted by Hoeltje—it may have been
    ¶3—"White Beans." Thoreau's Aunt Maria writes to Pru-
    dence Ward, "He is preparing his Book for the press, and
    the title is to be, Waldien (I don't know how to spell it) or
    Life in the Woods."
21? March 1849—Lecture No. 1
    Repeated in Portland, Maine.

22 March 1849
> "I shall advertise another [book], 'Walden, or Life in the Woods,' in the first" (*C* 214).

20 April 1849—Lecture, No. 1
> Repeated in Worcester, Massachusetts.

27 April 1849—Lecture, No. 2 (?)
> Sequel or possibly repetition at Worcester, Massachusetts.

? April 1849 (after the 27th)—Lecture, No. 3
> "Beans" at Worcester—probably "Bean-Field."

30 May 1849
> James Munroe and Co. publishes *A Week* with notice, "Will soon be published, *Walden, or Life in the Woods*. By Henry D. Thoreau."

1850–1851
> Thoreau adds quotations from Chinese and Hindu writings to *Walden*.

22 January 1851—Lecture, No. 1
> "Life in the Woods at Walden" at Medford, Massachusetts.

Early 1852 to September 1852
> D version.

? April 1852—Lecture
> "Reality" at Mechanics Apprentices Library.

July 1852—Magazine Publication
> "The Iron Horse" in *Sartain's Union Magazine*, 11:66–68—"Sounds" paragraphs 5:13.

August 1852—Magazine Publication
> "A Poet Buying a Farm" in *Sartain's Union Magazine*, 11:127—"Where I Lived" paragraphs 1, 2, 3, 5.

September 1852–1853
> E version added chapter divisions and titles.

Late 1853 to Early 1854
> F version.

February or March 1854
> G version.

28 March 1854
> "Got first proof of 'Walden'" (*J* 6:176)—finished work in May.

February or March to April or May 1854
Eighth version of *Walden*—printer's copy (now lost).
29 July 1854—Magazine Publication
Excerpts from *Walden* published by Greeley as "A Massachusetts Hermit."
9 August 1854—Book Publication
"'Walden' published" (*J* 6:429); Ticknor and Fields publishes 2,000 copies.
4 March 1862
To Ticknor & Fields: "I wish to make one alteration in the new edition viz, to leave out from the title the words 'Or Life in the Woods'" (*C* 639).

The Development of "Ktaadn"

[Additional sources: Robert C. Cosbey, "Thoreau at Work: The Writing of 'Ktaadn,'" *BNYPL* 65 (1961):21–30; Joseph J. Moldenhauer, "Textual Introduction" and "Textual Notes" to Princeton *Maine Woods*.]

1–10 September 1846
Travel to Maine with cousin George Thatcher, a break during Thoreau's residency at Walden.
September to December 1846
Contemporaneous account in the Berg Journal; started during the trip.
5 January 1848—Lecture
"Ktaadn" at Concord Lyceum (probably not the whole essay).
3 April 1848—Magazine Publication
Manuscript mailed to Greeley. Eventually in *Sartain's Union Magazine* in five installments (July to November 1848), with extracts in Greeley's *New York Tribune* (November 1848) and *The Student* (January 1849).
1864—Book Publication
The Maine Woods, published posthumously by Ticknor and Fields (earlier typographical errors corrected and some material added from Thoreau's reading after 1848).

The Development of "An Excursion to Canada"

September–3 October 1850
> The excursion. Upon return, Thoreau begins to read about Canada.

July–August 1851
> Journal entries as preparation for lectures; early lecture draft (Huntington HM 949).

6 January 1852—Lecture
> At Lincoln.

7 January 1852—Lecture
> At Concord.

17 March 1852—Lecture
> At Concord.

March 1852
> Manuscript to Greeley.

January–March 1853—Magazine publication
> Most of chapters 1 to 3 in *Putnam's Monthly Magazine*; rest of manuscript withdrawn after Curtis' censorship.

1866—posthumous publication
> *A Yankee in Canada, with Anti-Slavery and Reform Papers.*

The Development of *Cape Cod*

9–17 October 1849
> First excursion, with William Ellery Channing, probably at the end of work on the C draft of *Walden*.

23 January and 30 January 1850—Lectures
> Separate lectures at Concord Lyceum.

18 February 1850—Lecture
> Combination of the two lectures at Danvers, Mass.

May 1850—Lecture
> At Worcester, probably about Cape Cod.

ca. 25 June 1850
> Brief visit (second).
> Account in *J* 2:11–80, passim.

6 December 1850—Lecture

At Newburyport, Mass., probably about Cape Cod; may include material from the second trip.

1 January 1851—Lecture
At Clinton.

25 July–1 August 1851
Excursion to Hull and Plymouth, soon after the "Wild/Walking" lectures. Account in *J* 2:341–60.

16 November 1852—Magazine publication of Ch. 1–4
One hundred pages of manuscript to *Putnam's*, with "The Beach" (Ch. 4) to follow—this is "not yet half the whole" (*C* 288–89).

13 April 1855
Letter to Curtis of *Putnam's* concerning revision.

5–19 July 1855
Third excursion, with Channing. Account in *J* 7:432–464).

June-August 1855—Magazine publication
Chapters 1–4 published in *Putnam's*.
8 Aug.: letter concerning revisions to "The Beach Again" (Ch. 6) at *Putnam's* (*C* 379); the manuscript was withdrawn (later).

12–22 June 1857
Fourth excursion; account in *J* 9:413–55; material not used in *Cape Cod*. Presumably the manuscript was completed before this time; Journal evidence suggests the fall of 1855.

October and December 1864—publication
"Wellfleet Oysterman" (Ch. 5) and "The Highland Light" (Ch. 8) in *Atlantic*.
Cape Cod posthumously edited by Ellery Channing and Sophia Thoreau, published by Ticknor & Fields.

The Development of "Wild/Walking"

January-March 1851
Journal passages, used extensively in the lecture.

April 1851—Lecture
"The Wild" at Concord lyceum.

May 1851—Lecture
"Walking" at Worcester.

May 1852—Lecture
"Walking, or The Wild" at Plymouth.
20 or 21 November 1854—Lecture
"The Wild" at Philadelphia.
2 November 1856—Lecture
"Walking" at Perth Amboy, N.J.
18 December 1856—Lecture
"Walking" at Amherst, N.H.
13 February 1857—Lecture
"Walking" at Worcester. Letter to Blake, 6 February, explains that the lecture is divided into two parts and that the public would hear new material.
1862—Magazine publication
Revised for *The Atlantic Monthly*.

The Development of "Slavery in Massachusetts"

[Additional sources: Wendell Glick, General Introduction and Textual Introductions to Princeton *Reform Papers*.]

12 April–May 1851
Simms affair. Contemporaneous account in *J* 2:173–85.
May–June 1854
Burns affair. Contemporaneous account in *J* 6:313–70.
4 July 1854—Lecture
Framingham.
21 July 1854—Magazine publication
Liberator (Vol. 24, No. 29). Reprinted in *New York Daily Tribune* (2 August 1854) and *The National Anti-Slavery Standard* (12 November, 1854).

The Development of "Life without Principle"

[Additional sources: Wendell Glick, General Introduction and Textual Introductions to Princeton *Reform Papers*.]

June 1850–June 1854
Journal passages which represent two-thirds of the essay,
most of which come between January 1851 and August
1852.

20–21 November 1854—Lecture
Philadelphia.

26, 28 December 1854—Lecture
"Getting a Living" at New Bedford, then Nantucket.

4 January 1855—Lecture
"Connection between employment and the higher life" at
Worcester.

14 February 1855–Lecture
"What Shall it Profit?" at Concord.

? 24 October–1 November 1856—Lecture
At Perth Amboy, N.J.

9 October 1859—Lecture
"Life Misspent" at Boston.

9 September 1860—Lecture
"Life Misspent" at Lowell.

October 1863—Magazine publication
In *Atlantic* 12:484–95. Original title, "The Higher Law" (*C*
638).

The Development of "Chesuncook" and "Allegash and East Branch"

[Additional source: Joseph J. Moldenhauer, Textual Introduction
and Textual Notes to Princeton *The Maine Woods*.]

13–27 September 1853
Travel to Maine (second trip), probably at the end of work
on the E draft of *Walden*. Joe Aitteon as guide. Account in
Journals (see 5:424 and 456).

2 December 1853
57 pp. article (probably "Chesuncook) submitted to Underwood (*C* 308).

14 December 1853—Lecture
"Journey to Moose Head Lake" at Concord Lyceum.

20 November 1854—Lecture
  "Moose Hunting" in Philadelphia.
5 December 1854—Lecture
  Probably the same topic at Concord Lyceum (*MW* 360).
27 October 1856—Lecture
  "Moose Story" in Perth Amboy, N.J.
20 July–8 August 1857
  Travel to Maine (third trip). Joe Polis as guide.
  Account in Journals (see 9:485 and 10:53).
1 January 1858
  Draft of "Allegash and East Branch" announced (*C* 502).
25 February 1858—Lecture on Allegash
  Delivered at Concord Lyceum.
June-August 1858—Magazine publication of "Chesuncook"
  In *Atlantic* in three installments; Lowell's unauthorized ed-
  iting angered Thoreau.
1864—Publication
  The Maine Woods published posthumously by Ticknor and
  Fields.

The Development of John Brown Pieces

[Additional sources: Wendell Glick, General Introduction and
Textual Introductions to Princeton *Reform Papers*.]

  (1) "A Plea for Captain John Brown"
  (2) "Martyrdom of John Brown"
  (3) "The Last Days of John Brown"

16–17 October 1859
  Brown's raid in Harpers Ferry, Virginia.
19–28 October 1859
  "Plea" written.
30 October 1859—Lecture
  "Plea" at Concord Town Hall.
1 November 1859
  "Plea" at Tremont Temple, Boston.
3 November 1859—Lecture
  "Plea" at Washburn Hall, Worcester.

2 December 1859—Lecture
   "Martyrdom" at Concord Town Hall, on the day of Brown's
   hanging.
February 1860
   "Plea" and "Martyrdom" in James Redpath, ed., *Echoes of
   Harper's Ferry.*
4 July 1860—Lecture
   "Last Days" delivered in absentia by R. J. Hinton at Brown's
   grave in North Elba, N.Y.
27 July 1860—Magazine publication
   "Last Days" in *Liberator* 30, No. 30.

Index